THE LIFE & TIMES OF JULIUS CAESAR

THE LIFE & TIMES OF

Julius
Caesar

BY
A Noble

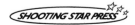

This edition printed for, Shooting Star Press Inc, 230
Fifth Avenue, Suite 1212, New York, NY 10001

Shooting Star Press books are available at special discount
for bulk purchases for sales promotions, premiums, fund-
raising or educational use. Special editions or book
excerpts can also be created to specification. For details
contact – Special Sales Director, Shooting Star Press Inc.,
230 Fifth Avenue, Suite 1212, New York, NY 10001

This edition first published by Parragon Books
Produced by Magpie Books Ltd, 7 Kensington Church
Court, London W8 4SP
Copyright © Parragon Book Service Ltd 1994
Cover picture & illustrations courtesy of: Mary Evans
Picture Library; Christies Images.

ISBN 1 57335 038 9
A copy of the British Library Cataloguing in Publication
Data is available from the British Library.

Typeset by Hewer Text Composition Services, Edinburgh
Printed in Singapore by Printlink International Co.

Gaius Julius Caesar, a member of the Julian family, was probably born in 100 BC, though some sources say he was born two years earlier. Very little is known of his childhood and events in his life are only reported when he reaches his late teens.

We do know, however, that he was born into a time of strife. Rome had been in a constitutional crisis for almost two hundred years, and this had come to a head a generation before Caesar. The crisis was ultimately due to the rapid expansion of the Roman state, as it took over the Italian peninsula and fought wars abroad, notably that with Carthage.

The image we have of the Roman Empire is one of stability and power. But the institutions that made it so did not exist before Caesar's time. To understand Caesar, we need to understand the world into which he was born.

ROME IN CRISIS

Originally, government positions in Rome – consuls, praetors, tribunes, etc. – were elective, to be held for one year. This short term of office prevented the holders from accumulating too much power – holders of offices could not be re-elected the following year. Also, by ensuring that several of the major patrician (aristocratic) families held offices in turn, it damped down internal rivalries. The only exception to these rules was in times of extreme crisis when the

3

imperium would be granted to an individual; the *imperium* meant absolute power and the person so endowed was known as the dictator, effectively the one whose word was law. Governors also held the *imperium* in their provinces.

Rome had been ruled by an Assembly, where all citizens could vote, in which the main posts were those of consul and tribune. Two consuls were elected and ten tribunes. The consuls shared ceremonial duties and command of the army, even commanding the army on alternate days in some cases. The tribunes had to come from the *plebs* and had the right to propose and veto new laws in the Assembly, but had no other responsibilities. The route to consul was via quaestor, with financial responsibilities, aedile, responsible for public works and games, and praetor, whose role was to act as a judge. Consuls were judges and had administrative and religious duties. Consuls and praetors were also expected to assume the senior military commands in time of war – and Rome was at war somewhere or other for almost all of its 1,000-year history.

All the preceding roles came under the general heading of magistrate, which then had the broader meaning of office-holder. All magistrates automatically became members of the Senate. The role of the Senate was to debate proposed laws and actions on behalf of the Republic. In time, the ascendancy of the Senate over the Assembly became complete. Its edicts became law and it started to issue commands under the slogan 'SPQR' – *Senatus Populusque Romanus* the Senate and People of Rome.

All this started to change as Rome expanded both in Italy and overseas. New posts were created to rule in the provinces and colonies – proconsuls and propraetors. (The distinction between a province and a colony was that provinces were not settled by Roman farmers – ex-soldiers – whereas colonies were). Because of the difficulties of travel – either on foot or slowly by sea, with journeys to colonies often taking several months – it became impractical for proconsuls and propraetors to hold office for only one year. Once the one-year rule was broken, the consequences were predictable. Proconsuls and propraetors began to attract loyalty to themselves rather than to the Roman Republic. This was especially dangerous as one of their tasks was to raise armies to control and/or expand their governorships. These armies were loyal first to their leaders, then to the Republic.

In Rome itself, the electoral system was utterly corrupt. Candidates required huge sums of money, both for putting on spectacular games to win over the population, and to directly buy votes as they progressed up the political ladder. This meant that many senators went deeper and deeper into debt. The only means of paying back such debts was to conquer new territory and seize booty in enormous quantities. This meant that, ideally, one had to get oneself appointed as a proconsul or propraetor and raise an army. As there were too few positions to go round, there were always frustrated senators and tribunes hugely in debt, and thus ready to resort to desperate measures, including *coup d'états*.

The army had originally been a citizen army, essentially a militia, and this had been adequate when Rome was fighting to achieve dominance in Italy, where distances and campaigns were relatively short. Once, however, long campaigns began to be conducted at greater and greater distances from Rome, it changed in character and became professional, with soldiers serving long periods (up to twenty-five years), at the end of which they expected to be settled on land to farm, and during which they hoped to gain the spoils of battle. Marius was the first consul, towards the end of the second century BC, to recruit volunteers rather than conscripts. Unlike the militia who only wanted to return to their farms, these professional soldiers were loath to be disbanded at the end of wars and lose the prospect of plunder. This meant large standing-armies came into being.

And if they owed loyalty to rival generals, then the consequences were obvious.

Rome also suffered from having an enormous mob (some 320,000 by Caesar's time), paid for by the city with grants of free corn. Its existence had been caused by the dispossession of smallholders throughout Italy by the ancient equivalent of agribusiness – landholders who had made their wealth through war and the extortionate tax-farming of provinces, and who had, by the same means, acquired large numbers of slaves who worked the land for free. These smallholders had flocked to Rome but there was no work for them there, as the urban economy was also slave-based.

All these fundamental flaws in the constitution and state of Rome came to a head with

Marius and Sulla. Marius was elected consul an unprecedented five times between 105 and 101 BC, having already held the post in 107. The Cimbri and Teutoni, two powerful German tribes, had already defeated three Roman armies, and were threatening to advance on Rome. Marius destroyed the Cimbri at Aquae Sextae (Aix-en-Provence) and the Tentoni Vercellae. He then disbanded his army, but the Senate did not honour his promises of land to his men. This naturally led to extreme disgruntlement on his part, and he entered politics on the side of the *Populares* (the People's Party). On his re-election as consul in 101 BC, he introduced laws to ensure that his veterans received land and also claimed further colonies in northern Italy and Gaul to settle them. He also enfranchised the Italian population (many of his soldiers were

Italians rather than Romans), which theoretically diluted the power of the Roman populace. This last measure was not well received by the *Optimates* (the 'best' people's party), a conservative, aristocratic group. The *equites*, the 'knights' who comprised the rich merchant-class and who monopolized tax-farming and agribusiness, ceased to support the *Populares*. The Roman population did not like Marius's reforms either. The result in 99 BC was rioting, murder and general disorder, including the murder of a consular candidate. Marius was temporarily made dictator. He suppressed the rioting and then left for the East, realizing he had the support of none of the parties in Rome.

In 91 BC trouble flared up again with the murder of Livius Drusus, a tribune. Rome's Italian allies, disgusted at the increasingly

Julius Caesar

Roman foot soldiers

outrageous state of Roman politics, rebelled. Rome immediately offered full citizenship-rights to those states that abandoned the revolt, known as the Social War, and sent two consular armies against the others. The legates (seconds in command) were Marius and Sulla. When the rebellion was nearly extinguished, Sulla was given the task of subduing Pontus (a kingdom on the north coast of modern Turkey) where Mithridates VI, the king, had taken the opportunity to overrun Roman possessions and kill all the Roman tax-collectors there. Marius, though, wanted to take over from Sulla so that he could reap the benefits of conquering Pontus. With the help of P. Sulpicius Rufus, a corrupt tribune, Marius had a law passed appointing him to command the campaign. But Sulla was in an invulnerable position and refused to obey the Senate's order that he

hand his army over. And Sulla's men, recruited under Marius's volunteer system,
were loyal to their general, not Rome, and
as keen as Sulla to plunder Pontus. Sulla
marched on Rome and occupied it. Marius
fled and his laws were repealed. Consular
elections were held and L. Cornelius Cinna
and Gnaeus Octavius were elected in 87 BC.
Sulla did not fully trust Cinna, but nonetheless left Rome for the East.

Virtually as soon as Sulla was gone, Cinna
contacted Marius, who raised an army of
slaves and brigands and seized Ostia, the port
of Rome, thereby cutting off its food supply.
Octavius's soldiers deserted to Marius and
Cinna, and these two then seized Rome. An
orgy of terror then ensued as Marius's men
went on the rampage and slaughtered their
enemies. Marius and Cinna then declared

themselves consuls for 86 BC. They reversed
Sulla's legislation, confiscated his property
and caused his family to flee to Greece.
Marius then died, shortly into his seventh
consulship.

Sulla meanwhile carried on his campaign
against Mithridates, successfully concluding
the war in 85 BC. He had reaped untold
riches from the campaign: after paying
himself and his soldiers, he still contributed
15,000 pounds of gold and 115,000 pounds
of silver to the Roman treasury. He now
announced that he would be returning to
Rome, and landed unopposed at Brundisium
(Brindisi) in early 83 BC. He was joined by
many *optimates*, including M. Licinius Crassus and Gnaeus Pompeius – Pompey the
Great. Sulla defeated Marius the Younger,
Marius's son and the other Marian generals.

(Cinna had perished in a mutiny, trying to persuade an army to go to Greece to prevent Sulla returning to Italy.)

When Sulla retook Rome he began a systematic programme of exterminating his opponents by proscription, slaughtering several thousand senators, exconsuls and knights. He seized their property and distributed it among 120,000 of his soldiers. Some Italian states lost their Roman citizenship and others were ravaged as punishment. Sulla also formed a bodyguard from 10,000 freed slaves, a forerunner of the Praetorian Guard. He then had the Senate declare him dictator for life, effectively making himself king in all but name, thus paving the way for Julius Caesar and Augustus. Much of the system he left untouched, apart from making it impossible for consuls, praetors and tribunes to be re-elected within ten years of holding their posts. The governors of the provinces were also forbidden to leave their provinces or go to war without the approval of the Senate.

Julius Caesar was lucky to survive this period: his aunt had been married to Marius and he was a recognized member of the Marian party. It was only through the intercession of the Vestal Virgins that he survived.

THE 'GREAT' RIVAL

Sulla died in 78 BC, having resigned the dictatorship. Almost instantly, Rome subsided into chaos again. Q. Lutatius Catulus and M. Aemilius Lepidus were the consuls in 78 BC. Lepidus wanted to restore the fortunes of the Marian party. This encouraged the Italian states, and one, Etruria, which had lost Roman citizenship under Sulla, rebelled, throwing out those veterans of Sulla's army who had been settled there. The Senate ordered Lepidus to crush the rebellion, but instead he switched sides and marched his army on Rome. In desperation, the Senate called on Pompey to defend it.

In short order, Pompey took to the field and defeated Lepidus, but failed to stop him and his army escaping to Sardinia. Lepidus died shortly thereafter and his army then sailed to Spain under Vento Perpenna to join Sertorius, an able Marian general, who was in effective control of the province. Pompey left for Spain in late 77 BC, crossing the Pyrenees in early 76 BC. As with so many campaigns in Spain, it was a guerrilla war, and Pompey only really achieved victory in 72 BC with the assassination of Sertorius at the instigation of Perpenna.

Pompey's star glowed more brightly, though, with the Spartacus Revolt. Spartacus, a Thracian gladiator, had escaped with seventy comrades from gladiatorial school in Capua. He and his followers sheltered in the crater of Mount Vesuvius, where they were joined by many escaped slaves and other criminals. Soldiers were sent against them, but were defeated, which encouraged many malcontents to join the revolt. Spartacus eventually commanded 70,000 men. A consular army was defeated and the Senate had to call on Crassus, who was a praetor in 72 BC, to raise six new legions to destroy Spartacus's army. Crassus managed to hem Spartacus in the toe of Italy and then defeated him in Lucania. Pompey's army met up with fugitives from this battle and wiped them out. Crassus meanwhile crucified 6,000 captives along the Appian Way between Capua and Rome. This left two armies in Italy, Pompey's and Crassus's, but

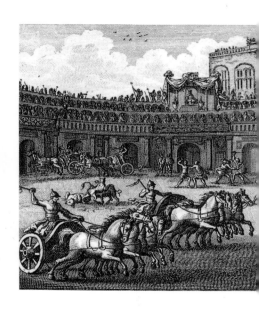

Caesar was responsible for the public games

The luxuries of the imperial court

despite the personal dislike of the two men for each other, they did not want to fight a civil war. Crassus, an immensely rich man, had the support of the Senate, half of whom owed him money, and Pompey had the support of the people for his successes in the field. The two men camped their armies outside Rome until they were elected consuls. They successfully disbanded their armies, and proceeded to reverse the legislation of Sulla. Both men retired when their consulships terminated at the end of 70 BC.

Pompey then spent the next two years in private life before coming up with a plan that would restore his fortunes. Because of the chronic strife in Rome, piracy in the Mediterranean had become a major problem: pirates had banded together and had a fleet of 1,000, with headquarters in Crete and Cilicia (south-eastern Turkey). They were strong enough to attack coastal towns and kidnap locals for ransom. More importantly, they threatened the corn supply to Rome, which was transported from Sicily, Sardinia and the northern coast of Africa. Because shortages of corn had been the cause of much unrest in Rome, the pirates had become a major political issue. Pompey had a supporter propose in the Assembly that a dictator of the seas be appointed, to command 200 ships, with responsibility for the whole Mediterranean. This would have been the largest command ever held by a Roman general. The Senate opposed this, guessing correctly who expected to be the appointee, but the people forced Pompey's election. Pompey immediately proposed that the fleet be increased to 500 and that he receive an army of 120,000. This bill was carried and the price of grain fell. Pompey then set sail and, within three months, swept the pirates from the sea.

He finished his campaign in the eastern Mediterranean and then took over there from two ineffectual consuls who were struggling with Mithridates. Within two years, Pompey had taken Syria and Pontus and Jerusalem, and had effectively created a lasting eastern empire for the Romans. He returned to Italy in triumph at the end of 62 BC, having promised to generously reward his men with land and money. The Senate quaked at news of his approach, but Pompey disbanded his army. The Senate refused to ratify any of the grants of land that Pompey had made. Caesar would not repeat this mistake.

THE MANTLE
OF THE GODS

The family of Gaius Julius Caesar was an ancient one. It was patrician, and as such mostly supported the *optimates*, but Julius was a *popularis* due to his aunt Julia having married Marius. Caesar's tutor was M. Antonius Gnipho, a well-educated Gaul, who passed on his knowledge of Roman and Greek culture to his able student. Caesar's first post was that of *flamen dialis* (Priest of Jupiter), to which he was appointed by

Marius and Cinna in 84 BC. He also married Cinna's daughter Cornelia, to cement the families' political relationship.

On Sulla's return, Caesar was lucky to escape with his life. Sulla had ordered Pompey and Caesar to divorce their wives, but Caesar refused. Suetonius, writing 150 years later, but with access to contemporary records, has it that Sulla predicted that Caesar would be the ruin of the *optimates*, being much greater than Marius. Shortly after his near-fatal encounter with Sulla, Caesar obviously thought it wise to put some distance between himself and Rome. He joined the staff of Minucius Thermus, the praetor in Bithynia (north-western Turkey), in 81 BC. During this period, he received a civic crown for saving a soldier's life at the siege of Mitylene. He then moved to Cilicia for a brief period

under the consul Servilius Isauricus, returning to Italy only when he heard that Sulla
had died. He toyed with the idea of joining
Lepidus in his rebellion but wisely thought
better of it.

Back in Rome, Caesar decided to establish a
reputation as a jurist, and acted for the
prosecution in the case of C. Cornelius
Dolabella, laying a charge of extortion.
Although Dolabella was acquitted, Caesar's
eloquence gained him many admirers. To
polish his rhetorical skills, he left Italy in 75
BC for Rhodes to study under Apollonius
Molon. On his way there an incident occurred that illustrates his character. He was
captured by pirates. They proposed a ransom
of twenty talents, which Caesar told them
was too small a sum – he was worth at least
fifty. He stayed with the pirates for six weeks,

A Roman provincial town

A Roman general's tunic

waiting for the ransom to arrive. During that period he bantered with them, saying that he would return and crucify them (the standard punishment for piracy) as soon as he was free. Once out of their hands, he hired some galleys with crews, returned, and captured the pirates, regaining his ransom and other booty besides. He then kept his word and crucified his prisoners; not being vindictive, he had their throats cut so that they would not suffer a lingering death.

Little is known of the next few years. He was involved in the Third Mithridatic War with some success, being elected a military tribune on his return to Rome – the first example of public recognition in his life. In 69 BC he was elected quaestor, and in 68 BC he was on the staff of C. Antistius Vetus, praetor of Further Spain. While in Spain, at Gades (Cadiz), he saw a statue of Alexander the Great; reflecting on his comparatively slow progress, he decided to return to Rome to seek greater opportunities. *En route*, he took up the cause of the Transpadane Gauls, who were seeking full Roman citizenship. When back in Rome, he married Pompeia, Sulla's granddaughter. She was a rich heiress and this was a great inducement to an aspiring politician; also, it may have indicated that Caesar wished to conciliate the *optimates*.

Crassus now sought out the political aid of Caesar; although he was immensely rich, he was not particularly popular. Caesar was quite popular because he had supported Pompey in his eastern ventures, but needed money to pay for the games he would have to put on if he were to become an aedile. In 66 BC, Crassus was elected censor; and Caesar, aedile. Caesar then proceeded to put on spectacular games, surpassing in scale and expense any that had gone before, presumably using Crassus's money. The result was a great increase in his popularity. Crassus meanwhile proposed granting the Transpadane Gauls their citizenship. This was opposed, but Crassus knew it would make allies for him of the Transpadanes. He also proposed the annexation of Egypt, which usually had a large corn surplus. It would have given Caesar a reasonable pretext for raising an army. But, since Pompey had secured grain supplies by defeating the pirates, there was little interest in this project, and the knights had enough to plunder in the new provinces he had added in the east.

Crassus and Caesar then attempted to revive the scheme by getting two of their supporters, Catiline and Caius Antonius, elected consuls in 65 BC. Catiline had led a conspiracy to murder the consuls of 66 BC; he had only been absolved by the Senate on Crassus's intervention. Catiline was violently opposed by Cicero, who was elected instead with Antonius. This virtually put an end to the scheme: Cicero was adamantly against it and able to persuade the Senate to reject it in whatever guise it was presented. But Caesar was elected Pontifex Maximus, a life position.

The consular elections for 62 BC were held in October 63 BC. Catiline was now desperate to be elected consul as he had run up spectacular debts; if he was not elected, he would attempt a *coup d'état*. He hoped to call upon others in a similar situation to his own. When he was again not elected, he imme-

diately put his plan into action. His colleague
Gaius Manlius was to lead a revolt in Etruria,
where most of Sulla's men had settled, and P.
Cornelius Lentulus was to seize Rome.
Cicero heard of the scheme from the mis-
tress of one of the conspirators – and from
Crassus and Caesar, who were eager to
distance themselves from the conspirators –
and convened the Senate, which granted
him the power to raise an army to defeat
the rebels. Manlius rebelled, Catiline fled to
join him in Etruria, and the slaves in Capua
and Apulia revolted. Lentulus was arrested.
Caesar then argued clemency for the rebels
but was opposed by Cato, who won the
support of the Senate. Cicero had Lentulus
and his accomplices strangled without trial.
News of their deaths disheartened the rebels
and Manlius's army shrank from 12,000 to
3,000. It was cornered and destroyed by

Cicero, and Catiline's head was sent back
to Rome for display.

Caesar became praetor in 62 BC, and was
appointed propraetor of Further Spain at the
end of his praetorship. This was his first
independent military command, and he
made the most of it. In summer 61 BC he
set off, after Crassus had settled most of his
debts (25 million sesterces). Immediately he
took the field, suppressing the local tribes in
Lusitania (Portugal), and sending the booty
back to Rome. At the end of his propraetor-
ship he went back to Rome to seek a
consulship. His popularity was almost
bound to ensure his election. To become
consul, Caesar had to enter Rome; but to
receive a triumph (a celebratory parade to
mark military successes), a general had to
remain outside Rome until granted the right

to retain his *imperium* within the city. The Senate, rather than viewing Caesar as a counterbalance to Pompey, rejected his request for permission to enter the consular race by registering by proxy. The Senate also made sure that M. Calpurnius Bibulus was elected – he was an enemy of Caesar – and converted the Civil Department of Forests and Cattle Drifts into a joint consular province, thereby depriving Caesar of the normal consular income.

Caesar immediately began talks with the disgruntled Pompey, whose men had not received the land he had promised them because of the hostility of the Senate. Caesar co-opted Crassus, and the first triumvirate came into being. Crassus had money; Caesar, popularity; and Pompey, soldiers – a potent combination. Caesar then proposed a bill to ensure that Pompey's men received their promised reward: in the Senate, Cato began to obstruct the bill. Caesar had him dragged out of the Senate; but when other senators followed, he adjourned the Senate and put the measure to the people. He knew he had popular support and Pompey had secretly arranged for some of his veterans to be present at the Assembly in the Forum. Crassus and Pompey spoke for the bill, but the tribunes vetoed it. In the ensuring uproar, Pompey's soldiers cleared the opposition from the Forum, a bucket of dung was poured over Bibulus, and the bill was passed. The Senate was completely wrongfooted by the triumvirate, whose existence it had been unaware of, and they could not get Bibulus to crush it as he had no soldiers.

Caesar now prepared for the next stage of his career, the acquisition of a province. Through his placemen, he was allotted Cisalpine Gaul and Illyricum (Yugoslavia). By a stroke of good fortune, the new governor of Transalpine Gaul died and Caesar was granted this governorship as well. Because of his control of the Senate, he ensured too that his proconsulship was for five years instead of the usual two. Before leaving, he dealt with his opponents: it was made a retrospective crime to execute suspects without trial, as Cicero had done with Lentulus. Cicero fled into exile. To deal with Cato and other senatorial opposition, Caesar ensured that Publius Clodius, an odious and ruthless patrician was appointed a tribune.

Caesar now heard that the Helvetii (a Swiss

tribe) were about to migrate into Gaul. With Titus Labienus, he raced off to Geneva. Fortune beckoned and Caesar answered her call.

Caesar crosses the Rubicon

A Roman centurion's helmet

GALLIC VICTORY

Gaul in Caesar's time extended from the Province (Provence) to the North Sea, including parts of modern Switzerland, Belgium and Holland. It was populated by Celtic tribes, from two to three hundred of them, and was considered quite a rich area at the time. It was semi-civilized, farming and trading with many other lands. Central control by chiefs was not very efficient, as every village had its own interests. The only unifying factor was the

Druids, who elected a Chief Druid for life.
The Druids met once a year, when they
would often adjudicate on tribal disputes.
The nobles spent much of their time attacking other tribes.

The Germans were much tougher: they
despised the agricultural life, considering it
too peaceful and sedentary. They preferred
hunting and war. They considered raiding
and plundering as healthy exercise. They
were also excellent horsemen, which gave
them great mobility for surprise attacks,
though they often fought on foot.

The Helvetii, a people numbering some
368,000, including 92,000 warriors, according to Caesar, wanted to leave western
Switzerland as they were worried about
the presence of Ariovistus, a successful Ger-

man war-lord, who had established himself
in Gaul by defeating several Gallic tribes.
They wanted to move to western Gaul, to an
area bordering that of the Tolosates (who
lived round modern Toulouse). This posed a
threat to the Province. He managed to
prevent the Helvetii crossing at Geneva,
whereupon they headed for a northern
route via the territory of the Aedui, a tribe
friendly to Rome, and the Sequani. Caesar
pursued them with five legions and some
Gallic cavalry under Dumnorix. He managed to bring them to battle: the battle was
conclusive as Caesar seized the supplies of
the Helvetii and the 130,000 survivors had to
surrender. Caesar ordered them to return to
their lands as he did not wish a tempting
vacuum to be left open to greedy Germans.

The Gauls were greatly impressed by Cae-

sar's success. The tribal chiefs, with Diviciacus, the Chief Druid, as their spokesman,
appealed to Caesar to rid them of the scourge
of Ariovistus. This project met his approval
as German tribes, such as the Cimbri and
Teutoni, frequently irrupted into Gaul,
sometimes travelling as far as Italy. He
approached Ariovistus for a parley, but this
was rejected. He then sent an ultimatum
forbidding Germans to cross the Rhine, to
which Ariovistus replied that he would do as
he pleased. News also arrived that the Suebi,
another German tribe, were gathering and
would be joining Ariovistus. Caesar had to
move fast. He now heard that Ariovistus
intended seizing Vesontio (Besançon),
which was well fortified and supplied; by
forced marches, he beat Ariovistus to it. The
two armies then circled warily around one
another, until Ariovistus began to run out of

POMPEY'S HEAD
shewn to Cæsar.

Pompey's head is shown to Caesar

Caesar returns to Rome triumphant

supplies and offered battle. The Romans managed to destroy the left wing of the enemy, but then their own began to fall back. Publius Crassus, Crassus's son, restored the situation and the Germans fled back to the Rhine. A few, including Ariovistus, managed to get across, while the rest were slaughtered by Caesar's cavalry. It was a stunning victory. As soon as the Suebi heard of it, they scurried back to their homes. At the end of 58 BC, Caesar headed off for Cisalpine Gaul to deal with his administrative responsibilities there, and to be in closer touch with events in Rome.

In the north of Gaul, the Belgae, a part-Germanic tribe, were growing alarmed by developments to the south. They feared, with good reason, that they were next in line for being pacified, and had no intention of losing their independence. Accordingly, they prepared for war. As soon as Caesar heard of this, he took two new legions north to Vesontio. After he had ensured his food supply, he quickly moved north to the Marne, the southern border of Belgae territory. There, the Remi, a tribe living round Reims, under the control of another tribe, the Suessiones, sought protection from this unexpected deliverer, and this was granted. The Remi told Caesar that the other Belgic tribes were ready for war and were being joined by Germans from over the Rhine. Galba, king of the Suessiones, was in command of over 300,000 warriors, including 60,000 Bellovaci, 50,000 Suessiones and 50,000 Nervii, the last of whom were actually trained.

The campaign began with much skirmishing

as the Belgae ravaged the lands of the Remi
until Caesar drove them off. He also asked
Diviciacus to attack the home territory of the
Bellovaci, and this threat caused the latter's
departure from the Belgic army. The two
armies then sat facing each other, separated
by a marsh which neither wanted to be first
across. Eventually the Belgae withdrew as
supplies ran low, promising to gather again
to protect any tribe that might come under
threat. As soon as Caesar realized their
withdrawal was not a ruse, he began to
pursue them and seized Noviodunum
(Pommiers) from the Suessiones. He then
took Bratuspantium from the Bellovaci.
Shortly afterwards, Caesar was nearly am-
bushed successfully by the Nervii, the Atre-
bates and the Viromandui while setting up
camp. Luckily, his men were sufficiently
disciplined to resist and Labienus saw what

was happening and led his legion, which had been capturing the enemy camp, back into the rear of the Nervii, who were wiped out. Shortly afterwards, the other Belgae surrendered, while Publius Crassus suppressed the tribes on the Atlantic coast.

Caesar returned to Italy where he was voted a fifteen days' thanksgiving, an unprecedented honour.

56 BC opened with bad news. The Veneti, a tribe of skilful seamen, who had a virtual monopoly of trade with Britain, heard that Caesar was contemplating an invasion, which would ruin them. The Britons were also aware of this potential threat and, the previous year, had sent contingents to Gaul to help in the struggle against the Romans. In the previous year, the Veneti had surrendered

hostages to the Romans after their defeat;
now they seized Roman corn collectors sent
out by Publius Crassus, so as to have something to swap for their own hostages before
they went to war. By doing so, they played
into Caesar's hands: he knew he would have
to completely subjugate them if he wanted
control of the Channel and a safe base in
northern France and Brittany, and this was a
perfect cause for war. He ordered a fleet to be
built and set about reducing their towns – no
easy task as many were virtually surrounded
by sea, and impregnable when the tide was in.
Eventually the Veneti took to the sea in about
220 ships. The Romans were initially non-
plussed as to how to deal with them – the
Veneti's craft were much more seaworthy
than the Roman galleys, and too strongly
built to be affected by the galleys' rams. But
the Veneti did not use archers and their ships

were sail-powered. As the galleys were faster, they were able to draw alongside the Veneti's ships and, with a specially developed pole and hook, grapple on to their rigging and, with a bit of strenuous rowing, pull them overboard, rendering the Veneti helpless. When a fortuitous calm fell, the Veneti were totally at their mercy, and their ships succumbed. Without ships, the Veneti had to surrender. Caesar put the Veneti's senate to death, saying that the corn collectors had been ambassadors, and sold the population as slaves.

The following year, 55 BC, two tribes displaced by the Suebi, the Usipetes and the Tencteri, moved into Belgic territory, where they were welcomed. This posed a major threat to peace in Gaul and Caesar realized he would have to nip it in the bud. He caught up with the German army and

C.CAESAR.DICT.PERPETVO.

JULIUS CÆSAR,
Founder of ye Roman Empire,
was born at Rome, reigned
3 Years, 11 Months, 15 Days,
was kill'd 44 Years before CHRIST.

Julius Caesar, Roman Emperor

The Emperor at recreation

ordered it to return over the Rhine, offering at the same time to settle it in the territory of a friendly tribe, the Ubii. During a day's truce, to give the two German tribes time to discuss the proposal, Caesar's Gallic cavalry, some 5,000 men, were attacked and dispersed by 800 Germans. The following day, a large delegation of German chiefs arrived at Caesar's camp to apologise for breaking the truce. Caesar immediately seized the lot of them, and rushed out with his troops to the German camp, eight miles away. The German warriors were astonished to see them and, leaderless, panicked. The legionaries slaughtered all whom they found in the camp – the Germans had not even taken up arms – while the cavalry pursued the women and children who had managed to escape. They did not get far, for they soon reached the point where the Meuse joins the

Rhine, which was impassable. Those not
already cut down were to drown in the
river. Caesar followed this up by building
a bridge over the Rhine and devastating the
lands of the Sugambri, who had given shelter
to the Usipetes' and Tencteri's cavalry.

Despite the lateness of the campaigning
season, Caesar decided he still had time to
invade Britain, and set of at the end of
August, landing between Walmer and
Deal. The Britons resisted the landings
unsuccessfully, but Caesar did not have the
time or the men to properly subdue them.
He took some hostages after besting the
Britons in several minor battles, but in
mid-September decided to return to Gaul
before the weather got worse. He then
returned to Italy, having ordered the building of a fleet of special transports that could

be loaded and beached more easily (several unbeached ships had been destroyed in a gale the previous summer) and more galleys. In the spring of 54 BC he returned to Portus Itius (Wissant) where he ordered the Gallic chieftains to present themselves, which they duly did; he then took them hostage, apart from Dumnorix, who escaped, but was pursued and killed. He then set out with 800 ships for Britain. The size of the fleet completely terrified the Britons and they fled inland. But defeating them was not as easy as expected, because their leader, Cassivellaunus, was extremely resourceful, resorting to guerrilla warfare. Caesar eventually wore him down, and he surrendered, promising hostages and tribute. The promises were worthless, being unenforceable, the minute Caesar left British shores.

While Caesar had been away in Britain, the Gallic chieftains began to plot how to throw out the Romans. Caesar's legionary camps were scattered in the territory of the Belgae, unable to come to each other's aid quickly. Ambiorix, chief of the Eburones, exploited this and managed to lure out and ambush the garrison of one, virtually wiping it out. The Nervii and the Aduataci were inspired by Ambiorix's success and laid siege to one of the other camps – they had learned well from their Roman conquerors the art of siegecraft. Caesar managed to drive off this assault. He then attempted to pursue Ambiorix, but the latter always managed to evade him, fleeing to the German forests which were too dangerous for the legionaries. Caesar managed to destroy the crops and homes of the Eburones and had one rebel leader flogged to death, but he did not end the revolt.

It blew up again the following year, when Roman corn-traders were massacred in Cenabum (Orleans) by the chiefs of the Carnutes, Cotuatus and Conconnetodumnus. Within hours, the news was relayed to Vercingetorix, a chief of the Arverni. He immediately set about preparing for war, rousing the other tribes, some of whom he sent to attack the Ruteni, a tribe just outside the Province. Caesar was cut off from his legions as he had been in Italy, but managed to traverse the snow-bound Cevennes, and put together a makeshift army which he led to the territory of the Arverni (now, in turn, cut off to the south). The Arverni now called off the attack on the Ruteni and moved north. But Caesar was ahead of them and managed to surprise and sack Orleans. He then besieged Avaricum (Bourges), the capital of the Bituriges, allies of Vercingetorix.

After a hard-fought siege, the town was taken and its population massacred. The Gauls had practised a scorched-earth policy to impede the Roman advance, but, because of the capture of Avaricum, Caesar was able to replenish his supplies and pursue Vercingetorix to his capital, Gergovia. Gergovia was sited on a 1,200 foot hilltop; the town was walled and the hill steeply sloped, and Caesar was unable to capture it and had to withdraw. Vercingetorix then assembled the Gallic chieftains and was elected supreme commander. He decided to move to Alesia (Mount Auxois) to gather his forces. Caesar pursued him there and built 25 miles of earthworks to hem Vercingetorix in. A relieving army was unable to dislodge the Romans and eventually the gauls were beaten. In their flight, they were slaughtered in large numbers. Vercingetorix sur-

Caesar is assassinated in the Senate

Public grieving at Caesar's funeral

rendered to Caesar. Caesar imposed the relatively light tribute of 40 million sesterces on the Gauls. He also allowed the Gauls to retain their existing forms of government, and released many prisoners: his clemency was motivated by the idea of winning the Gauls' loyalty. Apart from mopping up, the revolt was at an end.

THE CIVIL WAR

While Caesar had been in Gaul, events in
Rome had led to a resurgence of chaos.
Pompey and Crassus were unwilling allies,
and neither had the military forces to control
the city. Consequently, the city was under
the sway of Publius Clodius and Titus
Annius Milo, with their 'Blue' and 'Green'
factions, respectively supporters of Caesar
and Pompey. In 57 BC a new consul,
Lentulus Spinther, proposed Cicero's recall. With the support of Pompey, Cicero

returned. Cicero proposed that Pompey be given control of Rome's corn supply and an army and fleet to secure this. He also tried to break up the triumvirate by advocating that Caesar's laws be repealed. But Pompey and Crassus knew how powerful the triumvirate was as a group and met Caesar at Luca, where they agreed that Pompey and Crassus should be consuls for 55 BC and thereafter be assigned the important provinces of Spain and Syria. Caesar's governorship of Gaul was to be extended by five years. Not surprisingly, when Cicero heard this news, he tacked around and proposed a thanksgiving service for Caesar's victories.

Crassus and Pompey ensured that the measures confirming the triumvirate's decisions were enacted through a mixture of violence and bribery. Even so, the consuls elected were Domitius Ahenobarbus and Appius Claudius, opponents of the two leading triumvirs.

In November 54 BC, Crassus left for Syria. In May 53 BC he was defeated at Carrhae, the worst defeat for the Roman army since Cannae (against Hannibal), and killed. This ended the triumvirate. Also Pompey's wife, Julia, Caesar's sister, had died, thus snapping the family bond between the two men.

In Rome, political violence continued: Clodius was murdered by Milo in a brawl, the Senate was burned to the ground and senators were struck down. To restore order, Pompey was elected sole consul. Caesar was in a difficult position. If he wished to become a consul he would first have to become a private citizen again, and this would expose

The ruins of the Colosseum in modern Rome

Shakespeare's dramatization of Julius Caesar

him to prosecution for acts he had committed during his first consulship. The Senate was also agitating for successors to be appointed to Caesar's governorships. This would lead to him being without an army and put him in a very weak position. To prevent this, he bribed Gaius Scribonius Curio to veto any hostile legislation being passed. His faction was not strong enough, though, to prolong his governorships. Finally, when Curio's tribuneship was about to expire, Caesar sent an ultimatum to the consuls, Lucius Cornelius Lentulus and Gaius Claudius Marcellus, that he would return if Pompey were to disband his troops at the same time as he did. Caesar also ensured that Mark Antony and Quintus Cassius, two supporters, were elected tribunes, through bribery. Mark Antony and Cassius were thrown out of the Senate and fled to join Caesar in Ravenna. The Senate then proscribed Caesar. They thought he would await the arrival of his legions stationed in Gaul, but Caesar was always one for striking hard and fast.

Caesar gave the order to march, ordering his men to occupy Ariminum (Rimini). *En route* was the Rubicon, the border between Cisalpine Gaul, his territory, and Roman Italy. Apparently he stopped at the stream, lost in thought. He is reported to have said, 'Comrades, if I stop here, it will be the beginning of my sorrows; if I cross over, it will be such for all mankind.' Civil war was an appalling thought. He began to cross on 10 January 50 BC.

Pompey had more legions but Caesar had more prestige, with his recent conquest of

Gaul. He also understood that in a civil war it is vital to win the support of the populace. This would help him gain the upper hand and also demoralize enemy troops, who could provide a rich recruiting ground, especially if their cause was not clearly winning.

In the event, Pompey abandoned Rome, knowing that he could still count on the support of his legions in Spain, Macedonia and the East, but not on that of his legions in Italy. Rome was thrown into uproar and panic on Caesar's approach. Caesar ignored Rome as he wanted to bring Pompey to battle before he could escape to Macedonia. He spared the leaders of Pompeian garrisons, even allowing them to keep their property, and his invasion was almost bloodless. He just failed to trap Pompey in Brundisium

(Brindisi). Returning to Rome, he reassured the Senate of his good intentions and prepared to pursue the war abroad. In Spain, he managed to surround the Pompeian army and cause its surrender almost without any bloodshed. He then disbanded it, and returned to Rome, where he had been made dictator in his absence. As this was unconstitutional, Caesar had himself elected consul and settled affairs in Rome for the coming year.

Caesar then pursued Pompey over the Adriatic. Pompey did not expect Caesar to cross at this stage. Caesar's admiral, C. Cornelius Dolabella, had been defeated by Scribonius Libo and Marcus Octavius, and the remains of his fleet were no match for Pompey's. The bold step was to sail, even though he was virtually unprotected, so as to

surprise his enemy and this step Caesar took.
He then laid siege to Pompey in Dyrrachium
(Durres, Albania) on the coast, so as to
deprive him of an important naval base
and open up the Adriatic to his troop
transports. As Pompey had command of
the sea, he was able to circumvent Caesar's
work and gain access to supplies. An inconclusive battle was fought: Caesar's troops
were routed, but luckily Pompey did not
pursue. Labienus, a lieutenant of Pompey's,
killed all the prisoners.

Caesar's army managed to escape successfully
and, more by luck than judgement, met up
with Domitius Calvinus, who had been
dispatched with two legions to contain
Metellus Scipio in Macedonia. Pompey
marched to Scipio's aid, apparently with
the aim of waging a war of attrition against

Caesar, but he was persuaded to seek battle. At Pharsalus (Fersala, Greece) the two armies met. Pompey's was riven with disputes over how to divide the spoils of victory, whereas Caesar's was refreshed, having retreated to the fertile fields of Thessaly. Caesar had 22,000 men, Pompey 45,000. Pompey tried to outflank the right wing of Caesar's army with his cavalry, but Caesar spotted this ploy and hid six cohorts of infantry behind his own cavalry. When Pompey's cavalry charged, they broke on the ranks of infantry and, in their retreat, disordered and abandoned their supporting light infantry, who fled in panic. The six cohorts then turned in on Pompey's line, already engaged with Caesar's, and put it to flight. The battle was effectively over.

Pompey went to Egypt and requested the

king, Ptolemy XIII, to protect him. Ptolemy was at war with his sister, Cleopatra VII. By a ruse, Ptolemy lured Pompey ashore and had him murdered and beheaded. When Caesar arrived, Ptolemy had the head presented to him. According to Plutarch, Caesar was disgusted and wept.

Instead of returning to Italy and ending the Civil War, Caesar now decided, rather quixotically, to sort out the Egyptian Civil War. This episode lasted eight months, longer than the conquest of Italy and Spain, or the campaign in Greece.

Caesar's absence from Italy was leading to a resurgence of unrest and a decline in authority. Elsewhere, Pharnaces, son of Mithridates the Great, had overrun Armenia Minor and Cappadocia. The two states appealed for help and Domitius Calvinus, now stationed in Pontus, responded. Pharnaces defeated the Romans and their allies, and Caesar rushed to Pontus to stop the rot. At the Battle of Zela (Zilleh, Turkey), Caesar destroyed Pharnaces's army, and uttered the immortal words, '*Veni, vidi, vici*'.

Caesar was now supreme in the Roman world.

A GOD ON EARTH

On landing at Tarentum (Taranto, Italy) in September 47 BC, Caesar found he had been elected dictator for the second time. Back in Rome, he restored the Senate to its normal size, and placated those who were expecting to be rewarded at the expense of the Pompeians. Discipline in the army was collapsing, as his soldiers had not been paid their prize money or discharged. Eventually they camped outside Rome, where Caesar shamed them into line, by addressing them as citi-

JULIUS CAESAR

zens, not soldiers. He needed them for his next campaign in Africa, where Cato, Scipio, Pompey's two sons, Gnaeus and Sextus, and others, had raised the Pompeian standard. The delay in sorting out problems in Rome had allowed them to accumulate a considerable force – ten legions – allied to the four legions of King Juba of Numidia (Algeria). They had laid in stores and fortified the towns.

Fortunately for Caesar, they had also alienated the local population by seizing goods, and King Juba had angered Bocchus and Bogud, the kings of Mauritania (Morocco). Scipio also ignored Cato's wise advice to wear Caesar down by endless marching, rather than face him in battle with his untested recruits. Even so, at one battle, Labienus nearly succeeded in destroying Caesar's army, and it is not clear how Caesar escaped. Caesar retired to Ruspina (Monastir, Tunisia), fortified it and sent for reinforcements. Scipio and Labienus camped outside, awaiting the arrival of Juba. Supplies ran low in Ruspina, and Caesar became more and more impatient of rescue. At the end of January 46 BC, a corn fleet arrived, followed by a troop convoy ferrying two legions from Sicily. Juba aborted his attempt to link up with the Pompeians, as Bocchus had taken advantage of his absence to destroy and plunder the richest town in Numidia. Two more legions arrived shortly after. Caesar decided to break out of Ruspina. Near Thapsus (between Sfax and Sousse in Tunisia) the two armies collided. Scipio had been rejoined by Juba with his Numidian cavalry and elephants. After a few days' manoeuvring, the armies drew up in lines of battle. For some reason, Scipio's front line

did not organize itself in a disciplined way.
Caesar's troops could not restrain themselves: they rushed forwards, against orders.
Caesar's archers and slingers assaulted the
elephants, which were terrified, wheeling
round and trampling on their own troops.
The Numidian cavalry panicked, and, within minutes, Scipio's army had become a
terrified, fleeing rabble. Caesar's troops, be-
side themselves with blood-lust, pursued and
massacred them. For the loss of about 50
Caesarians, 10,000 Pompeians are said to
have died. The Pompeian generals escaped
only to perish shortly thereafter, with only
Labienus living to fight another day.

On his return to Rome, Caesar promised
clemency, and proceeded to lay on extraordinary and lavish games. His power was
absolute.

Trouble now broke out in Spain, where Gnaeus and Sextus Pompey commanded several legions. Caesar travelled there as quickly as possible and eventually brought them to battle at Munda (site unknown), and after a particularly hard-fought struggle, prevailed. Labienus was finally killed and, shortly afterwards, Gnaeus Pompey was hunted down and beheaded. All opposition was at an end.

After Munda, Caesar received a fifty days' thanksgiving and received the title of imperator (supreme commander) for life. He was deified and elected consul for ten years. He shared power with no one, needing no one's support. He was incredibly rich from the spoils of his campaigns, so he could bribe anybody and everybody, and he had a loyal army behind him. He enlarged the Senate

JULIUS CAESAR

from 600 to 900, and packed it with his
supporters, including Gauls, which caused
great resentment. He gave Latin rights to
Spain, Sicily and Gaul, and reformed the
tax system in the East, so that it would not
be too oppressive. He ordered the establishment of colonies to settle his veterans. His
plans were equally monumental: the rebuilding of Carthage and Corinth, the defeat of the
Parthians, and the construction of vast mu-
nicipal buildings and temples in Rome itself.
He had also drawn up his will, leaving his
estate to his great-nephew Gaius Octavius
Thurinus, who adopted the name Gaius Julius
Caesar Octavianus, later to be Augustus.

A craven Senate fuelled his vanity by naming
him *Pater Patriae* (Father of the Country),
and putting his head on coins, usually a
monarch's right. He was declared a god.

They renamed the month of *Quintilis* (the fifth month), *Julius* (July). The title of king was offered to him at the *Lupercalia*, a festival in honour of Pan, but apparently he rejected it when the crowd did not seem to approve. The other side of all this flattery was the growth of a conspiracy, probably led by Cassius, and involving Marcus Brutus, two forgiven Pompeians, and about sixty others. The pretext for the conspiracy was tyrannicide. In fact, they probably wanted to restore the Senate to its previous power.

On the ides of March (15th), Caesar set out for the Senate. He was probably aware of the conspiracy, but relied on the senators' oath to protect him. Antony was detained at the entrance to the Senate and Decimus Brutus had placed some gladiators in the Theatre of Pompey in case Caesar was too well protected. Caesar entered the Senate and sat in the gilded regal chair that the senators had awarded him. Tullius Cimber approached him and appealed for the recall of his brother. Caesar refused this. Cimber grabbed his purple toga and exposed Caesar's neck. At this signal, C. Servilius Casca rushed forward and tried to stab Caesar in the throat, but missed, causing a minor wound in the neck. Cimber grabbed Caesar's hand but Caesar leapt forward and hurled Casca to the ground. The other murderers closed in while the senators watched, aghast. Caesar was stabbed twenty-three times.

Suetonius declares that, because of failing health, Caesar had no particular desire to prolong his life. His only fear was that his untimely death would lead to a civil war worse than that he had won.

LIFE AND TIMES

Julius Caesar
Hitler
Monet
Van Gogh
Beethoven
Mozart
Mother Teresa
Florence Nightingale
Anne Frank
Napoleon

LIFE AND TIMES

JFK
Martin Luther King
Marco Polo
Christopher Columbus
Stalin
William Shakespeare
Oscar Wilde
Castro
Gandhi
Einstein

FURTHER MINI SERIES
INCLUDE

HEROES OF THE WILD WEST

General Custer
Butch Cassidy and the Sundance Kid
Billy the Kid
Annie Oakley
Buffalo Bill
Geronimo
Wyatt Earp
Doc Holliday
Sitting Bull
Jesse James

LUX

HERE IS INFORMATION.

MOBILISE.

Selected writings by IAN WHITE

edited by Mike Sperlinger

Frontispiece: Ian White, *Trio A Practised Three Times on
the Beach*, photograph (2004) (from the installation, with Jimmy Robert,
6 things we couldn't do, but can do now, 2004)

Contents

Ian White performing *Hinterhof feat. James Richards Untitled Merchandise (Trade Urn), 2008*, KUB Arena, Kunsthaus Bregenz (2010)

Inevitably Making Sense: An Introduction to the Writing of Ian White

Mike Sperlinger

Anything made is a lie. I want to be a problem. A generous snare.
Ian White, from an unpublished notebook

I still remember being at the Tate Triennial in 2003 and hearing Ian White's voice on the soundtrack to Oliver Payne and Nick Relph's video *Gentlemen*, asking, rhetorically, 'Where do you end and Prince Charles begin?' The script was Payne and Relph's, but the voice was very much White's – an inimitable voice, witty, warm, camp, and more than a little querulous.

That sentence comes back to me now in another tenor, because I would struggle (like many others, I know) to say precisely where I end and Ian White begins. Editing this book, writing this introduction, I'm faced with the fact that I am to some degree the product of the writings here – of the arguments and ideas they transmit, of the person whose voice they recollect. This is a personal observation of sorts; but it is also a simple recognition of the character of White's own life, which was lived furiously in collaboration, dialogue, argument.

In the earliest text collected here, from 2002, White writes that the work of the late New York artist David Wojnarowicz 'mounts as radical a challenge to the containment of commentary as it does to personal and cultural commodification'. White's own work, his own life, perhaps represents a similar challenge – not least because, like Wojnarowicz, White died absurdly young (Wojnarowicz was thirty-seven, White was forty-one). White's practice as a whole still seems uncategorisable. It included, amongst other things, scores of curated film programmes and events, a series of solo and collaborative performance works, a hugely influential teaching career and a substantial amount of writing. The process of thinking, collectively, about what this body of work might mean – or whether it can even be reconstructed as 'an integrated whole predicated on biography', as White suggests in Wojnarowicz's case – has barely begun.

Writing was integral to White's work. He never merely recorded or commented upon; rather, his writing was catalytic. In the words of his essay 'Foyer' (2011), 'it is where things happen(ed)'.[1] His texts were also enormously important for others, but they had been published in very diverse contexts, sometimes in quite ephemeral forms, so the idea of a collection seemed obvious. White and I worked a little on this book in the last year of his life, whilst he was being treated for lymphoma; but he was busy with other projects and we planned to revisit it later. In the event, when later was no longer a possibility, we spoke about the principles of selection, and he suggested some of the texts which might be included. The final selection and all of the detailed work of editing I have done without him. I have tried as much as possible to follow in the direction we had mapped out, but I am under no illusion that this is the book we would have made together had he been able to work on it longer.

This account – this introduction, this book – is, then, as White noted of his account of Wojnarowicz, 'doubly partial'. Firstly, in the obvious sense: it is a selection, compiled posthumously, which omits a number of perhaps equally important pieces of his writing.[2] The selection was driven by a desire to show both the variety of White's writing and the development of his thinking around a particular constellation of ideas about theatre, cinema, performance and politics – a constellation which seems important to me as a continuing challenge to our present. But it is also partial in the sense of partisan: the choices I made were inescapably subjective, based on a shared history – of curating, teaching, writing and making together; of friendship and conversation – extending from when White and I first started working together at the Lux Centre in London in 2001 until his death in 2013.

I will not attempt to give a detailed account of either White's life or his artistic practice here; both of these tasks would feel impossible

10

for different reasons. Instead I am going to try to trace one selective path through his writing and to read these very various texts – written at different times, for different reasons – through the prism of my experience of his work, and of him. In doing so, I will suggest that the writing's often varied terminology refers, ultimately, to the same thing – that there is a coherent and tightly woven net of ideas behind what may appear to be quite different kinds of texts. What follows is, therefore, avowedly and unashamedly a construction: 'something made', a readerly speculation, a shoring of fragments. A desire, mobilised.

✳

In notes for an artist's talk he gave at the Ruskin School of Art at Oxford University in 2011, White addressed how he inhabited the roles of artist and curator. He speculated that while there are valid reasons for distinguishing them – biographical, economic, ethical – ultimately,

> ... they are both the means by which I am personally able to get through life, to navigate, think, be – they are processes of negotiation ... they are indivisible.

The texts in this book reflect that indivisibility. Spanning just over a decade, as of 2002, and organised chronologically, they are drawn from a wide variety of sources: magazine articles, texts for exhibition and film festival catalogues, blog posts, talks, press releases, etc. They are slanted somewhat more towards the curatorial and critical side of White's work, and many focus on artists with whom he worked in his groundbreaking film programmes, beginning in the mid-1990s, at, amongst other venues, the Horse Hospital, the Lux Centre (later LUX) and the Whitechapel Gallery in London; the International Short Film Festival Oberhausen; and Kino Arsenal in Berlin.

White's own artistic practice developed in parallel to his curatorial projects, and traces of his performance work – at least half a dozen solo pieces as well as his collaborations with Jimmy Robert, Emily Roysdon and others – are to be found throughout his writings. Although I have not included his performance scripts, for example (three are already published in another volume),[3] the writings here offer numerous reflections, whether in passing or in detail, on the ideas and influences behind his own work. They include the texts of two performative talks ('A Life, and Time' and 'Hinterhof', both 2011) and two collaborative texts related to performances developed with others (Martin Gustavsson and Jimmy Robert). Moreover, White's texts themselves tend to render such distinctions irrelevant and demand to be considered as a whole. As the late text 'Division' (2013) puts it: 'Any extraction is a picture, a story(line), lies.'

For the reader of this book, the indivisibility is likely to manifest itself more immediately as an experience of form: these texts constantly collapse critical distance and insist instead on a kind of present tense of writing and reading, an active encounter in which something is being *produced* rather than transmitted – a performance, in other words:

> I am writing this. You must be reading this, but you do not have to.
> ('Yet But If But If But Then But Then', 2003)

This gesture of readerly interpellation recurs frequently, in different forms, but always as a claim on (and about) us, as singular or collective readers – readers who are not being offered an idea or a programme to assent to, but are rather being solicited to become actively complicit in the making of meanings. 'Complicity too is participation', White writes in 'One Script for *9 Scripts from a Nation at War*' (2008). That demand simultaneously 'lays US on the line', as the Wojnarowicz text puts it, which also means a constant need to negotiate what kind of 'us' we are or might wish to be.

White's style is idiosyncratic in other, related ways. It is often dense and grammatically complex, with peculiar emphases, nested quotations and counterintuitive formulations. For example, there are the slash signs which constantly threaten the proliferation of (sometimes incompatible) meanings: 'is/was', 'a/our condition', 'the/her body', 'art from/of this life', 'a problem solved/exposed', 'installed/dismantled', 'wrong/right', 'other than/as well as/because of'... As a result, sentences become like electrical circuits, rerouting and flipping the currents of thought: present, past and future oscillate wildly; causality flickers like a promise, the fragile product of his/our interpretation.[4]

12

In some ways, the writing here is a kind of 'museum without walls': a catalogue for a virtual collection of works, a partial record of White's enormously influential curatorial projects ('Kinomuseum', 2007, being a case in point). It should already be clear, however, that when White writes about artists, artworks, ideas, lives, etc. that there is never simply exposition or transmission of knowledge – information is never neutral or merely given. Rather, for White writing is radically productive and the category of 'information' is always to be treated like the promptings of a gallery wall label: partial, selective, prescriptive, authored.

In the script for his performance *Black Flags* (2009), White draws on phrases from his interview with a Curator of Interpretation at Tate about the function of museum wall texts and audiences' supposed desire for 'neutral' information about artworks. Through White's script, this emerges as the defining institutional fantasy of 'bodiless information':

> [...] unobtrusive, unnoticed expressions of institutional authority/ their invisibility defines institutional authority which functions by not being seen or felt: it is nothing.[5]

For White, this fantasy – of authority that functions *because* it is not consciously experienced – is both ludicrous and dangerous. Information is always bodily, factitious, intentional, something that only comes into existence when it is thrown or projected: 'Look at a reel of film, a tape, a hard drive and you cannot see with the eye alone the information' ('Foyer'). Nor is any content or information stable and pre-existing; rather, it comes into existence contingently each time it is enunciated or performed. Only the recognition of that – of our own agency as viewers, listeners, readers – allows for 'change beyond that which occurs through information' ('Palace Calls Crisis Summit', 2003). The phrase which recurs in differing formulations in White's late writing, and which gives this volume its title, seems to condense this idea into an imperative: 'Here is information. Mobilise.'[6]

The form of such a mobilisation might start from the recognition that, as White puts it in relation to the work of Gerard Byrne, 'context... becomes content' ('The hole's the thing...', 2011). This formulation is not esoteric, and White suggests what it might mean in a number of

13

other ways, from his account of how the TV news he has watched in a film festival hotel room affects the films he subsequently sees ('Palace Calls Crisis Summit'), to his allusions to John Cage's silence,[7] or his various readings of Morgan Fisher's radically site-specific film *Screening Room* (1968–). It is there, too, in his account of 'expanded cinema', a term which is normally an art historical label for a particular set of performance/film practices from the 1960s, but which he expands in turn to encompass something more utopian:

> expanded cinema could be considered as a practice that extends or multiplies the frame of the screen to incorporate what is happening in the screening room itself, to include space, movement, live speaking, to incorporate the corporeality of the spectator as also constituting the work itself through relative, physical positions in space.
> ('Performer, Audience, Mirror', 2012)

White is clear on the genealogy of this idea: it begins, in essence, with the polemical appropriation of critic Michael Fried's 'brilliantly unsuccessful denunciation' of Minimalist art as 'theatrical' in his famous essay 'Art and Objecthood' (1967), which inadvertently 'defines what it attempts to denigrate'. Byrne's multi-screen video installation *A thing is a hole in a thing it is not* (2010) – which White describes as a 'continuous representation, examination, extension of and participation in' Fried's text – becomes an occasion for White to explore this ('The hole's the thing...'). Elsewhere, White spells out more precisely how he understands this inversion of Fried's argument:

> What Fried denounces we might celebrate as a liberating self-reflexivity: the viewer becomes the activating agent – simultaneously a player and an audience – in a theatre without stage, props, costumes, etc. The meaning of these indivisible shapes is entirely constituted by their equal indivisibility from the room which surrounds them and their relationship to the viewing body which sees – experiences – both these things and itself.
> ('Death, Life and Art(ifice): The Films of Sharon Lockhart', 2009)

14

Throughout the course of White's writing, we can see the gradual elaboration and complication of this basic argument, his mapping of a series of transpositions from theatre and Minimalism (read in Friedian terms) onto the conditions in which we experience artists' film and video – or as he puts it in 'Wishful Thinking' (2012), his essay on the work of Oliver Husain, 'the political imperative of theatricality, of theatre, of cinema read as theatre for the sake of new social formations'.

White draws on an extraordinary range of thinkers – Samuel Taylor Coleridge, Yvonne Rainer, Bertolt Brecht, Roland Barthes (on Racine), Dan Graham (on architecture), etc. – in order to develop a genealogical concept of 'theatre' which perhaps relates less to most of what is currently produced under that name and more to a certain history of performance art. Another way to think of it might be in terms of camp, as in White's provocative description of Fisher's *Screening Room* as 'a theatricalising (camp) gesture' ('Wishful Thinking'). This is certainly not, however, the kind of camp that Susan Sontag could insist was necessarily 'depoliticised', a sovereign aestheticism.[8] Instead, White's camp theatricality mobilises an apparently formalist, tautological conceit like Fisher's (the audience watching a film of the space in which they are sitting) to create a flash of insight into our bodily present, the psychic-physical conditions of our own spectatorship. For White, such camp would be less a question of the 'failed seriousness' of any particular artwork, as Sontag would have it; rather, it would be a name for our experience of the ultimate failure of the institutional frames for *all* artworks, and the process of discovering, each time anew, that perhaps it is *we* who are in fact producing the work – together, here and now, in the auditorium. Hence the task becomes, as 'Recording and Performing' (2008) urges, 'to replace the question about where the meaning of a performative artwork might be located by reconstituting this "location" as the question itself'.

This leads White to make some very unexpected conjunctions: the unities of classical Aristotelean theatre, for example, can come to rhyme with a certain kind of austere filmic structuralism through their shared insistence on a conspicuously unbroken time frame. This paradoxical affinity is expressed most clearly in 'Death, Life and Art(ifice)',

15

his incisive account of Sharon Lockhart's films, and how what might appear as a kind of literalistic minimalism – for example her fixed-frame shots, held for the length of a reel of 16mm film – becomes, oddly, a device which heightens the viewer's awareness of the constructedness of the image and, crucially, their own relationship to it. Formalism at its most rigorous and rarefied sometimes flips into something entirely, shockingly familiar – or vice versa. White describes this reversal elegantly, for example, in a comparison of Yvonne Rainer's dance works with Chantal Akerman's films in relation to their apparently untheatrical 'everydayness':

> By definition, the everyday would seem to be something done which is not thought (as in planned). But by definition also it is something that is repeated to an extreme degree – every day, in fact. ('Death, Life and Art(ifice)')

What becomes apparent is that this is not simply a question of art and spectatorship. In White's writings, 'theatre' is a term which implies a whole set of political subjectivities, a way of figuring individual and collective agency in the production of the present – and this idea is one bridge between his more evidently critical/theoretical writing and the more diaristic texts, such as those from his blog *Lives of Performers*. It is why, for example, he can describe a hospital, in a post written during the period of his treatment, as being 'theatre of the worst kind' – because hospital is a kind of perverse and alienating stage for the isolated patient, who is figured as a passive non-performer, with 'no audience or no one who wants to be one' ('In. Adequate. Time. (Prisons 1)', 2012).

In order to begin to conceive what another kind of theatre and another kind of audience might be, White asks us to think about our bodies, assembled, in space. The physical and conceptual space of the auditorium becomes key because, in relation to the body of works White is interested in, it represents 'context' in its most concrete, historically and socially specific terms. (In a different formulation, in 'The Projected Object', 2004, the auditorium becomes a 'social metatext'.) Part of the presupposition of an auditorium, in both theatre and cinema, is a single, unitary perspective – but this is belied in reality, for example by

16

the deceptively obvious fact that we are distributed around the space with different sightlines, often with a hierarchy of perspectives based on the price of the seats. Discussing how the theatre director Robert Wilson 'organises his stage as a picture designed and choreographed to be viewed from the middle of the stalls (from where it was directed) for optimal impact', White remarks that 'sitting at the back of the auditorium, on the end of a row – in a cheap seat – throws the picture into radical relief. The power structure breaks down because the lines of persuasion effected by perspective are broken'[9] ('Performer, Audience, Mirror'). In other words, the embodied experience of the auditorium viewer is no less divisible from what they see than that of Fried's spectator of Minimalist art. One important imperative then becomes to examine precisely the 'aesthetic, economic, critical and political' determinants of the auditorium in all its forms, from the Greek amphitheatre to the modern museum's screening space.

Audience for Ian White's project *Richard Serra's Hands* at lab.oratory, a Berlin gay sex club, in 2011. The event involved several of Serra's 16mm films of his own hands, including *Hand Catching Lead* (1968) and *Color Aid* (1970–71), being sequentially projected onto paper screens stretched over the club's furniture.

White explored this idea throughout his curatorial work in many different ways, the traces and implications of which are everywhere in this book. If the project is to devise forms which dramatise what White calls the 'unstable present' of performance for the audience – to present the work so that they become aware both of its physical/institutional framing and their own agency in deciding the value of that framing – then I think we can find a number of different names for that ambition throughout these texts: 'Kinomuseum', 'artists' cinema', 'differentiated cinema', 'the foyer', 'liveness'...

What all these concepts point to is a form of radical production and exhibition which refuses any simple distinction between those two terms – or between an inside and an outside, whether that refers to what is within/without the frame, or what is within/without the art historical canon. The (cinema) auditorium becomes the fulcrum for this, and, in White's understanding, the auditorium becomes activated when we realise how continuous it is with everything we think it excludes, so that

> the frame of the work is multiplied and extended not only into
> the room where the work is viewed but also disintegrating these
> physical limits to occupy the world at large – life, itself, material.
> ('Performer, Audience, Mirror')

In this way, the space of viewing – that paradoxical space we are supposed to forget when the lights go down, where we go, in Jean-Luc Godard's phrase, '(together) to be alone' [10] – becomes something else, something more: 'a productive limit or a dialectical location' ('Performer, Audience, Mirror').

The limit becomes productive, for White, when we realise that 'LIMIT IS MATERIAL' ('F R E E (Prisons 2)', 2012); that is, when we become conscious of the limits imposed on our experience by framing, of whatever kind, then those limits can be made into the material (content) of our experience. [11] This, I think, is why White returns repeatedly to the image of 'occupation', conceived – as he puts it in 'I and I/12 to 12' (2005), his text on the Copenhagen Free University – as 'the occupation of a form conducted to make its organisational and operational

18

principles apparent'. White does not advocate a turning away from compromised forms – whether political, social or artistic – but rather a conscious attempt to occupy them, to inhabit them, in such ways that their limits could be revealed and challenged, and perhaps overcome.

Occupation is necessarily something provisional, tactical and temporary; it turns what it occupies (theatre, cinema, the auditorium) to use. And in case this sounds too militaristic, perhaps it is simply an attempt to redeem another militaristic concept, that of the avant-garde, by virtue of a gesture of (camp) appropriation – not forging ahead to seize new territories, but rather trying to rescue a productively ruined present. Meaningful political agency is to be sought by claiming and inhabiting the ruins of institutions or ideas, or what the filmmaker Lis Rhodes called 'a crumpled heap': [12] the disorder of hierarchies and histories in the moment we refuse them. One of White's favourite words is 'collapse', as in:

> The collapse of: political regimes, private ownership, 'passive' reception (being told), narrative, hierarchical order, the Institution, exclusion, lies. ('Foyer')

Possibility resides in ruins. That is why occupation is linked in White's writing to 'evacuation', which functions both as occupation's opposite – an institution or convention which is no longer legitimate, whose meaning has been hollowed out – and its condition of possibility – the way in which the self-conscious *experience* of evacuation might become the productive experience of a limit: 'evacuation is made material' ('The hole's the thing...').[13] Perhaps this idea marks the beginning of a politics we might call queer?

It is the emphasis on forms of fleeting, fragile, negative freedom which makes this politics so radical. White's model of occupied ruins and permanent provisionality resists even the fatalistic comforts of Robert Smithson's idea of entropy. In his 1967 essay 'A Tour of the Monuments of Passaic, New Jersey', Smithson famously imagined a sandbox neatly divided into white sand and black sand, mixed into grey by a child running clockwise; if the child is then asked to run counterclockwise, 'the result will not be a restoration of the original division but a greater degree of greyness and an increase of entropy'.[14] White offers a simple response to Smithson's allegory:

> Seen in this way, all systems are processes of disintegration, the circulation of parts towards their indivisibility, invisibility. This degenerative spiral into sameness is erasure, producing an inertia even in the act of looking. But move closer. Get really close. Step into the box and bend down. What is there is not what you saw before. The individual grains of sand in Smithson's pit are not grey, but still black and white. The analogy only holds for as long as we occupy a fixed position of inviolable, immaterial perception. 'Greyness' is the impression of a colour from a fixed perspective. Only in this way does looking become blindness. ('What is Material?', 2012)

In White's writing, the collapse of divisions, the dissolution of the frame, the abandonment of a unitary perspective – however momentary or provisional – is a negation which functions as promise. The/our world in a grain of sand.

⁂

One marker, perhaps, of the effect that White's writing and thinking has had on me is the realisation that I cannot conclude this introduction without allowing a little for its possible collapse. Because there is a problem here – a trap White himself named, repeatedly, insistently. As he succinctly puts it in the text written with and about the painter Martin Gustavsson: 'narrative is an inevitability'. We lay things end to end and want to call them a story, a train of thought, a life. Especially now, with his death still relatively recent, I find myself tempted to search for a single thread of meaning on which all of White's ideas and practice can be neatly strung – to want him to have been one thing. This is what he called, in relation to Wojnarowicz, for example, the 'common cultural lie of consistency' – and yet it is also, as he says, unavoidable. 'Inevitably making sense.'

White prized fidelity, but not consistency. Talking with me about the rationale for this book, when it was still at an early stage, he stressed the need for it to acknowledge repetition and failure – the way in which the texts might contain redundancies, or, conversely, might try, and fail, to repeat themselves. (The passage on Smithson's sand, for example, occurs twice.) This is perhaps one way of naming the searching, compulsive quality of White's writing which, as he emphasises about Wojnarowicz's work, 'DEFIES ASSIMILATION' and demands that the reader engage it without any guarantees, in the present tense of an act of reading.

It is important not to underplay either the very different tones of the texts included here, or the degree to which White's ideas were often developed polemically, in the process of attacking unthinking orthodoxy or intolerance. The later texts, particularly those written in the last year of his life, necessarily take different risks than the earlier ones and often adopt very different voices. Their preoccupations are more explicitly personal; or rather, they attempt more radically and explicitly to expand the frame of the writing until it becomes coterminous with 'the world at large – life, itself, material'. More than any other writing here, they make a mockery of any too clean or conceptual account.

White's writing is often savagely funny, too, as in his reviews of an experimental film conference or a Jack Smith seminar, or the camp observational comedy of 'First, Six or So People' (2012, shades of Kenneth Williams's diaries). There is a failure to suffer fools gladly, and an occasional waspishness, which those who knew him will recognise instantly, and which are just as characteristic as the more considered critical judgments. But equally, many of these texts are really a kind of indexical record of the love he felt for colleagues and friends, or of the mark that certain works had made on him. He makes himself vulnerable, wonders if he has gone too far. And sometimes the voice that we hear from this writing can be heartbreakingly simple and direct, as in some of the very last texts.

Conversely, I have passed over some parts of his texts which remain enigmatic to me. To take just one example: the extraordinary page of capitalised terms that concludes 'Performer, Audience, Mirror' (a text he once described to me as his favourite amongst his own writing). The subheading has an underlined blank between the ellipses where we might expect the final term to appear, the 'solution' to the question of cinema/theatre/liveness (the ultimate term to unify all those disparate concepts I have been trying to insist are secret homonyms). Instead we have this strange, compelling, tabulated list of terms ending with

WITHDRAWAL.

His text has reached this point by a series of deft and cogent steps, and it draws, in particular, on a text I had written in relation to the artist Lee Lozano and her notorious withdrawal from the art world. And yet every time I read it, I have the same sense of vertigo, of an ecstatic insight which I experience powerfully in the moment of reading but can't quite crystalise. The nature of White's thinking and of his writing resist capture or paraphrase.

So it's simple: in the face of withdrawal, we will have to occupy these terms, these texts. To put them to use ourselves.

Here is information.

Stuttgart, August 2016

A note on the text

The original context of publication is given at the beginning of each text included here. Wherever possible, I have checked the texts against earlier published versions. In one case, the essay on Ruth Buchanan called 'What is Material?', I have reconstructed, at Ian White's suggestion, an earlier and longer draft than the one first published.

The footnotes that appear at the end of each chapter are White's, unless marked by square brackets, in which case they are my own clarifications.

In copy-editing I have tried to strike a balance that respects White's idiosyncratic grammar and usage and my desire to correct for any obvious mistakes, malapropisms, etc. that were not picked up by his original editors (often texts were written quickly to meet deadlines, or edited by non-native speakers, or not edited at all). I have tried to keep a lighter touch in particular for the texts drawn from the *Lives of Performers* blog, in order not to smooth off too many of their characteristic edges. My experience of working with White to edit several of his texts for previous publications gives me some confidence that, here at least, I have not departed from the spirit of his writing.

1. The phrase occurs at the conclusion of 'Foyer', and refers in that context to Roland Barthes's concept of 'the Antechamber' in his book *On Racine* (1987); but as White's quotation of Barthes makes clear, the Antechamber is explicitly 'the site of language'.

2. In particular, I would point to his monthly columns for *Art Review* (2003–06); the extraordinary collaborative texts he wrote with the artist Emily Wardill for their book *We are behind* (2010); 'Who is Not the Author? Gerry Schum and the Established Order' (2005), his strange and wonderful piece on Schum's *Fernsehgalerie* project, written for an anthology I edited on early conceptual art, which he later disavowed; essays on other artists with whom he had long and important working relationships, such as Rosa Barba and Klaus Weber; and a few longer, more academic essays, such as 'Life Itself! The "problem" of pre-cinema' (2009) and 'Signs of the (Other) Times: Television, video, representation' (2009). See the bibliography at the end of this volume for further publication details.

3. See *Ian White: Ibiza Black Flags Democracy* (Berlin: Deutscher Akademischer Austauschdienst Galerie, 2010).

4. One especially notable influence on White's style, as well as his thinking, was the filmmaker Peter Gidal. See, in this volume, 'Yet But If But If But Then But Then: Peter Gidal' and 'Death, Life and Art(ifice): The Films of Sharon Lockhart'; and also Gidal's recent collection of writings, *Flare Out: Aesthetics 1966–2016*, ed. Mark Webber and Peter Gidal (London: The Visible Press, 2016).

5. Ian White, 'Black Flags', in *Ian White: Ibiza Black Flags Democracy*, op. cit., p.81.

6. Variations of the phrase appear in 'Statement for *Appropriation and Dedication*' (2013) and '(I Am) For The Birds' (2013), both in this volume. The phrase also featured in White's *Trauerspiel 1* (performed at HAU1, Hebbel-Am-Ufer, Berlin, 2012).

7. See White's account in 'The Projected Object' of the problem of translating the 'silence' of T.J. Wilcox's film *The Little Elephant* (2000) from gallery space to cinema auditorium. White also addressed the analogy with Cage's silence more explicitly in an

essay on the artist Paul Pfeiffer (not included in this volume): 'If the lesson of John Cage is that there is no such thing as silence then there are no empty spaces either. There are no neutral spaces. Especially if they are not literally framed, artworks are framed by the journeys we take to see them and everything that we are given, plus everything that is in us which we use to read them; so I wonder if the art gallery (or its proxy) is not always – at least in part – a certain kind of psychic-physical theatre' ('Situation Cinema: Models of spectacle, empty spaces and *The Saints*', in *Paul Pfeiffer: The Saints*, exhibition catalogue, ed. Britta Schmitz [Heidelberg: Kehrer Verlag, 2010]).

8. Susan Sontag, 'Notes on Camp', *Against Interpretation and Other Essays* (New York: Picador, 2001), pp.275–92.

9. In relation to the question of unitary perspective, White was long interested in Hans Holbein the Younger's painting *The Ambassadors* (1533), with its famous anamorphic skull. In an earlier draft of the essay on Peter Gidal included here, he drew on Stephen Greenblatt's account of how the painting forces us to acknowledge that 'the limitations of vision are... structural' so that the viewer's movement becomes 'an anti-representational, physical act, an effacing of the portrait'.

10. See Colin MacCabe, *Godard: Images, Sounds, Politics* (Bloomington: Indiana University Press, 1980), p.139.

11. The idea of limit-as-material was important to White in his later thinking; see, for example, his discussion of his own performances in *On Performance*, ed. Eva Birkenstock and Joerg Franzbecker (Bregenz: Kunsthaus Bregenz, 2011): 'I think for me in the work I made, I was trying to construct a situation, not in an absolute sense but in a way where limit becomes material' (n.p.).

12. The phrase comes from an essay which he returned to repeatedly: Lis Rhodes, 'Whose History?' (1979), in *Film as Film: Formal Experiment in Film, 1910–1975*, exhibition catalogue, ed. Deke Dusinberre and A. L. Rees (London: Hayward Gallery, 1979), pp.119–20. See, for example, 'History is Written for Historical Reasons' (2008) and 'Performer, Audience, Mirror', in this volume.

13. Regarding the image of ruins, Douglas Crimp's famous essay 'On the Museum's Ruins' (*October*, vol.13, Summer 1980) was another obvious and important influence on White's thinking.

14. Robert Smithson, 'A Tour of the Monuments of Passaic, New Jersey' (1967), in *Robert Smithson: The Collected Writings*, ed. Jack Flam (Berkeley: University of California Press, 1996), p.74.

Film Art Life (Death, Sex, Social History):
David Wojnarowicz

Each painting, film, sculpture or page of writing I make represents
to me a particular moment in the history of my body on this planet,
in America

David Wojnarowicz, 'Do Not Doubt The Dangerousness of the 12-Inch Politician'

Expression without compromise, David Wojnarowicz's work mounts as radical a challenge to the containment of commentary as it does to personal and cultural commodification: totemic, narrative and metaphorical paintings; iconoclastic photographs and montages; gory, transgressive multimedia installations; transient performances; fine art graffiti; diaries, political journalism, semi-fictionalised stories, imaginary monologues; collaborative films; finished/unfinished personal films; political video. Defying assimilation with the wild rigour of autobiography, it's a body of work that lays the body of the artist on the line, lays US on the line.

The diary is pivotal for Wojnarowicz. His scrapbook-style journals ricochet into the rest of his writing as his super 8 diaries, shot between compulsion and intent, ricochet into a comparable visual lexicon, and the two are intrinsically linked. Images are translated from super 8 into the iconography of his paintings, frames become photographic stills, sequences are used and re-use in performances and installations. Journal entries detail primitive storyboards, re-document and mirror films already shot, repeat themselves, are repeatedly translated into other written works, and spiral into images which resonate and repeat in turn.

27

First published in *Untitled*, 28 (Summer 2002).

Four of Wojnarowicz's personal films have recently been reconstructed (as yet minus their soundtracks) by the Estate Project: *Heroin*
(originally 1979), *Fire In My Belly* (originally 1987), *Peter Hujar* (originally 1987–88) and *Howdy Doody Goes for a Ride* (originally 1989, the
only one of the four significantly dependent on absent dialogue).

Wojnarowicz witnessed the AIDS-related illnesses, hysterical and
desperate searches for cures, and eventual death of photographer
Peter Hujar, one of his closest friends, in 1987, and within a year was
himself diagnosed as HIV+. The most tender of extended, furious lita-
nies, between text and image, across space and time, Hujar's (life and)
death is but one paradigmatic event that literally and ritualistically
figures and reconfigures:

> I can't form words these past few days. Sometimes I think I've
> been drained of emotional content, from weeping or from fear.
> Have I been holding off full acceptance of his dying by holding
> a mane camera – that sweep of his bed, his open eye, his open
> mouth, that beautiful hand with a hint of gauze at the wrist, the
> color of it like marble, the full sense of it as flesh?
> (*In the Shadow of the American Dream: The Diaries of David
> Wojnarowicz*)

> I can't form words these past few days, sometimes thinking
> I've been drained of emotional content from weeping or fear.
> I keep doing these impulsive things like trying to make a film
> that records the rituals in an attempt to give grief form.
> (*Close to the Knives*)

> It's a dark and concrete bunker. There is a clump of three guys
> entwined on the long ledge. I had an idea that I would make
> a three-minute super 8 film of my dying friend's face with all
> its lesions and sightlessness and then take a super 8 projector
> and hook it up with copper cables to a car battery slung in a bag
> over my shoulder and walk back in here and project the film
> onto the walls above their heads.
> ('Spiral', *Memories That Smell Like Gasoline*)

No super 8 reel of the dead photographer has been found since Wojnarowicz's death, remarkably throwing it into question. The classicism of the reconstructed film *Peter Hujar* is aesthetically akin to the tone of Hujar's work itself; dark stylised blacks, discreetly composed and juxtaposed images. The film resonates with the photographic, an insistence that Hujar's work is seen; long, deliberate sequences of hands flipping through Hujar's photographs, of Hujar as a child (in his journals Wojnarowicz describes returning to Hujar's apartment after he died and spreading the photographs out on Hujar's bed), reproductions of paintings of St Sebastian (an echo of the earlier painting *Peter Hujar Dreaming/Yukio Mishima: St Sebastian*, 1982) and then a panning shot, not actually of Hujar on his death bed but of the contact sheet of 35mm stills Wojnarowicz shot on that day. Rain falls into darkened puddles, onto already drenched streets, sheets of grief.

The unfurling of Hujar's memorial quilt (with designs by Wojnarowicz, a close-up of a faceless man hugging a tree trunk in midair), a seemingly alien ritual that it's terrifying to realise feels so historical. A William Burroughs/Antony Balch-like dream sequence of a man sitting up in bed wearing a gas mask; a man, his head wrapped in bandages, walking up a staircase, is unbound in the glare of a light. Wojnarowicz made numerous super 8 reels and photographs of Mexican mummies (one of which is the hidden key to the as-yet-unrestored super 8 film *Beautiful People*, 1988).

Overwhelmingly, there's a powerful determination of Hujar's existence (work, life) and a painful, profound fury at his death through the act of its telling and retelling. Vehemently, Wojnarowicz WITNESSED.

The circuit board of the painting *Wind (for Peter Hujar)* (1987) becomes a cycle of destruction, consciousness, creativity and rebirth that modifies traditionalist approaches; a set of personal signs manifesting, metaphysically, the whole of Hujar and social rage – a visual map that's the site of politics, as indivisible as experience and expression, the acts of looking, feeling, of documenting, themselves political action.

As time goes on I have come to believe that all things are not
necessarily what they appear if you judge them only by their
silence or invisibility.

('Do Not Doubt The Dangerousness of the 12-Inch Politician')

Heroin is a stylised apocalypse of addiction. A gang of people shoot up
and variously collapse, compounding prophecy, the record of a state
of emergency, humour, profundity. In the seminal photographic series
Arthur Rimbaud in New York (1978–79), the romantic similarly collapses onto reality; a guy wears a crude photocopied mask of the nineteenth-century French Symbolist poet and poses at various locations
around New York: eating cake at Tiffany's, at peep shows, on Coney
Island, in the meatpacking district, shooting up in a Hudson River
warehouse.

Much of *Fire In My Belly* is from Wojnarowicz's many trips to Mexico.
With overwhelming prescience, it's divided into sections by the found
drawing of a steam train (again, an icon repeated: *Crash: The Birth of
Language/The Invention of Lies*, 1986; *Some Things From Sleep*, 1986;
Time, 1988–89) that rushes closer and closer, and a growing number
of tarot cards; a young kid breathing fire on the streets, Mexican wres-
tling, the circus, newspaper headlines of death, murder, destruction,
Mayan temples and camera-wielding tourists, cockfighting.

A painted burning eyeball revolves like the earth against a bright
blue background. A dirty hand catches money falling from just behind
the camera lens. We think of the painting *Fire* (1987) (smoking vol-
cano, a snake eating its own tail, a car battery, cartoon flashes, 'wanted'
posters), the sculpture of the pig's skull covered in dollar bills and
maps, an upside-down globe between its jaws (*Untitled*, 1985), the shot
of bandaged hands barely cupping coins in the photomontage *Silence
Through Economics* (1988–89). The discretion of the film's cultural
and social rage, the drive for an alternative, is enormous, imagination
becoming the collation of evidence, a system defiantly flipped back on
itself, a language.

We are born into a preinvented existence within a tribal nation
of zombies. Some of the tribes are in the business of sucker-
punching people's psyches. Then there are the tribes that suckle

30

at the breast of telecommunications every evening after work.
Day after day they experience waking nightmares but they've
bought the con of language from the tribe that offers hope,
or they're too fucking exhausted or fearful to break through
the illusion and examine the structures of their world.
(*In the Shadow of the American Dream*)

Without apology or concession to the common cultural lie of consistency, Wojnarowicz was a WITNESS, driving against a corrupt system of social control, legal, political and religious hypocrisy, railing violently against Cardinal John O'Connor's Roman Catholic Church, Reagan's America, his 'One Tribe Nation' and famously against the censorious National Endowment for the Arts. Articulated as lived (hustler, addict, artist), his means of expression were equally a means of resistance, subjective impulse and disjunction of register staking out a radical formalism.

This has been a doubly partial account: the provocation of Wojnarowicz's body of work through a tiny proportion of reconstructed films and a few of their intersections. Relentlessly, that body reflects itself, refracts himself, his witnessing, his body, our structures. It DEFIES ASSIMILATION, constructing instead an integrated whole predicated on biography that's by turn insistent, disarming, comprehensive. Radical, romantic formalism.

Jet-Packed Nomads:
Mark Leckey, Nick Relph & Oliver Payne

There's no better signifier of exquisite taste than those collections that re-imagine the potential ugliness of seemingly disjunctive aspects into a new and brilliant coherence. It is perhaps no coincidence that artist Mark Leckey's band DonAtella takes the first name of Gianni Versace's sibling heir and turns it into the nom de plume of a swaggering, sub-fashionista Don (like Juan or Quixote). In Versace's well-photographed New York mansion, 5 East 64th Street, Lichtensteins are framed by Russian crystal sconces and pop-coloured French glass-works, and the Schnabel-furnished Elton John guest suite pitches the artist's raw *Paradis* with a gold sleigh bed, Empire tables and an imported Italian ceiling. *LONDONATELLA* (2002), DonAtella's first 'promo', which consists of a collection of liminal television ads, soap-opera titles and feature films of a pastiche London conquered by two impeccable modern-day dandies, is engorged with a similar classy-dirty baroque. Moreover, like Gianni Versace, Leckey himself has always been a gleaner-grafter, apparent ever since his magical video dossier *Fiorucci Made Me Hardcore* (1999), which skimmed and scrabbled through the luxurious pockets of pop-cultural lives left after *Smash Hits* had done its worst.

33

First published in *ArtFoto*
(*ArtReview* annual supplement), vol.1 (2002), pp.30–33.

LONDONATELLA is in fact more a non-promo-cum-archaic sci-fi manifesto, its disarming and naïve surrealism fantastically melding past, present and future into part-narrative, part-videolog. Its protagonists fall from the sky like angel-aliens, omnipresent in the tourist traps, backstreets and skyscapes of the capital like peculiar avatars of the band's formidable namesake: 'like a Michelin for our times, a jet-packed nomad with suitcases full of La Prairie creams and 40 pairs of candy-coloured mules' (Cathy Horyn on Donatella Versace, *Vanity Fair*, June 1997). The video opens with a title plaque over sepia-stained glass. Eyes appear in the postcard-blue sky between Tower Bridge; then we see Piccadilly Circus (perhaps in the 1960s, but we're not sure) and the caption 'LONDON' (as if we needed telling – but then again, there's something already implicit that suggests in fact we do). What ensues is the dandies' torrid psycho-destruction of a futuristic Victorian London made plastic by our disorientation: a blood-red sky over St Paul's and Canary Wharf; looting, fire, mayhem; astrological sky showers. Lightning strikes Big Ben, its clock faces spectacularly blown out by flames. A bombed-out London gives way to celestial flood-lights from rooftops and a camped-up version of Leonardo's *Vitruvian Man* hovering between tower blocks. The earth's new occupants enjoy a Hogarthian sunset, and pealing bells (the already borrowed escape-route of the Lars von Trier film *Breaking the Waves*), superimposed over the opening title map from the tawdry soap *Eastenders*, leave us beguiled and entranced, wishing the revolution were true, feeling like everything's going to be OK.

LONDONATELLA can only be read through the opulence of its own telling: sexy straight-boy camp as revolutionary fantasy. The band's (cover) song, pitching reinvented 'found' tracks against each other, likewise takes no prisoners. As a whole it's extraordinarily allusive: *The Day of the Triffids*, *War of the Worlds*, *Oliver Twist* and *Spider Man* via Tsukerman's *Liquid Sky* courtesy of Jack the Ripper and Eliza Doolittle, a brash national anthem for the alternative cultural truths it festers and champions.

While one wouldn't describe *Mixtape* (2002) as brash, Nick Relph and Oliver Payne's latest work is certainly audacious. The video, like

LONDONATELLA, is made to a specific track – Terry Riley's 'You're No Good' – sound and image both twisting inside out, back on themselves and into another dimension, making them impossible to separate. Whilst referencing Relph and Payne's previous work, *Mixtape* goes further in its direct engagement with spectacle, 'entertainment', and expressions of boredom, beauty and lyrical resistance. Briefly, their debut trilogy (*Driftwood, House & Garage, Jungle*, 2001) begins in the inner city, moves to the suburbs and ends in the 'jungle' of the English countryside, a stunning formal collapse occurring as the artists move further from home-base. The same actor from the trilogy's central video reappears in *Mixtape*, again as a muse, an ubiquitous nomad loose in the city, again the embodiment of something private, adrift and hoping.

From its juddering, epic opening – reminiscent of Angus McBean's stark surrealism – announcing a eulogy, to the spectacular release of a high-camp B-movie ending, *Mixtape* makes for a disjunctive journey that not only provides a psychological correlative to Riley's music, but also to the mess of life itself. There's futility as a Starbucks employee disfigures her facial piercings with blue plasters; mute desire as our muse kisses the lips of a stone statue, watches his sweetheart tap dance in an enclosed railway bridge; pure love as skate-kid twins ride a micro-scooter on a running machine. A tripped-out, friendly policeman waves like a demented toy in front of Buckingham Palace and New Scotland Yard. There's fury and loss as music and image glottal- stop into a cluttered interior of taxidermy birds and animals and a couple kissing on the sofa, a high-pitched industrial scream and deer being hunted on the television (a repeat from *House & Garage* turned profound horror movie), close-ups of a smug Home Counties hunter laughing and his small son, blood coagulating on his cheek.

Mixtape's onslaught and hallucinogens act by stealth as it shifts through layers of performance (boys jam in a studio, playing a track that's different to Riley's but seemingly closer to its meaning than a lip-synch) and artifice (a ridiculously lurid kid clutches the lead of a tortoise wearing rhinestones). Our genuine and psychological disorientation is perversely resolved and blown wide open as a day-glo

35

old lady steps from her mini-cab, paying the ferryman of her own River Styx and, pure radiance, removes her shades, picks up her suitcases and walks into a leafy cemetery, consumed by private rapture. The soundtrack winds itself out as it wound itself in, like a plane taking off, and, finally, there's a strobing shot of a gravestone, only maybe saying 'TO DIE IS GAIN'.

Perhaps *Mixtape* is a rites-of-passage essay, though its action is more metaphysical than storytelling, its duration a complex of component parts. Shooting largely (and for the first time) on 35mm, Relph and Payne seem to turn this conceivably commercial filter into a comment on itself and on what an audience expects from TV ad-land 'production values'. The repeating high-energy soul mantra of the lyrics 'you're no good' turns angst and 'success' brilliantly on their heads, reconfigured as an unapologetic and bravura declaration of intent.

While their formal concerns are more separate than synchronous, there are other aptly camp correlatives between these two videos and Versace than an obviously shared canvas: I first saw DonAtella play live at Gavin Brown's Enterprise, New York, three days before Relph and Payne's debut there last year. The Versace jacket loaned to Leckey for the gig was sported by Mr Brown himself for Relph and Payne's love-drenched opening bash. Nick Relph is currently a member of DonAtella (though has yet to figure in a performance), and when *Mixtape* had its New York debut at the same gallery last October, its soundtrack was played through Leckey's massive resident sound system. Oh, and *Mixtape*'s breathtaking and joyous iconoclasm, as breakdancers hit the deck of a full-colour pavement reproduction in chalk of Botticelli's *Venus*, is not so far away from Gianni Versace describing how he used to play football on a Medusa's head mosaic in a dried-up fountain that he could see from his bedroom window when he was a child.

Romantic, Beyond, Impossible and Heartbreaking: An open response to Tilda Swinton's 2002 Vertigo address 'In the Spirit of Derek Jarman'

Dear Tilda,

We met once, you and I, a dinner at Casale Franco. Though that was ages ago and I think I was very different.

I wrote to *The Guardian* last year when I read the version of your *Vertigo* Edinburgh lecture that they published, asking them for a right of reply... I'd written something for them about a year before that, when the Lux Centre (where I worked) was shut down and all the staff made redundant on the spot. Actually they asked me to do it, they seem to like post-facto laments from the frontline. What I'd wanted to write in response to your lecture, by my own pitch, was quite the opposite. It's not all *Sunday Times* 'digested opinions about marketable artistic endeavours' that makes the papers like you said in Edinburgh. It's also quite a dash of misery, the erosion of independence measured in column inches or a double-page spread. So *The Guardian* never replied.

I'm interested in change. We've been thinking a lot recently about the relationship between cinema and change. I wonder how strange it must be, the avant-garde in waiting for access to the Royal Festival

37

First published in *Vertigo*, vol.2, no.5 (Summer 2003).

Hall. Renegade 'punk-spunk nonsense' waiting for its BFI [British Film Institute] DVD release. And what happens when that happens? Maybe one accepts invitations.

So this then, my letter, is like an invitation. What I want you to know is that there are pockets of resistance. That the terms have changed. That in fact we're finding alternative structures, not completely free of the institution but much freer of the film industry than you seem to think possible. Of course we're angry, and we all have reason to be, but actually right now there is optimism. People working together, in the mess of all this life.

Do you know the videos of Nick Relph and Oliver Payne? This is an England. Do you know the films of Jimmy Robert? This is romantic, beyond, impossible and heartbreaking. Have you been to see anything outside of what we think of as The Cinema? This form, Cinema, is one way. There are others, moreover there are other ways of understanding the auditorium and it's these alternatives we're mining nowadays. Nostalgia may exist but it rarely does anyone any good. It's like still looking at the Pre-Raphaelites in the Tate – they change nothing.

I curate the film programme for Whitechapel Art Gallery. What we're trying (and I should emphasise, trying) there is to build an artists' cinema. A place of questions, of new work, old work, but a site where things can happen, shifts might occur. It doesn't always occur, but that's the beauty of the effort that is shared and made with an audience.

For the past few months a group of us have been working on a project with the women's film agency Cinenova. They're now under threat, but more of that in a paragraph. This project we're working on is called 'Mary Kelly'. It's organised collectively, around the work Cinenova distributes; a series of screenings, a publication, discussion. The first was a showing of Lizzie Borden's *Born in Flames* (1983). Do you know this film? A feminist revolution has occurred in New York

38

that touches on every aspect of work, life, culture, politics. The screening took place at the re-branded Other Cinema. You know, the one that used to be the Metro.[1] We sat in the auditorium afterwards and volunteers from the audience read out two statements from members of Other Cinema staff and one from a disgruntled customer. We talked for a long time about working conditions there at the cinema. Not confrontationally, just together. We began to explore ideas.

The Mary Kelly Project is attempting to pose radical questions about working practices, not just what it means to sit in an auditorium and take part in that experience, but what it means to programme film/video, to organise outside of Cinema, to find alternatives to the received structures of all this instead of waiting and working until we gain entry into a system that we profoundly doubt, that has been constructed, like most systems, around illicit notions of self-protection, mainly by men.

In the meantime, in the course of my thinking about writing to you, the BFI, who were housing the film prints that Cinenova distributed, decided they just didn't want to do this anymore – the room they had they don't have any more, mysteriously. They are returning them. Cinenova is run by women and engages with women's film and video. A close friend of mine, an artist called Emma Hedditch, manages it and she does this on a voluntary basis – that is, she gets no money. Which isn't the point of my grist but it is important you know it. We're now working on saving Cinenova in the face of no current public funds but with the energy of belief and conviction. Theory/ practice. Organisational structures. Imperative we sort these out, we claim them, they reflect the politics of our work – artists, curators, managers, collectives, people – if we can get there, and, crikey!, maybe we can?

There's something altogether more fluid going on today. Like with raves in the 80s we're all on the motorway waiting for the call to the next point for the next call, and we're keeping on moving but growing with it. It's a shame you missed the screening of Anthony McCall and Andrew Tyndall's film *Argument* (1978) in 2001 at Pentonville Prison, because that made some sense. Maybe you'd like to come to Emma Hedditch's project-based exhibition at Cubitt Gallery in September? Maybe you'd like to come to Whitechapel? At the end of this year we're starting a new project there – 'Utopia' – an assessment of the no-place, art/film/anthropology, politics actually, challenges, attempts to move beyond the audience kept in rows receiving the screen like we are too often expected to receive the decisions made by governments.

There's more to say but less to no space left to say it in, but do also go visit The Horse Hospital, check the Lux's calendar. I'll jot some web addresses below, just in case. And this is, of course, an open letter and an open invitation.

Yrs, Ian

1. [The Other Cinema was a brief-lived arthouse cinema in Soho, Central London in the early 2000s run by the longstanding, eponymous political film collective. It closed in 2004.]

40

Experimental Film Today

The University of Central Lancashire has the look of a business park of mildly designed pseudo-Docklands buildings in split sites that sprawl across the post-industrial urban landscape of Preston. Out of term time and in the more traditional English summer which August's heatwave might make us forget, the grey skies, quick chill breeze and occasional drizzle did nothing to alleviate a pervasive sense of desolation. This does not make it a more or less likely pioneer in the world of experimental film, though it is here that a new MA begins this autumn in that subject.

To mark the inauguration of this new course, the conference 'Experimental Film Today' was convened. This was the potential first of a biannual series, much as Tate convened an International Council to discuss the role of film and video in the gallery two years ago. This event was inextricably linked to the appointment of its Kramlich Curator, the increased focus on this work in the permanent collection and its presentation in their exhibition spaces. If the fact that the university is only now working on acquiring its first 16mm projectors caused some confusion as to the depth of their intentions (those used for the accompanying screenings were shipped from London with a projectionist to operate them) then the conference proper provided scant reassurance. Papers ranged from Malcolm Le Grice's

41

First published in *Art Monthly*, 269 (September 2003), p.42.
The conference 'Experimental Film Today' was held
at the University of Central Lancashire, 4–6 July 2003.

erudite though basic history and three-category definition of the field (a generic, undergraduate staple) to the artist-theorist R. Bruce Elder's impassioned convolutions about the haunted world of late modernity and the profound formal instability of an incredibly stable canon made up of Picasso, Gertrude Stein and Stan Brakhage.

The ghost of Brakhage loomed large throughout, and while one hesitates to claim that his recent death alone had precipitated a particular panic as to where the film avant-garde might now be located, it was ironically one of the rare contemporary events considered in Preston. A seance for the maestro was not an idle thought that some of us explored while walking past a dead rat in the halls of residence's car park (our observations prompting images of Brakhage's famously deceased dog Sirius). It was actually a redundant thought when, after a memorial screening in Brakhage's honour, R. Bruce Elder became the conduit between us and the artist, fantastically answering questions on Brakhage's behalf that had not been asked of him by the conference delegates while he was alive ('What would Stan think about Sonic Youth using his films as part of their stage show?').

Anecdote notwithstanding, it was exactly these troubled, directionless relations to the artist-monoliths of experimental film for which the conference's general quibbling over terms ('avant-garde'/'vanguard' 'experimental'/'artists'' film/video etc.) was an unnecessary smoke screen. A number of speakers clutched at the straws of recent, gallery-based exhibitions. This either marked a continuing divide between 'art' and 'cinema', in part a historical-political prejudice between diametrically opposed systems of production, exhibition and ownership, or attempted to yoke together relationships between current art trends (i.e. video installation) and past experimental film practice (Chris Meigh-Andrews on experimental film's relation to video art, Jackie Hatfield on expanded cinema). Paris-based filmmaker Pip Chodorov spoke on the new French lab scene, locating experimental practice firmly within a traditionally orientated, craft-based tradition, entirely separate from the art gallery and kept alive by his incredibly focussed, almost messianic support for this work as a teacher-cum-technical guru. Much as Le Grice attempted to distinguish experimental film from commercial cinema along economic lines, Chodorov lamented the organisational shift in the sector between artist-run distributors to financially viable ones, the French company Light Cone in particular.

Le Grice's binaries, equated with the difference between the experimental and the corporate (the marketing and branding biases of feature film production), were aligned to the difference between art and commercial cinema as a validating definition. Such a summary position fell disappointingly short of acknowledging the gallery system's own commercial onus – a rose-tinted view omitting the branding and marketing strategies of our public spaces, the leisure economy specifically targeted by the current proliferation of live art events that is no less fuelled by the acceleration of artists' film and video screenings. For traditionalists the concept of entertainment never figured, leaving the feisty Duncan Reekie (a founder member of the collective Exploding Cinema, ironically scheduled against the showing of R. Bruce Elder's *Eros and Wonder*, 2003) finally to mount his broadside against the state-constructed, self-industrialising avant-garde on behalf of the underground. Reekie lambasted rarified and cosseted film-as-film as 'handicraft', calling for the avant-garde to unravel itself, to dissolve under the embarrassing weight of its incestuous self-invention, against the delegates' reply that underground culture remains entirely dependent on the status quo of the dominant culture for its very definition.

Mark Webber's important touring series of screenings that mapped the 'first' ten years of avant-garde film in Britain, 'Shoot Shoot Shoot' (2002), was well-acknowledged in Julia Knight's financial analysis of its benchmark funding structure (straddling the impact of actual screenings and the long-term gains of new prints struck for the project), though the David Curtis-curated display at Tate Britain, 'A Century of Artists' Film in Britain', has yet to enter the discourse. Nevertheless a special screening of Le Grice's new work, *The Cyclops Cycle* (1998/2003) (a five-section, triple-screen video work that moves at times quite beautifully from abstraction to narrative to diary), clearly passed the mantle of responsibility from Curtis (to whom the first section is dedicated) to Webber, whose profile touchingly figures in the final part. Jackie Hatfield was not wrong to comment on this sector's tendency to self-historicise and its generally irregular relationship to women artists.

With all the introspective, meandering self-questioning and limp clamouring for positions, the absurdity became painfully apparent of a sector adrift, looking for its leaders in the face of an expansion from the co-operative structures of its 60s and 70s legacy into the public playground of major art (and educational) institutions. The subtext of this quest for the holy grail of a current avant-garde felt more like self-protectionism than meaningful exchange.

Only in the inspiring paper given by Dennis Hopkins and Will Rose, of Leeds-based Lumen and the Evolution Festival, was there a genuine cause for optimism. Hopkins and Rose detailed their recent curatorial work with mainly American artists engaged with video-gaming experiments and computer modifications – Cory Arcangel, Tom Betts, Jodi, Joseph DeLappe and more – whose work not only transcends the staid parameters of experimental film while correlating to its genesis in structural cinema, crossing between auditorium and gallery space, but is also a testament that work made means nothing without being alive, now. Instead of listening to the University of Central Lancashire's John van Aitken's final comments of the conference, hoping it had not 'put us off' experimental film, that perhaps we should all go home 'have a bath and watch some television', I felt more inclined to act, to abandon academia's limiting frustrations, leave the cloisters and quite frankly go out more. 'Today' might just be staring us in the face.

Palace Calls Crisis Summit

I'm in Oberhausen. It's 2002. 'Katastrophe' is the festival's special programme; an epic, exhaustive selection of film and video works that unpick, map and re-invent the catastrophe, historically and in our time, cultural products of a social obsession, of a collective unconscious willing the catastrophe into being, for art, for entertainment, perversely as some indicator that we might be alive. We respond to the information presented in a way prescribed by already being in the cinema auditorium. Moral outrage, validation, political unrest – as an audience (audiences interest me a lot), we are complicit in the spectacle: thrilled, appalled, challenged, frustrated. Under the occupation of the screen...

Film festivals can be lonely places, the auditorim also prescribing isolation. My hotel room, its satellite TV, becomes both a friend and the site of private communication, between oneself and oneself, between oneself and the memory of a world. Events unravelling on the English-language news channels are conversations that I am carrying with me during the day, from the television into the auditorium in increasingly bizarre correspondence, like a growing community. Israel is holding Yasser Arafat hostage in his Ramallah compound. Over the course of these days he is released... I meet Alia Arasoughly, who lives round the corner from Arafat but has just about made it to Germany.

45

First published in *Film [lokal] (Dominique Gonzalez-Foerster, Markus Schinwald, Thomas Steffl, Costa Vece, Albert Weis)*, exhibition catalogue, ed. Markus Heinzelmann (Frankfurt: Revolver, 2003), pp.40–46.

She presents her film *Hay mish Eishi* (*This Is Not Living*) (2001) and she is talking about news footage, about the margins of the frame and it's the first time I understand this. News reports for Alia are not about the content of an interview but about attempting to see literally beyond their subjects to check on the conditions of the surrounding buildings, houses of her friends, her own house, whether they are still standing, occupied, looted...

On CNN, the Dutch right-wing independent leader Pim Fortuyn is assassinated. In the auditorium, Hamburg has been rebuilt after World War II. Le Pen on the television is celebrating record election results and the people of France begin a public protest. We watch the Hindenburg's collapse and crash in luxurious, horrifying flames. An EgyptAir plane has crashed somewhere. A few hours later the plane hasn't crashed, it's just made an emergency landing. Mediated. *The Eternal Frame* [Ant Farm, 1976] is shown, an incredible, hysterical re-document, re-performance of JFK's assassination in which Dallas residents photograph this re-enactment as if it is real, their belated souvenir. On TV, a Dutch man is interviewed and says 'we used to be a nice, funny country'. Italy refuses Palestinian exiles.

Jump cut. Six months later. Now I'm back in London. November, the London Film Festival. At the Gala screening of Peter Mullan's 'The Magdalene Sisters' there are mob scenes outside the cinema. Police, crash barriers. Based on ('inspired' by) a profoundly shocking television documentary, this feature film re-creates (with some concessions to hair and make-up) the abuses carried out on women in Ireland punished by their own society's adherence to an extremist Catholic doctrine and imprisoned in the vicious correction centres called Magdalene laundries. The director and his cast appear on stage at the end of the film to answer questions and from the floor something incredible is happening. A series of women stand up. They lived through this experience, for real. They are grateful for the film, but their memories are insufferable and they are listing the actual abuses carried out against them which go much further than narrative; this film is only the tip of an iceberg they say. 'The Catholic Church makes the Mafia look like a child learning to walk.' Suddenly something becomes clear.

46

This is absolutely vital, watching the film together. Catharsis through collective re-experiencing, something that did not happen when however many viewers tuned in to the television documentary, despite it being actually more graphic, more disturbing – inspiring, even. The feature film came close to social work. Ground swell. Two days later and Alexander Sokurov's new film *Russian Ark* is being screened in the same cinema. No crash barriers, but the audience is full of royalty – Prince Michael of Kent is present. Brian Eno is sitting in the row behind. Sokurov genuflects magnificently, repeatedly. Introducing the film he is saying that cinema is a secondary art form, because it is young, compared, say, to oil painting. The Ark, for Sokurov Saint Petersburg's Hermitage museum, is like the actual vessel of salvation. Art (the art the Hermitage contains) will be our salvation and this is Russian. By implication, cinema is not salvation. This is perverse. The idea that art in a national museum is not there because of political, economic, social engineering, is not representative of agendas that museums everywhere would rather viewers (audience) were not aware of. Today's headline on London's local newspaper *The Evening Standard*: 'PALACE CALLS CRISIS SUMMIT'.

With the waves from documenta 11 now crashing on our beaches, Oberhausen's 2003 special programme 're<local>ization' (2002) is a timely investigation, via cinema, of precisely this ricocheting between the auditorium and the outside world, the seemingly new role of the artist in this context; the meaning of the local in the face of global culture, a frame within the frame, a pocket of resistance? Thematically, a collapse is precipitated, between art and news, between auditorium and television, information and emotion, that in the form of the installation works included also becomes a collapse of space, modes and registers of exhibition. This precisely counters Sokurov's misaligned equation, the festival's line of enquiry becoming a spot marked with and by a brand new 'x': $x = art + cinema$.

Given the urgency being attributed to artists operating as social commentators, analysts, documenters, and given that the gallery readily adopts the look of the cinema to facilitate their work, one wonders less about art and more about *cinema*: *cinema* = *?* ... Social change?

Information? Collectivity? That is, not only what does it mean for a piece of work to be shown in an auditorium but where are the limitations of this, what is the allure of its co-ordinates, where is the auditorium sited in relation to the world outside itself, how might the equation be unravelled?

Sited in a studio cinema with its seats removed, the works by Dominique Gonzalez-Foerster, Markus Schinwald, Thomas Steffl, Costa Vece and Albert Weis represent as much of an enquiry into the film festival context, as they question the limit of experience itself. Removing the auditorium's seating is an evacuation of the physical determinant that orders how we ordinarily view work in such a space, turning the room into a reference that the installations themselves oscillate around. With each piece shown for a single day, the viewer is able to enter the installation room at any point, repeatedly, and to stay for an indeterminate length of time. This temporal removal from the ticketing and fixed start times of the festival's film programmes is nevertheless within earshot of the café's cash tills, the queues of people waiting to enter the other auditoria and the generally frenetic activity of traditional festival-going. The installation room is also one which members of festival staff move through as a shortcut from foyer to projection box. It is a transitory space precisely because of the terms on which it attempts to assert its refuge. In short, the dialogue that for me was previously conducted between the hotel television's news channels, newspapers, the 'real' world and the resulting response to the content and function of 'film', the auditorium, is shifted into a more discrete dynamic, or, even, contained within and summarised by a shifting space that is much harder to define than the auditorium. In fact this dialogue is localised, encapsulated.

Viewed as a series or as individual works, my response hovers around a particular romanticism. As five frames of a curatorial narrative, the series begins and ends with a storm. From Costa Vece's lighthouse, illuminating disasters on our horizon line, to Dominique Gonzalez-Foerster's *Sturm* (1996), we as viewers shift from witnesses to players, through Albert Weis's *disposition* (2003), from a position of silent looking, to one of acting.

48

Vece's *La Fin du Monde* (2003) clearly marks the installation room as a sanctuary that is no less emphasised by the local noise of the festival's patrons just outside the door. Sweeping classic cinematic images of space explorations, computer malfunctions, collapsing buildings and explosions on the black walls, as if to illuminate rather than project them; a rough-shod lighthouse, made from cardboard boxes foraged from local shops, is stood on a makeshift plinth of pallets. At the calm centre of this horizon-line destruction, the base materials of Vece's sculpture are in themselves also a reassurance that is not without a sense of melancholy. The boxes of the lighthouse are stamped with their products: 'Procter & Gamble', 'Made in Belgium', 'Pistachios'. The technological failure inducing the videos' apocalypses is thrown humbly into relief, into a correspondence with an imaginary origin of these boxes; mass production, international trade and the local supermarket. And at that moment a festival technician appears from a door at the back of the previously infinite room, crosses the floor and exits into the foyer, another trader, a vessel.

Acts of intrusion. Progressively the act of intrusion becomes increasingly content. Intruding into Albert Weis's constructed metal-lined corridor we find our shadows projected onto the screens that block off each of its ends. A puppet show for our own entertainment, like a James Bond opening sequence, these shadows are the opposite of the surveillance footage that Weis shot in the streets and precincts around Oberhausen, where people pass by, irradiating whiteness due to the heat-sensitive camera he used for filming. The same camera in fact that the coalition forces used to seek and destroy in Iraq, that makes Oberhausen's urban-scape immediately as unfamiliar as Basra at night, an unrecognisable locale that shifts from theatre of fear to playground. The inhospitable is here made safe, celebrated paradoxically by trapping its viewers for the sake of their own release.

Gonzalez-Foerster's *Sturm* turns the installation room into a make-shift studio. To intrude (to view simply, even) is impossible in this room turned inside out. *Sturm* is such a functional collection of components that it flips from object into experience, as if the work rebounds its audience out of its installation space, back through the foyer, into an

49

auditorium and through to the flipside of a screen showing amateur yet well-lit drama. Well-lit dramas though are few and far between in the Oberhausen context (this is not so much the commercial territory that the *Sturm*-machine re/de-constructs) though what is made clear is another trajectory. When art meets cinema it generally takes its raw material from the commercial mainstream, repositions it, reframes it, re-enacts it: *La fin du monde*, Markus Schinwald's *Diarios* (2003), *Sturm*.

Schinwald's *Diarios* is in fact the closest of the five installations to the look of the cinema. Faced with a screen and a fragmented narrative, the surface of this piece is so acutely replicate of the traditional mode of exhibition as to belie its complex revelry. Schinwald's point perhaps is that there is a direct relationship (obliquely manifested) between a diary made public, the camera's ability to turn an object into its opposite, a set of hermetically sealed signs and the cinematic imperative to communicate. It is through information extraneous to the piece for example that we know the military bunker we think we are seeing is in reality a modernist church. A figure, so reminiscent of Richard Prince's photographs of the American archetypal Marlboro man (who looks like the generic hero of this story) was actually photographed on the outskirts of Vienna. Everything here which is exotic can in fact be found around Vienna, where the artist lives. That the private can become, in a frame, our unfamiliar universal, in much the same way as Costa Vece's lighthouse is not illuminating just any disasters, but our own and in turn, civilisation's.

From Schinwald through Vece's destruction to Thomas Steffl's idyll. *Helikopter* (2003) is no less than the explicit summation of the romantic (as process, as politics) that seems to me to permeate each of these works, as they localise a dialogue with the world by holding a mirror to their local context, their proximity not just to 'cinema' but to our experience of an actual cinema. *Helikopter* is a simplistic extreme of mimesis and abstraction. Transcendental, cognitive, emotional, it is a specific blueprint that is equally elemental. Steffl places a monitor outside the installation room. The festival places monitors outside its auditoria to display the progress of each film programme, relaying a video documentation of the screen to prevent audiences

50

entering mid-film. On Steffl's monitor is a red helicopter, at the point of take-off, blades pulsing at full speed, yet going nowhere, perfectly stationery in a green field. Projected onto a large, partially translucent screen inside is a silver helicopter, set in the same landscape though shot from a more stylised perspective, its blades also at full speed, overwhelmingly present. Monitor outside, screen inside. Touchstones. The shift in perspective, the red helicopter replaced by a silver one, mimics the semantic shift between outside and inside the auditorium (exterior/interior), between document and experience. Hearing the meticulously remodulated pulsing of the helicopter's blades as we face the screen is nothing short of induced meditation, an acoustic portal into the sublime. The longer I choose to stay in this space the more profoundly affecting this hallucinatory pulsing becomes. The more I choose to suspend myself in this space, the more this suspension effects a cognitive shift, an investment of energy, a removal from the outside world that reaffirms presence. The excitement of this impossibly minimal content is overwhelming. I leave the room convinced of something. I've changed. Social change. Change beyond that which occurs through information. The experience of a perfectly integrated Elysium from which there is no going back.

This is where I began writing, from a position of rethinking. A modification of experience, a movement inside precipitated by all the things outside. A hunch about Coleridge defining the romantic as the willing suspension of disbelief, that space, for Coleridge the theatre, modifies experience but that it's more complicated now than just theatre, sitting in rows, in silence, in darkness, for the prescribed time. That if change is to occur, Coleridge commenting on theatre provoking a leap of faith is as binary as the auditorium, while the process is in fact as nebulous as personal choice, as an extension of being alive. Choosing in fact to enter a space marked 'x' for crossroads.

Yet But If But If But Then But Then:
Peter Gidal

Using language isn't often (or always) easy.

Peter Gidal, 'The Anti-Narrative', *Screen*, vol.20, no.2 (1979)

As I say what one repeats is the scene in which one is acting the days in which one is living, the coming and going which one is doing, anything one is remembering is a repetition, but existing as a human being, that is being listening and hearing is never repetition. It is not repetition if it is that which you are actually doing because naturally each time the emphasis is different just as the cinema has each time a slightly different thing to make it all be moving.

Gertrude Stein, 'Portraits and Repetition', *Lectures in America* (1935)

It (unending duration) positions the viewer in a place of seeing, i.e. perception, without conflating that into knowing (as it is one extreme function, not the whole), without mixing the two up. The separation of the two underlies avant-garde film from Warhol on.

Peter Gidal, '*13 Most Beautiful Women* and *Kitchen*', *Undercut*, 1 (Spring 1981)

53

First published as 'Peter Gidal' (2003), *Luxonline*,
www.luxonline.org.uk/artists/peter_gidal/(printversion).html>
[last accessed on 10 January 2016]. (The title used here is from a late draft of the text, probably discarded for reasons of house style in the published version.)

This was where I started: with a question about what it means to make Peter Gidal's films the subject of a piece of writing, with the inevitable process of translation or evidence of 'understanding' that this incurs. This becomes a problem because of the way in which it implies a potential re-inscription onto the films (in somehow 'explaining') of the very modes of knowledge which they construct themselves against – the works themselves attempt to defy, structurally, any received notions about how, traditionally, 'cinema' might operate, and by doing so question also the ways in which cinema is described, inscribed, 'read' by standard interpretative practices.

Peter Gidal is a (self-theorising) theorist as well as a (self-defined, structural-materialist) filmmaker. Yet there is no indexical relationship between his writing and films, exacerbating a simple matching between theory and proof, so the problem becomes how to describe when the films themselves are precisely not about description, but about process, about something being produced not reproduced: not representational (although they do show recognisable things, sometimes) but anti-representational, anti-narrative – structural. In as much they are like a resistance, an exclusion zone, engaged in manifestations of 'unpleasure' that effectively block normative response instead of facilitating it, and this attempt is political, a resistance to capitalist (patriarchal?) structures through which 'cinema' might be otherwise understood (capitalism and patriarchy). So should this process of questioning not extend to the business of me writing this? Should it not question this business, what this (critical/cultural) 'industry' is also about – would this not be the best way to 'describe' the films, to raise a question about this piece of writing as you are reading it?

※

In the first draft of this essay the opening paragraph would have read:

> Peter Gidal's writings are not Peter Gidal's films. I am writing this. You must be reading this, but you do not have to. Reading is different to watching. To write this is an implicated activity, about to be necessarily non-descriptive, just ____ ; resistance, something, nothing. To know (each word implicates), for me to know,

is prescribed by its refusal, specifically, by the films of Peter Gidal, because they cannot be 'known'. Peter Gidal's films are not Peter Gidal's writings, which have already fed into, back to, reading (writing) that is not watching, is not Peter Gidal's films, nor Peter Gidal's writing. So I am writing this, caught because: if there is not knowledge but there is perception there also cannot be a translation (description) because there is not representation...

That was one start point that was not liked editorially (and I did not necessarily disagree) because of the imperative to communicate, i.e. because of how things in this 'business' of education must be organised, because of the already inscribed ways of knowing or coming to know that Peter Gidal's films attempt to challenge. Another start point, the first-draft second paragraph, was more narrative:

> Peter Gidal came to England in the summer of 1968, just days after Andy Warhol was shot, steeped in philosophy, a fine canon of European existentialist writers and playwrights, and having studied theatre directing himself...

It would have been a deliberately truncated (begun to be abandoned) narrative imposition, a reproduction.

⁂

At the end of *Conditions of Illusion* (1975) a quote from Louis Althusser's 'On the Materialist Dialectic' scrolls slowly from the bottom of the screen. It is meant to be read, not made impossible to read like the flying quotations he uses in *Assumption* (1997, 1 min). The quotation is also found in Gidal's seminal 1975 text 'Theory and Definition of Structural/Materialist Film', neither necessarily coming before or after the other – that is, the text not describing the films but being of the films. In part it reads:

> A 'theory' which does not question the end whose by-product it is remains a prisoner of this end and of the 'realities' which have imposed it as an end.[1]

If '"theory"' is the (/one?) 'by-product' of an end, by implication it must question this end rather than effect its summation, be equally of process or it will let the 'real' in by the back door, the 'real' of course which is unknowable.

Peter Gidal was a pivotal member of the London Filmmakers' Co-op and taught at the Royal College of Art from 1971 to 1983.

1. Louis Althusser, quoted in Peter Gidal, 'Theory and Definition of Structural/Materialist Film', in *Structural Film Anthology*, ed. Peter Gidal (London: British Film Institute (BFI), 1978), p.12.

56

The Projected Object

Advance-guard cinema. Artists' film. Avant-garde film. Experimental film. Film Art. Independent film. Personal film. Serious film. Short film. Underground film. [~ and video]: Artists. Filmmakers. / Formal-Political, Historical-Contemporary, Lost-Found. / Festivals, Cinemas, Galleries (Backrooms, Bedrooms, Community Centres). Collectives, Curators, Auteurs. / Budget/no-budget, state-sponsored/self-funded. / Ownership-Distribution.
} Inclusion/Exclusion.

The words used to describe a field of activity perhaps have never been less stable than those applied to people making moving images which are not commodifiable feature films. Perhaps this is not incidental. Instability is not commercial and, predicated on guarantees, not risks, 'wise' investment forces the imperative of containment and definition (ownership and/or consumerism). The artist working with moving images defines a position within, against or circumnavigating the particular economic structures of distribution, exhibition, production, often as the form and content of their work. Strategies are multiple, conscious and deliberate, as multiple in fact as the various political sets and subsets, practice-based micro-pockets, cultural, sub-cultural and personal divisions that are more characteristic of the 'short' history of artists making moving images than an institutional drive towards cohesion. It seems more and more characteristic for the moving image outside of the cinema mainstream, then, that the preferred position is one of argument; opposition, resistance, struggle, abandon.

57

First published in German as 'Das projizierte objekt', trans. Gaby Gehlen, in *Kurz und Klein: 50 Jahre Internationale Kurzfilmtage Oberhausen*, ed. Klaus Behnken (Ostfildern-Ruit: Hatje Cantz, 2004), pp.191–96.

For this piece of writing I veer towards the terms 'artist' and 'artists' film' (as an abbreviation for – rather than a formalist elision of – 'artists' film and video'). Choose any words from the list and they ricochet back through the practice they attempt to describe. Both here and in general, 'artist'/'artists' film' have come to feel closest to the territory which interests me and closest also to the conundrum of practice/production and exhibition(-distribution) in our current climate. These tags might open more areas of difference than represent a particular closure. My point is that the instability of terms is not confined to semantics, but is interconnected with the crisis and culturally prescribed agendas of where artists' filmworks are shown and the literal, conceptual and economic implications of these physical spaces: namely, the institutional wrestling between gallery and cinema. Furthermore, my lines of reading the situations I aim to outline are consciously investigatory, deliberately attempted to provoke questions. It feels as necessary to complicate what some might understand as a binary opposition between white cube and black box as it does to mark the factious nature of artistic practice. Gallery/Cinema? Artists' film.

Moving beyond the binary, then. Nothing strikes me as a straightforward difference between the gallery and the cinema, though of course obvious differences do exist: access, economy, cultural status, history.

There are public galleries and there are private galleries. The cultural status that the (contemporary) public gallery seemingly bequeaths is more often than not prefaced by the commercial gallery system. That is, public galleries buy works once they have a proven economic status within the commercial system – meaning that they have been bought by enough private collectors within the commercial sector, or even quite directly bought by private collectors for the public gallery. Yet the economic history of works of art in public galleries is never made clear to their visitors; never will there be a room that we are told contains 'commercially successful work from the 1990s' even though this might be both exactly what we are seeing and its reason for being there.

This general picture serves as both metaphor and context for gallery-based artists' film. The line between film/video installation works

58

and single-screen projections in the gallery may be finer than it seems at first – though, already referring to a subset, I mean predominantly here those works presented in the gallery on a single screen, generally in a black box, faced by rows of viewers. Like the Hollywood feature from which the artist's work diverts, the public gallery is dependent for its cultural success on the masking of its structures (or even, to borrow a term so predominant in an 'experimental film' history, its *material-ity*). Aspiring to the look of the cinema in the gallery space, this reference point is merely that: an image that elides the associated economy of the cinema. In commercial art, and/or the public gallery upon which it relies for ultimate status, a single piece of work may be seen by many but it will be owned by the wealthy few. This is the diametrical opposite of cinema's economy, where the audience equally invest the price of a ticket in an altogether different (utopian?) model of financial sustain-ability. Within the gallery, the economics of cinema are always masked in its presentation, its *re*-presentation, in the way that public galleries always mask the relations between works of art and the 'validating' commercial strategies which bring them to account.

This *partial*-general allows dividing lines to be drawn that may also be refuted by example. The work of film or video made for distri-bution against the work made in a limited edition for the consump-tion of the private collector may be conceptual opposites, but they are not in practice always simply mutually exclusive. Matthew Barney's *Cremaster Cycle* (completed 2002, full duration 397 mins) remains impossible to programme in the cinema without gallery endorsement, although the work is exhibited by the 'gallery' in an actual cinema auditorium, rather than a re-created one. The buyer of one 35 mm print of its editions invests in the invisible object (the work actually is the projected image) and its imaginary audience – in one film can is the *idea* of cinema. Obversely, the films of Sharon Lockhart, an equally successful gallery artist, are intentionally traditionally distrib-uted in Europe and America. Matthias Müller and Christoph Girardet may make installation works together or separately, though extracted from these may be videos that appear in the Oberhausen Short Film Festival competition programmes. While there are general models for conceptual difference, there might also be cultural prejudice, but there are no rules. While there are economies, in the equation between making work and making a living, there are also sensibilities.

Despite the shudder that runs down the spine of some at the most recent development of the editioned *videotape*, the practice of artists making film/video that nowadays sells successfully through the gallery system stands an infinitely greater chance of financial independence and sustainability than those who rely exclusively on the distribution model for artists' film developed at the inception of the famous 'co-operatives' in the late 1960s. Independence, that is, from income exterior to that generated by the work made – and sustainability in terms of facilitated continued production. If organisations such as the (now dissolved) London Filmmakers' Co-op (LFMC) might have been characterised by their presentation of alternative models to dominant cinema culture, by a profound resistance to its terms and conditions, then there is a confusion about the exact terms of access to the dominant culture that such a legacy is now translated into: artists' film – significantly, materially *film* (as form and content) – transferred to digital formats for the ease, for example, of gallery exhibition, or retrospectively editioned film prints for the private gallery economy?

Is the increase of gallery-exhibited filmworks responsible for the lack of a sufficient artists' cinema infrastructure? Maybe we ought to think more about the ways in which we and other people choose to spend our/their money, or the ways in which this has changed. The collector's confidence in buying a film or videotape is actually a very recent phenomenon. To argue cinema's opposition to the gallery feels like something of a misnomer, presupposing as it must a discreet and coherent alternative. Almost like a rehearsal for the current anxiety surrounding the battle of exhibition spaces and their (socio-economic) structures, in fact the history of artists' film distribution is one riddled with not dissimilar issues of inclusion and exclusion. The LFMC might have originated as an open archive where membership entitled the subscriber's work to be included in the collection, but the patriarchal bias of its exhibition and promotional policies was already (historically) questioned from within when a focussed group of women filmmakers withdrew from that organisation, removed their works and formed an independent distribution and exhibition network, Circles, in the late 1970s. Visitors to Oberhausen in 2002 might recall Madeleine Bernstorff's catalogue essay accompanying her selection of two programmes of Joyce Wieland's work. Wieland's films were excluded from the 'Essential Collection' (basically a self-promoting repertory canon of works) of the contemporaneously formed New York Anthology Film Archives in 1970. Inclusion/exclusion. In the construction of its canons and in its modes of operation what might have been an alternative to the dominant culture of the past seems also, in retrospect, to employ enough of that culture's tropes to actually appear more like a replicant structure than a replacement one, something that is not least borne out by the current desire amongst some of those founding artists for assimilation into the gallery.

Once a year it may become an ark, but there is no Ship Lichtburg[1] in which the practitioners of artists' film have been happily sailing together all this time – I would suggest that the image of a flotilla of vessels, some with rudders, some without, some with oars and the occasional speedboat, sailing for a long time on a very large ocean is a better metaphor. Certainly the fluidity of positions, moving towards and away from the institution, is more accurate than the self-devised historical image of separation that so consciously benefits a wilful division between the gallery and the cinema.

If part of my intention is to move the multiplex-cinema style of the gallery system into a less ambiguous light, then it is also to push our understanding of alternative cinema practices into a more ambiguous one. I want to return to the fine line between the gallery referencing cinema and the artist making an installation work, and consider this in relation to the 'auditoria' of non-commercial cinema. The single-screen installed in the gallery is not a fixed entity; size, scale, positioning all vary. There is the flux of fashion, and there are also experiential differences. The projected image might fill a whole wall, floor to ceiling, edge-to-edge. Jane and Louise Wilson's work overwhelms in this sense, for example, resonates with an *exaggerated* cinematic (almost, perhaps, the image-made-object to make private ownership more conceivable).

61

The projected image might occupy a screen-space roughly equivalent to the dimensions, scale and positioning of the traditional cinema screen, say as in the work of Nick Relph and Oliver Payne. In fact, when their important video *Mixtape* (2002) was included in the Beck's Futures show at London's ICA in 2002, it was exhibited actually in the institute's smallest, 40-seat cinema (and shown at fixed times for the duration of the exhibition). For the viewer, this is already an alternate relation to that of the image-object. In both cases the screen may be single, but it is deliberately so.

The screen in commercial cinema *is* a fixed entity (excepting the shift in size of different projection formats), its authority confirmed by our experience of the building that houses it: box office, foyer, corridors, ushers. The exterior's self-promotional façade is broken down as we travel through the interior warren into the auditorium, and is then reinscribed by our relation to the monumentalist screen, an unquestioned frame, the standard format. We are experientially removed from life, through the movement of our own bodies. Dominant culture dominating.

It could be argued that physical space in these examples bears relation to our experience of the work shown, consciously or subconsciously. We could choose the gallery's strategy as an oppositional one based on elision, but I would rather suggest a similarity in difference that in turn opens yet more questions. The available auditoria for experimental works have generally been entirely other than the standard format that the corporate provides. Festivals are an exception to this, not least Oberhausen's Lichtburg, which might mark a critical interjection between spaces rather than the obliteration of one by the other. Imperative realignments start to occur from this point. The gallery refers more specifically to dominant cinema than to the legacy – meaning in part the physical locales – of experimental cinema. The 'found footage' in artists' work might be understood as the performance of this dynamic; from Joseph Cornell's *Rose Hobart* (1936) to Müller and Girardet's *Phoenix Tapes* (1999), where small sections of Hitchcock films are looped, slowed down, expanded, intensified into a crystallised psychological space-time. The footage is 'found' not in

62

the work of other artists, and permission to 'find' it is based on a distinction which is ultimately, I think, parallel to the division between 'art' and 'life', between maker and materials, 'art' indeed and 'cinema'.

By means of illustration it is interesting to consider the variety of screening venues used by the London Filmmakers' Co-op in its first twenty years as noted in A. L. Rees's text that accompanied Mark Webber's 'Shoot Shoot Shoot' survey in 2002:

> The LFMC was begun by a small group of such enthusiasts who screened films at an avant-garde book shop in Charing Cross Road in 1965–66. ... In 1968–69 the filmmakers were in control of the LFMC and more films were being made. When it moved north to Robert Street, on the fringe of Camden Town, in 1969, the LFMC ... was already developing its own ethos as well as the facilities to shoot, process and edit films. ... It [then] moved successively through a series of former industrial spaces: 'the Dairy', 'the Piano Factory' and finally 'the Laundry', its home in Gloucester Avenue for twenty years. In the crucial years of 1971–75, it occupied austere studios in Prince of Wales Crescent. *Each location stamped its shape on the films that were made there*, from the meltdown of media in the 'expanded cinema' of the two Arts Labs, to a more purist climate at Fitzroy Road. En route, the LFMC effectively invented a new avant-garde genre, the British Structural/Materialist film. Its tough and demanding screening programme often featured the latest work, straight from the workshop.[2] (Emphasis mine.)

'Each location stamped its shape on the films that were made there' might be extended into each location shaping the physical experience of the visitor/viewer into one of radical difference – an experience that is deliberately not foregrounded by mainstream cinema-going. Moreover, there came to exist a relation between these physical spaces and 'the films that were made *there*': places with not only technical facilities and collective interests but also an exhibition context. While sometimes questioning this model, the same might be said of any film club in Europe or America where the choice of venue can be as much a critical, entertaining, political or social metatext as the work shown.

63

What I mean is that the frame a building or screening space places around the work shown there is perhaps a pre-variation of the ways in which the gallery's installing of a single-screen work operates: namely, the determination of specific viewing conditions as an integral part of the experience (and meaning) of the work shown, while the gallery permits the individual control of the artist to determine these conditions as a microcosm within the institution.

There are other issues of control in these situations that should be noted. The artist filmmaker in a distribution collection, generally speaking, surrenders control of where their work is shown and in what context. This is true in particular of works that are shorter than the acceptable feature film length, the short film, artists' film exhibited within the confines of our current cinema structures. Curatorial process against cinema programming. Cinema curator? Actually this role, whatever we choose to call it, adopts a heightened significance in working with artists' film in the cinema, especially in accessing works from distributors rather than the makers. Distributors do not operate any kind of curatorial censorship in the ways that a private gallery (to serve the commercial imperative) would certainly guide all exhibition opportunities for the work of the artists they represent. Nor are gallery works always exactly or easily translatable into the cinema auditorium. The same of course might be said for cinema works translated into installations – and without commenting on their success, there are a number of precedents for this kind of activity: John Smith, Chantal Akerman, while Kutluğ Ataman consistently shifts between poles.

T. J. Wilcox's film *The Little Elephant* (2000) is silent. It was included in an Oberhausen competition programme in 2001 and was shown in silence, appropriately enough one might think. Yet Wilcox's works are shown in the gallery on freestanding projectors as 16mm loops. The viewer hears the sound of the projector. The silent film is not a silent room. Recently showing all of his films (and videos) to date at London's Tate Modern, Wilcox requested that the projector be removed from the projection box and installed in the auditorium itself. When this became impossible the compromise was to pipe the sound of the projector from the projection box into the auditorium instead. Of course, this had an effect, but it was not the same as the clearly visible though hermetically sealed system of projector/film loop/screen/image that occurs in exhibiting the same work in the gallery, and it is this system, predicated on the objecthood of its component parts, which informs our response to the image.

Meaning, space, context, necessities. Perhaps this example best typifies what I've been thinking about: that between the gallery and the cinema some things are clear and some things are opaque, and that transparency or mystification are equally self-serving, mirroring systems rather than opposing ones, in complicated rather than binary relations. Of course, there are other aspects of film viewing than the ones I have explicitly mentioned which are implicated in the act of exhibiting: duration, freedom/restriction of movement, repetition. There are more omissions too: the importance of expanded cinema in relation to the gallery installation, cinema in relation to performance art, gallery auditoria showing programmes of artists' film. What, though, I hope to suggest, in this writing's own context of the Oberhausen festival, through the gaps and fissures of language, is that the areas discussed might be nodal points from which to move forwards from, towards ways in which a radically re-imagined cinema might make itself known. Between the 'cinema' the gallery elides and the appalling multiplex culture it mimics. Beyond the traps of cultural (economic) status with which we are plagued, from this start point, not to replicate but to remember, replenish and communicate.

1. [The reference is to the Lichtburg Filmpalast in Oberhausen which hosts the annual Short Film Festival Oberhausen. This essay was originally commissioned for a publication celebrating the festival's 50th anniversary.]
2. A. L. Rees, 'Locating the LFMC: the First Decade in Context', *Shoot Shoot Shoot: The First Decade of the London Film-Makers Co-operative and British Avant-Garde Film 1966–1976*, exhibition pamphlet, ed. Mark Webber (London: LUX, 2002), p.8.

I and I / *12 to 12: Notes on* UtopiaLive

On Saturday, 18 June 2005, the home of Henriette Heise and Jakob Jakobsen, or the Copenhagen Free University, opened to a mass audience for twelve hours. That is, the cinema space at Whitechapel Gallery, London, was open from midday until midnight, receiving a durational live broadcast from the University – organised with friend and co-worker Emma Hedditch – that is based in the home of Henriette Heise and Jakob Jakobsen. What unfolded was a major work that shifted 'reality' into performance, sliding between spontaneous action and speech and rehearsed actions, scripted speech, between visible and off-screen decision-making: mundane and beautiful, an essay on television delivered through the aesthetic of cinema.

> *The Free University is an artist-run institution dedicated to the production of critical consciousness and poetic language. We do not accept the so-called new knowledge economy as the framing understanding of knowledge. We work with forms of knowledge that are fleeting, fluid, schizophrenic, uncompromising, subjective, uneconomic, acapitalist, produced in the kitchen, produced when asleep or arisen on a social excursion – collectively.*

So reads the entry under 'SLEEP', three-quarters of the way through CFU's 'ABZ' – the closest thing they have to a manifesto.[1] It is an oft-quoted statement in any description of their project, but is used invariably minus its critical section heading. That the self-consciousness of such a definitive paragraph be modified by association with its seemingly opposite state of mind is precisely the point.

The 'ABZ' is a strictly non-alphabetical, a-systematic collection of texts that outlines a field of activity and enacts a methodology. That is, it is a blueprint for a way of working which to be understood requires an

67

First published in 'Cram Sessions at the BMA: 04 Counter Campus',
exhibition brochure (Baltimore: Baltimore Museum of Art, 2005), p.4. The *UtopiaLive*
event with the Copenhagen Free University was part of a season of film
screenings called 'Utopia' that Ian White programmed for the Whitechapel
Gallery, London in 2004–05.

engagement with the very practices it attempts to describe. 'UNHAPPY CONSCIOUSNESS' is explicated by the sentence 'A motor running in the background'; 'CONTESTATION' equals 'Strike and disappear'; an entry under 'MESS' is specific, like the news, about the Danish elections on Tuesday 20 November 2001, which saw a government supported by the far-right come to power. Other entries list organisations with which CFU have a literal or symbolic allegiance (Black Mountain College, London Anti-University...), or promote the work of affiliates (www.andiwilldo.net),[2] while still others are disarmingly first-person ('We are both sitting at the table, with our hands under our legs, waiting for the food to arrive. I am not sure if I should speak...'). The 'ABZ' becomes, through the act of reading, information and poetry, didactic and performative. Its message is found as much in the actual and metaphorical spaces between its words as it is in any attempt to summarise (rewrite) it into something that reads like a cohesive argument or defines a position. And this too is precisely the point.

EXODUS
The active refusal of the present social relations of capitalism,
an evacuation of its means of support and the construction
of an alternative. Not a direct opposition or negation, but the
immediate evacuation.

What constitutes this 'immediate evacuation'? In part it is a particular combination of occupation and escape, where opposition is configured not as destruction but as revelation, the occupation of a form conducted to make its organisational and operational principles apparent.

During the live broadcast, the auditorium at Whitechapel became the site of multiplying occupations; the University itself occupied by its organisers and collaborators, under a peculiar self-determined house arrest, the auditorium occupied by the projected durational event. Television and cinema occupied each other, the former read through the codes of the latter by the wide-screen format of the projected image, the carefully constructed camera positions foregrounding formal composition as a key function, the immediacy of the live represented by the cinematic image to effect a continuous mental flickering, a constant reminder that the 'everyday' being witnessed was in fact both a construction and a live event in which the viewer as receiver became complicit, or occupied, in other words, by the request to spend some time with people.

> *EVERYDAY LIVES*
> *Our work is usually closely connected to the daily life we live.*
> *The Copenhagen Free University is, in fact, situated and func-*
> *tions within the framework of our flat and household economy...*

At 4pm London time, we (CFU and the audience in the gallery) watched together two videos – an extract from Yvonne Rainer's film *Lives of Performers* (1972) and Dan Graham's video *Performer/Audience/Mirror* (1975) – on a screen erected in the University. The tops of the University inhabitants' heads were just visible on the screen in the auditorium, a beguiling mimicry of Graham stood in front of a mirror in the presence of an audience whom he then described from their reflections through a series of instructions that inverted authority. When the camera in the video piece moved it served as a jolt of recognition that the camera relaying this image projected in Copenhagen was not moving, that no one from the CFU was in Graham's audience, but also that no one in the auditorium was in the audience in Copenhagen even though we were sharing the act of looking. The double mediation of a projected image displaying a projected image, like a double negative, cut through geographical distance.

> *The Copenhagen Free University guarantees a wide array of per-*
> *sonal, improvised and politicised forms of knowledge embedded*
> *in social practises around us – forms of knowledge we would*
> *like to make explicitly social and create communities around.*

In Rainer's film extract, discursive texts were being spoken about acting, about modes of speech, correlating to the intimate stylisation into which those in the University had situated themselves, exposing the

69

formal acknowledgement of being simultaneously personal and conscious. Both videos were exemplars, and an interview between Rainer
and the writer Scott MacDonald published in *A Critical Cinema 2* (1992)
that I re-read after the event provides a telling exchange. Attempting
to locate the 'personal' in Rainer's work, MacDonald notes the difference between her films and those of a self-mythologising avant-garde
typified by the work of Stan Brakhage. Brakhage proceeds by extending his eye to the lens of camera, by filming the marks of his own
hand on a strip of film. Rainer describes her non-'visual' filmmaking
perversely as playing a form such as melodrama back on itself, to the
extent that it exposes the form's defining tenets such as narrative and
identification, making what they signify (emotion) explicit by their
absence – a practice Rainer describes as an expression of 'the emotional life lived at an extreme of desperation and conflict', or, even, an
evacuation through occupation.[3]

The last entry in CFU's 'ABZ' reads, finally:

> *MANIFESTO*
> *Today there are loads of manifestos being produced promoting*
> *all sorts of ready-made subjectivities wanting to become gov-*
> *ernment. Our intention was to produce a power that refuses to*
> *become government.*

This 'power that refuses to become government' is dependent on
ellipses. Precisely those ellipses effected by the act of reading what, by
that process, precipitates itself into being a counter-manifesto. Not to
replace a social system with its inevitable double but to construct an
alternative through the instigation of shared experience. To approach
the whisper from a stack of speakers with something other than its
explanation.

> *SUBJECTIVITY*
> *Become one, become many. I and I.*

1. [See 'The ABZ of the Copenhagen Free University', <http://
www.copenhagenfreeuniversity.dk/abz.html> (last accessed
on 10 January 2016).]
2. [The former website of the artist Emma Hedditch, mentioned
above, a frequent collaborator of both Ian White and the CFU.]
3. From 'Yvonne Rainer (on *Privilege*)', *A Critical Cinema 2*, ed. Scott
MacDonald (Berkeley: University of California Press, 1992), p.347.

Occupation: Animation and the Visual Arts

In 1936 the German artist-filmmaker-animator Oskar Fischinger was denounced as degenerate by the Nazi government. With an already established aesthetic that was anchored in the often astonishing, resonant relationship between (largely abstract) images and sound, he left the animation studio he had established and emigrated to Los Angeles. He began work in the factory system of the Hollywood studios – Paramount, MGM – and in 1938 for Walt Disney on *Fantasia* (1940). At Disney he was respected as an artist (weekly screenings of his films were held for the staff's appreciation), belittled as an employee (earning $60 a week as a 'motion picture cartoon effects animator') and resented – if not hounded – as a co-worker who was overly celebrated. On 1 September 1939 Germany invaded Poland. That same day a swastika was pinned to Fischinger's door and he immediately sought the termination of his contract that was finally granted on 31 October.

How such an apparently bizarre collapse of political understanding intersects with the industrialised workplace is not entirely the subject of this essay. Nor is how art and the artist might be defined in the context of this political chaos – against, through or within a political system to which they are otherwise marginal. Rather, the essay presents a proposition about animation, and attempts to open up a definition of animation to incorporate visual art that would not ordinarily be considered as such.

73

First published in *The animate! book: rethinking animation*, ed. Benjamin Cook and Gary Thomas (London: LUX, 2006), pp.120–31.

In the most general of senses animation might be considered as the transformation of static, two-dimensional images or objects into motion, the illusion of life or abstract rhythm, the exploitation of the possibilities that such a process affords – fantasy, making the impossible imaginable, defying laws of nature and physical boundaries. The proposition I would like to make is supported by the application of this general definition to the work of the artists Paul McCarthy, VALIE EXPORT and Catherine Sullivan. In their different practices are examples of animation rendered physically (in the body) and conceptually (as part of the works' formal strategies) that are developed through the artists' common interest in the metaphor and the various actualities of occupation. In turn, the work of these artists opens the discussion to a political, social and aesthetic axis upon which animation might operate, and through this, to how animation might – perhaps surprisingly – define a/our condition.

In 2005 the American artist Paul McCarthy and his son Damon jointly authored an epic installation work, *Caribbean Pirates*, based on the theme-park ride 'Pirates of the Caribbean' at Disneyland in Anaheim, California. Four years in the making, the work was exhibited at the Haus der Kunst, Munich and later in a slightly reordered exhibition at Whitechapel Gallery, London (where I saw it) as the major component of a show that at both venues was called 'LaLa Land Parody Paradise. Caribbean Pirates' and consisted of large-scale sculpture, modified found objects and video projection. There were three boats: an adapted houseboat (*Houseboat*) with one side removed, a television set on a worktop playing a film noir; a massive, steel mock-up of a slightly scaled-down, rusting frigate (*Frigate*); and a mounted, moving ship constructed from a geometrical metal frame lined with wood (*Underwater World*), a fairground ride that the viewer could not enter. *Houseboat* and *Frigate*, along with an odd wooden platform and walkway (*Cakebox*), displayed signs of heavy usage – destruction, even. Smeared with Hershey's chocolate syrup, the empty cans of which littered these macabre structures, along with other dried fluids, half-destroyed furniture, the occasional, clearly fake, 'amputated' limb, the dormant machines, buckets and spray guns used to wreak this havoc

74

and other signs of former habitation, the whole felt no less terrible because of its simulated blood and film-set lighting rig. The scene was a typical yet still unholy reformulation of the all-American products that McCarthy has used in his work since the mid-1970s, when ketchup and mayonnaise replaced his own bodily fluids.

In London the installation was housed in a warehouse, a short walk from the gallery proper, where related drawings and objects were displayed. Not much other than the minimum required for safety reasons had been done to alter the original condition of this run-down, functional space. Derelict offices surrounding the main floor housed video projections of ersatz schmaltz (tropical islands floating in clear blue seas turning upside down and rocking from side to side, a group of day-glo, over-eager carol singers playing forwards and – satanically – backwards) which were asymmetrically thrown onto rough walls, across corners, over cutaways. Two specially constructed projection areas above and alongside the boats were made of gallery-standard white boards. One showed three images side-by-side, roughly lined up, sloppily overlapping. The other – three white-boarded walls of an adjoining room, the fourth side of which opened onto the main floor – showed four off-centre, angled and overlapping images, arranged across its corners, slipping onto the corrugated iron ceiling (*Pirate Party*). Such an ordered chaos of successive, if different, images looked like an arrangement borrowed from one of Eadweard Muybridge's nineteenth-century chronophotographs showing the passage of a body in motion over time. The coherent image appeared literally broken across a number of projection planes. The successive frames of animation.

What was being broken down by this manic exhibition of successive frames, of scenes that otherwise had a chronological relationship to each other being seen simultaneously, was the elaborate performance conducted on the pirate ship sets by Paul McCarthy in his role as First Mate, captured on video by Damon McCarthy. First Mate, a band of pirates and their acolytes (men and women, some in out-sized cartoon-inspired grotesque fake heads) invade, rape, pillage and occupy an island. The literal destruction they effect is mirrored and codified by their morally disintegrated, infectious behaviour, the physical abuse they inflict on the inhabitants, their gratuitous, rampant (and perverted) sexual appetites, gross exhibitionism and exploration/exploitation of their own bodies and the bodies of others, literally or by association. The exhibition catalogue reflects the excess. It is large, with a slightly padded cover. Page after opulent page shows details and images of seemingly crazed, pirate-themed drawings (ships and pirates' noses metamorphosing into penises, pornography, advertising), installation shots and video stills. In it, John Welchman reports from the set and lends a linear perspective to what occurred:

> We are in a village as it is attacked and occupied by the marauding
> pirates.... The boy is verbally abused, repeatedly asked about the
> whereabouts of treasure, then tied up and subjected to a horren-
> dous routine of torture and dismemberment. First a slice is taken
> out of his bulbous (fake) nose, then his (false) right ear is slit,
> and finally, the First Mate takes an axe to his fake but elaborately
> simulated left leg, smashing and hacking until he gets right
> through the 'bones'. The villager howls and wails, his stump
> spews blood... the pirates dance and cavort in voyeuristic ecstasy.
> Looking onto this scene are three village sisters wearing wench
> costumes.... They moan, writhe, chant, and grimace, like a cross
> between harpies, sirens, and a dissolute rendition of the three
> graces... their hollers and screams are accompanied by an increas-
> ingly gymnastic display of affected passion.[1]

What Welchman describes as linear, in the multiple projection of the exhibition, is itself dismembered. What he describes as present, in the exhibition, has actually passed. Damon McCarthy's wild video camera mimics the general state of disorientation, leering towards its subjects, turning them upside-down, casually, chaotically, relentlessly. The soundtracks from each projected image are mixed into a single source that can be heard throughout the whole installation, signalling and conditioning responses. Even from its beginning, with what is to come being seen alongside the planning of the pirates' assault, there are screams, yelps and human-animal wailing. While Paul McCarthy may have developed a structure for this improvised marauding and while First Mate may well have had a plan of attack, not only does the recorded action appear as destruction performed to its own spiralling volition, but its subsequent exhibition refuses the viewer the security of narrative. In this continuous, hideous charade there are no epiphanies, no Hollywood endings.

At the same time as we come to realise that everything in this used-up film set installation relates to something having happened, we become aware that it is a particular definition of our own witnessing that becomes the overriding content of the work. While the discarded props, the smell of rotting, smeared chocolate sauce, broken furniture, the vessels that display these things relate, like proof, to the world of the projected images. The two things together, the object and the image, establish truth values for each other (this is where they sat, this is what they used, here is the limb) that implicate the viewer as a necessary function of their construction. Being trapped between them effects the erosion of critical distance in favour of inane entertainment, the troubling aspect of which becomes the comparative ease with which we witness these things, the familiarity with what is expected of us and a curiously familiar pattern of indulgent reception.

The description of 'Pirates of the Caribbean' on the Disneyland Resort website entices us to 'Set sail from an 1860s Louisiana Bayou as a rag-tag band of marauding pirates has overtaken a Caribbean village, ransacking and setting ablaze everything in sight – including yer boat if yer not careful, matey!' In a bullet point we are encouraged to 'Revel in the comic fun of swashbuckling shenanigans.' *Caribbean Pirates* mimics and assimilates the ride's component parts, but is most truly horrifying in the content it makes of these promises. It is a strategy we could understand as extending to Paul McCarthy's practice in general. His studio adopts the form of the sprawling system of the Hollywood production machine in which Oskar Fischinger found himself,[2] and in the context of this work develops a grand metaphor of (artistic) production and (public) consumption. Welchman describes artistic practice, like the fake bodies of our protagonists, taken to the extremity of its own – and our – complicity:

> In *Caribbean Pirates* the studio [McCarthy's] becomes an
> enormous lair swarming with actors and extras, assistants and
> special effects people, film crews, technicians, and hangers-on.
> At some moments the professional apparatus is deployed as it
> would be in a Hollywood film set; at others the on and off-camera
> worlds merge without jurisdiction, just as the sets and props
> shift from backdrops and objects to the different valences of
> sculpture and installation.[3]

Carribbean Pirates not only plays out occupation as torture-by-comic-strip, it also occupies the forms of entertainment which are its content. This is the occupation of a form in order to animate it, and at the heart of this animation, in the installed work itself, the projected videos, we are not transported as in the theme park ride, but physically move ourselves. *We* occupy, *we* animate this animation in a double deathblow to the fantasy of escape that we would otherwise be sold.

The McCarthy-Disney equation then inevitably extends to government and a wider set of politics and contemporary international relations. Welchman cites Africa, Iraq, Haiti. *Caribbean Pirates* lends profundity to an anecdotal swipe at President George W. Bush that Dave Hickey takes in his *Vanity Fair* article on Florida's Walt Disney World. Hickey ventures to the animatronic Hall of Presidents:

> A music video about the constitution opened the show. Its broad
> generational appeal was followed by a softly lit tête-a-tête with
> a coterie of American presidents.... The avatar of our current
> president stepped up to the plate and delivered a short homily
> that, I swear, the man might have written himself.... Of all the
> animatronic presidents, statesmen, heroes and ordinary Joes we
> had seen, Dubya was the best. The oft-cited defects of animatronic
> technology, the fact that it makes characters seem stiff and
> only intermittently lifelike, were no problem. Dubya was born
> to the medium.[4]

And in the process of writing this piece, a report on the rebuilding of New Orleans following the unthinkable destruction wrought by Hurricane Katrina in *The Observer* newspaper echoed something I'd heard on the news a few days previously:

78

As images of Katrina start to fade, tourists will return. With the projects razed and criminals gone, big business will also return. In place of slums will be condos and cluster homes; where the Lower Ninth stood, golf courses. Mayor Nagin has even proposed a law permitting casinos in most hotels. Ten years from now, if Nagin has his way, New Orleans may be Las Vegas South.[5]

A society occupied, remodelled and (re)animated as an entertainment complex.

The deliberate lack of critical distance in the experience of the McCarthys' own theme park manifests a world without an exit strategy and a confusion of positions, between the viewer and the viewed. It finds its parallel in Stephanie Rosenthal's catalogue essay description of how Paul McCarthy's work tests the boundaries of the physical body to the point of dissolution. She constructs a metaphor between McCarthy's work as a physical body in relationship to, comparable to, the architecture of an idiosyncratic house:

> This house metaphor is, to be sure, only correct when one does not think of an ordinary house, but rather [one] with tilted floors, with holes in the floors and ceilings, and without a roof, so that the rain falls through all the levels. The water is then pumped back up from the bottom of the house and shot back in under high pressure through the windows and other openings.[6]

✳

It is precisely a dissolution between interior and exterior that VALIE EXPORT is concerned with in her feature-length film *Invisible Adversaries* (*Unsichtbare Gegner*, 1978). The film's protagonist – an artist named Anna – enacts this dissolution: (her) perception, knowledge, the/her body, city, by extension the state, are thrown into a nexus of relationships where mediation – the *mediated* self – and apparent mental instability, map onto each other. As in *Caribbean Pirates*, the linear arrangement of space and time collapses, though the moral disintegration that accompanies McCarthy's installation instead, in *Invisible Adversaries*, becomes the structured examination of a political and

79

social condition. VALIE EXPORT does not so much occupy and animate the forms of mass media (mass entertainment) as demonstrate the media's occupation of the world at large. The film in this sense forms an unlikely (historical) bridge between the work of Paul McCarthy and that of Catherine Sullivan.

The premise is this: Anna is convinced of having heard radio announcements amidst a string of national and international headlines that the world has been invaded – and people occupied – by invisible aliens called Hyksos that control behaviour. Whether this is insight or delusion remains ambiguous. Anna is VALIE EXPORT's avatar. Her practice is that of VALIE EXPORT, the actual artist's works appearing in the film as those of Anna. A discussion of the film and its strategies is also a discussion of VALIE EXPORT's practice, which is here presented as both precipitating, and as the symptom of, an obsessive, sometimes visionary spiral. Anna obsessively documents herself and her surroundings, her relationship/s; she photographs herself naked, emulating the poses of classical paintings in modern dress with everyday objects, wraps her body around street furniture, into corners, mediates a conversation with her lover using video monitors, makes video recordings of other women speaking, fixes her own shadow, photographs her own excrement, speaks her lover's name into a Dictaphone, makes herself a moustache from her pubic hair, sees a row of cardboard cut-out figures on a balustrade in a city square and falls down after circling them, herself become a two-dimensional image. Anna is seen photographing a building being torn down at the same time as developing its image in her darkroom. Two men walk down the street wearing sandwich boards made of mirrors, she looks at herself in a mirror at home and her reflection has a life of its own. A man is lying down in the middle of a road, slowly licking the tarmac.

Sound splits from image: a man's guttural, growling voice is heard over a photograph of a woman's vagina (as in VALIE EXPORT's short film *Mann & Frau & Animal*, 1973), the turning pages of a book sound like a machine gun. As Anna's partner is seen in an absurdist, Kafkaesque altercation with a parking attendant, we see close-up shots of salami being sliced until it is revealed that Peter is telling her this story as she prepares dinner. Their conversation descends into an argument that is apparently infectious. Everyone, everywhere across the city is arguing. War footage of running street battles, ravaged cities. The personal is utterly interconnected with the political.

Invisible Adversaries' complex balance of occupations is figured in the mind, the body and in the (perceived) social system. Shots of modern-day Vienna are accompanied by a voice-over that describes the city's history as one of 'oblivion and treason':

> In wickedness and brutality population and authorities are as one. The cultural climate of the Second Republic has heightened this continuum of corruption by its banality. The banality of evil is not Viennese dirty washing, but its very face. The Viennese golden heart, beating faster for a dog than for an artist, has been the death of many. If you're creative in Vienna the police suspect you...

A history of Viennese architecture ensues, with a list of the abuses conducted by the state on its architects. A disrobed, faceless priest is seen on a sun-lounger masturbating, echoed later in the film when Anna leaves her doctors and, walking home, passes a number of single men, 'police cadets', masturbating in doorways and stairwells.

Anna and Peter have a heated conversation over lunch. Peter insists upon the dominance of a socio-political system that is out of individuals' control, of which they are but a side effect. Anna asserts personal responsibility. This is the trajectory that *Invisible Adversaries* tracks: occupation against independence, agency against articulation. The film's metaphoric, surrealist coda details the Hyksos' greatest threat – the reduction of individuals to automata, occupation not as the opening (or the animation) of a form, but as depoliticising automation.

Instead of witnessing the whole of an action that has taken place over time, as we do in McCarthy's *Pirate Party*, *Invisible Adversaries* presents an action with its psycho-symbolic visual correlative, or simultaneously (inseparably) with its document. Anna's crisis, what plays upon (and is an extension of) her own nervous system, is VALIE EXPORT's enquiry. It turns upon questions of agency – intent, action/inaction, responsibility – and of systems played out and back upon

81

themselves. Transgression, in this context, is not the act of documenting, but of transcending the document; the film's final image a photograph ripped in two.

✳

Catherine Sullivan's *The Chittendens* (2005) was, ironically enough,
first shown in Vienna, at Secession. It is a six-screen video work. Like
McCarthy's installation, its exhibition in London (at Tate Modern, where
I saw it) was a reordering of its first manifestation. The piece comprised two projection rooms. An antechamber contained an elliptical
projection screen and a second room that was long and relatively nar-
row had screens on three sides. The audience completed the rectangle
on the fourth side, seated on benches facing three projection screens,
with one screen on each of the short ends of the room so that the experience was of confronting the proscenium arch, or at least the (projected) performance space (and the wings) of a theatrical stage. Unlike
McCarthy's belligerently positioned projections with their overlaps,
overhangs and angles, *The Chittendens*'s images are pristinely aligned,
fitting their screens perfectly, signalling the work's acute structure.
It is a complex work, the full exegesis of which is not my intent here
other than at some points of intersection with *Caribbean Pirates* and
Invisible Adversaries. Like Paul McCarthy, Catherine Sullivan too is
interested in the sea, its alternative sets of rules, in the past and the
present, occupation and animation, the occupation and animation of
these things.

In the antechamber, on an oval screen, a naval Captain in historical uniform is seen at sea, approaching an island. The scene is idyllic: blue sea, foliage, smooth camera movement and the gentle swell
of the ocean are matched by a lyrical soundtrack, and they describe
each other. The Captain looks through his telescope towards the island
with its lighthouse and we see what he sees. A woman, also in period
dress, is rocking backwards and forwards on the cliff, like a neurotic
siren. People dressed in pure-white overalls signify routine and seem
to be going about their daily work. The captain walks amongst these

82

workers, the two not acknowledging each other, as if they inhabit parallel spaces in parallel time zones. The Captain as a sign of hierarchy, the workers of the communal, preface and summarise the work's concerns: the co-existence of contrasting (social) systems.

In the main room, the co-ordination of sound, action, image across the four sections of the five-screen work is specific, choreographed to direct the gaze and to work symphonically, in stark contrast to the consistent, chaotic immersion of *Caribbean Pirates*. Sean Griffin's commissioned score moves from lyrical ballad to broken, industrial repetitions. Catherine Sullivan's performers occupy period and contemporary dress, sometimes a hybrid of the two, sometimes simultaneously, the same actor performing the same actions in and 'out' of costume, superimposed onto each other. They move mechanically, trapped in slapstick loops, expressive, repetitious, hysterical, abstracted, neurotic. A male voice talks about ancient watches that start to tick again, like the woken dead. Instead of ransacking a film set or exploring a city besieged by unseen invaders, *The Chittendens* occupies semi-derelict, half-furnished ex-insurance company offices, from which the piece borrows its title. The work's prologue maps its divisions (and differences) of labour onto them both by association and through the animated bodies of its surrealist, dysfunctional workforce.

It is no coincidence that Catherine Sullivan uses the verb 'to animate' throughout her own description of the piece, published to accompany the exhibition, in which process is critical. Each actor was ascribed fourteen 'attitudes', derived by the artist from her interaction with them. Each of these could, by her, then be:

- minimised or maximised in terms of dramatic stakes
- reduced or expanded in physical form
- abbreviated or extended in terms of time[7]

She goes on, 'The attitudes and their treatments were then assigned to a series of numeric patterns which could be executed rhythmically at multiple tempo.' The relationship between artist and performer occurs within and is regulated by a set of fixed terms. The performer's body, to the limit of its possibility, is mechanised. Psychological inter-action becomes the subject of a system that foregoes naturalism, exten-uating its own instance into stylised movement and (generally abstract) sound. In *Invisible Adversaries* Anna collapses twice, her body given over to the physical manifestation of her psychological condition. In *The Chittendens* this loss of control is harnessed and styled into arti-fice, while in McCarthy's *Pirate Party* physical abandon is a key func-tion of the performers' – and by implication the viewers' – collusion in moral decline. In each case it marks a deliberate removal of the body from normative patterns of behaviour. In each work, the relationship between (self-)expression and the body articulates central theses about (self-)control, variously unpicking, or re-describing, the/our social and moral fabric by eliding realism with strategies derived from or in met-aphorical relation to the abstracts of animation.

Catherine Sullivan details how her reading of Thorstein Veblen's *The Theory of The Leisure Class* (1899) threads its way into *The Chittendens*. Veblen constructs the 'leisure class' as a social grouping that emerges during the development of social relationships to owner-ship – during the 'unexplained' transition from 'peaceable savage' (no class divisions, simple social structures uninformed by private owner-ship) to 'predatory barbarian' ('defined by the maintenance of wealth and ownership acquired by unceasing force and predatory habit').[8] Industrial capitalism is equated with the high barbarian, and labour, in this context, becomes linked to exploitation, to the power of con-trol over animate things – ultimately, other people. Paul McCarthy's First Mate. Peter's system over Anna's personal responsibility. Against repression, *The Chittendens* is a chorus of neurotic habits, a multitude of classes occupied and venting, the inverse of the society from which Anna removes herself, engaged in a kind of automation, of animation, that is profoundly connected to a kind of psychotic liberation.

※

In the opening paragraph of his essay 'Will the Monster Eat the Film?, a dossier of artist-animators practicing between 1980–94 in the context of increasingly industrialised opportunities for the form, Simon Pummell evokes *Alien³*:

> In the Hollywood blockbuster *Alien³*... the monster eats all the characters the viewer can identify with or be interested in (excepting the heroine Ripley) in the first third of the film... the real thriller is whether the monster will eat the narrative before it resolves itself in a classical narrative fashion. It represents cinema teetering between the narrative... of classical cinema and the plastic spectacle (the monster) of digital and special fx cinema; in fact the cinema of animation.[9]

He concludes that 'the forms traditionally used to describe the monstrous... the magic... the marginal, childish and grotesque... are being used more and more to describe our experience as post-modern subjects'.[10]

Whether or not anyone wants to be a 'post-modern subject', it is not so much the way we are being described that feels at stake, but the ways in which we are behaving that have become monstrous, magical, marginal, childish and grotesque. And that these things are revealed through animation as strategy, and animation as metaphor, rather than masked by its complicity with illusion, fantasy or escape. Oskar Fischinger refused to be complicit in the macabre carnival of Disney's industrialised workplace; there is no little irony in that his contract was finally terminated on Hallowe'en.

85

1. John Welchman, 'First Mate's Bloody Flux', in *Paul McCarthy: LaLa Land Parody Paradise*, exhibition catalogue, ed. Stephanie Rosenthal (Munich: Haus der Kunst, 2005), p.192.
2. 'McCarthy's studio becomes more and more a constructed mimicry of a Hollywood film production company with no intention of making legitimate "Hollywood films".' Stephanie Rosenthal, 'How to Use a Failure', in *Paul McCarthy: LaLa Land Parody Paradise*, op. cit., p.136.
3. Welchman, 'First Mate's Bloody Flux', op. cit., p.196.
4. Dave Hickey, 'Welcome to Dreamsville', *Vanity Fair*, (August 2005), p.129.
5. Nick Cohn, 'The Day the Music Died', *The Observer Review*, 15 January 2006, p.6.
6. Rosenthal, 'How to Use a Failure', op. cit., p.130.
7. Catherine Sullivan, 'The Chittendens', in *Catherine Sullivan – The Chittendens*, exhibition catalogue (Vienna & Berlin: Secession & Revolver, 2005), p.16.
8. Ibid., p.23.
9. Simon Pummell, 'Will the Monster Eat the Film? or The Redefinition of British Animation 1980–1994', in *The British Avant-Garde Film 1926 to 1995*, ed. Michael O'Pray (Luton: University of Luton Press, 1996), p.299.
10. Ibid., p.313.

Richard Of York Gave Battle In Vain:
museums without walls, walls without corners
and words with no edges

You don't notice at first. One. Then another. They look handsome as concrete ledges with neon strip lighting. They look like the present. And then comes the skin, of glass, and the heart skids, slips around another curved edge just as they want us to. (Every street's a slip-stream.) And you don't notice it again, until the next one. The City is turning the dome of St Paul's on its side and making this weightless roof into an invisible wall. Every new building in the City is curved like a smoke screen of dynamism. Actually, designed to a generic architectural code, they are sold as something new, promise the future and deliver something not to be noticed. There are no dustbins on the street and all the corner shops are Tesco Express. And this is where I am happy to live.

The tower of Tate Modern is the extended middle finger of the building seen from the river and imagined as a fist, disingenuously shown to the City that replies to the blur of its Swiss Light with the crisp neon strip on the top of Tower 42. Inside, all of the floors in the stairwells, foyers and non-exhibition areas of the upper levels slope inwards to glass walls that overlook the Turbine Hall. They put art in it but the architecture asks us, really, to look at other people arriving. To look at us. An extraordinary escalator traverses two floors. Once you're on you can't get off and you are displayed in another glass box to the

87

First published in the press release for an exhibition by Oliver Payne
and Nick Relph at Herald St gallery, London in 2007.

floor you see passing seamlessly by. You can take a boat branded with Damien Hirst's dots direct from this Tate to the other Tate in Pimlico. The letters of the institution's logo are dissolving, smoke and mirrors, as if we might not notice.

Every spine of *frieze* is colour-branded. If you keep them on your bookshelves they look like a rainbow and you wonder if they'll ever run out of colours. You realise that there are an infinite number of colours. All the worry goes away. The front of their 100th edition included every other cover, cut into a tiny strip and collaged into a camouflage of stripes like a scarf from Gap or a rug from Habitat.

The Institute of Contemporary Art's new logo... Etc.

It is the proposition of André Malraux's 'Museum Without Walls' (1967) that through reproduction one thing might be compared with another, entirely different thing, these two things, by definition, never actually appearing in the same physical space alongside each other. Before that Walter Benjamin was worried that reproduction would disintegrate the original. Conceptual artists 'dematerialised' the object. Between these three is modern life and Oliver Payne and Nick Relph make art from/of this life.

Like buildings without corners, museums without walls are everywhere, even though we might not notice them. They are embodied in the idea of the agency that permeates structures as diverse as the (commercial) art gallery and the funding and advertising agency, but perhaps their apotheosis is the brand consultant. Agencies are diffuse structures that are successful because they sell something in addition to actual product, like the idea of something, which makes them all somewhat the organs of ideology. Even though Tate Modern was conceived long before New Labour soft-shuffled to Downing Street, the two share a prescient emphasis on mediation – in politics they call it spin – that in our time is manifested as much by a logo formed of letters you can barely read as it is by an official colour palette, a curved glass wall, a house font, gallery walls painted pink or a boat or a plane covered in dots.

Wolff Olins, brand consultants – a museum without walls par excellence – manifested Tate Modern as an institution by engineering how it looks, not architecturally but on the page, in its signs – as they did for Orange, First Direct, Go, Heathrow Express, the British Council, Renault, Tesco... and innumerable other companies that unnoticeably shape contemporary artistic practice. 'All our clients have the ambition to be the best... and the imagination to re-write the rulebook.' This agency-museum masquerades as the direct descendent of Samuel Taylor Coleridge's radical definition of imagination as an active force, perpetually destroying in order to re-create. Actually it reconfigures imagination as mediation. That is its content.

In [Oliver Payne and Nick Relph's video] *Round Writing* a set of images filmed in London in May 2007 is back-projected onto a screen, the front of which is obscured by a grid of mirrors catching another projection of abstract colour and light. The projections are not synchronised. Organised in this way its (video) collection of objects, scenes, texts is the cyclical taxonomy of mediation, organised, aptly enough, so that it can barely be seen, that is not to be noticed.

Camera Obscura

Pornography is like silent film. Both share a formal drive that turns action into a demonstration of itself for the sake of entertainment. When a door is opened in a silent film we see it opening not as if it is incidental, but as a pronunciation, as definite as an intertitle. Generically, the pornographic code is such that we do not simply see people fucking, but a formal demonstration of that, a formulaic series of shots that are the exegesis of foreplay, insertion, repetition, the display of male ejaculation. Such observations might seem an unlikely beginning to a consideration of the nineteenth-century photographic taxonomy of hysterics constructed at the Salpêtrière hospital in Paris in the name of science, but the profound confusion between the real and its document, between the natural and the artificial, pseudo-scientific document and visual pleasure are at the very heart of an argument about how these photographs were made, how they were and are read. They are also the terms that connect Jean-Martin Charcot and his colleagues' experiments at that hospital to cinema – especially the pre-cinematic – and they are nonetheless the first in my collection of other observations that throw these photographs into a discursive field of representation and (mis)recognition, actuality and manipulation.

There is one field in particular in which a confusion between a work of art and the reality of that which it depicts still seems to hold sway: portraiture. The back cover of Richard Brilliant's book *Portraiture*[1] declares it to be 'the first general and theoretical study' of the genre.

91

First published in a limited-edition booklet to accompany the debut screenings of Richard Squires' short film *Programme* at the Whitechapel and The Old Operating Theatre, London, 2007. *Programme* examines the history of the Salpêtrière Hospital, Paris and the practice of neurologist Jean-Martin Charcot.

First published in 1991 and reprinted in 1997 and 2002, it was surprising enough that such a study had not been existed before. Moreover, Brilliant's introduction is remarkable. He describes a response to the image of a sitter as genuinely oscillating between (collapsing) the actual presence of the person and their picture: 'It is as if the art works do not exist in their own material substance but, in their place, real persons face me from the other side or deliberately avoid my glance. Quickly enough the illusion dissipates; I am once more facing not a person but that person's image, embodied in some work of art...'[2] His comments strike a resonance with those of Robert Rosenblum in his essay for the catalogue of 'Citizens and Kings: Portraits in the Age of Revolution 1760–1830', a recent exhibition at the Royal Academy in London (to which I will return later). About Picasso's portraits Rosenblum writes:

> the deformation of Cubism... had so obscured the identities of the people who inspired Picasso... that they disappeared beneath the camouflage of his art. But today, these flesh-and-blood individuals have become visible again, each one a unique human being, with a real biography.

And on recent appraisals of the work of John Singer Sargent '...these tableaux vivants of a historical past, [are] the equivalent of seeing a Henry James novel come to life'.[3]

Is it this same oscillation that viewers of the camera obscura, known to us since Antiquity, also experienced? The pragmatics of the camera obscura are familiar and simple enough: a small hole in a wall will allow enough light into a darkened room to project an image of the exterior onto the opposite wall of that room. What is less simple is that this image is also, absolutely simultaneously, actually there, outside the room. Anything seen as an image is also, simultaneously, known to be happening in real time and space. This unique image is not a recording although it is practically at the root of the photographic. But is the complexity of this situation at the psychic, interpretive core of cinema? By which I mean narrative cinema, its own generic codes of identification with character, scene, plot, dependent on the screen functioning as a window onto a world that *could* actually exist.

92

The real and the imaginary – and their readings – become co-dependent in this sense.

Is Brilliant's oscillation the inheritance of something else? Something that connects the portrait as a work of art with voyeurism, with what we now call photo-journalism, the taking of images in the public interest because they are 'real' (as in, representations of something that actually happened and that because they happened we have a right to see). In eighteenth-century France, a century before Charcot's photographic project, Madame Tussaud was commissioned by the revolutionary National Assembly to record dramatic contemporary events. Working from life – well, death – she was commissioned to make casts directly from the heads of the guillotine's victims, of Robespierre as well as Louis XVI and Marie Antoinette. She is one entry in Marina Warner's *Phantasmagoria*.[5] Notably, Tussaud, at the request of the neo-classical painter Jacques-Louis David, made a cast of the assassinated revolutionary Jean-Paul Marat, stabbed to death in his medicinal bath – a waxwork that became a tableau of the death scene that is still displayed today, a model for David's famous painting *The Death of Marat* (c.1793) and an image that has peculiar resonance with Charcot's photographs of the sitter we now know as Augustine, herself a subject made macabre celebrity by the number and tenor of studies of her. The reality that Tussaud preserves is entirely fabricated.

As if to counter ambiguity (while in fact perpetuating such paradoxical co-dependence), the photographs that form the monumental volumes of the *Iconographie photographique de la Salpêtrière* are presented as if they are 'simply' the documentation of the various states and stages of hysterical attacks, and thereby define the condition. They are organised on the page as examples, listed and described with a classification that is inseparable from both the scientific impulse of the project and from the curiosity they arouse in the non-scientist as viewer (like the inscription on the plain wooden box that stands in front of Marat's bath tub in his death scene like a tombstone: 'NAYANT PU ME CORROMPRE / ILS M'ONT ASSASSINE' [unable to corrupt me, they assassinated me]). In Paul Regnard's Marat-like photographs of Augustine in the late 1870s, she is lit to chiaroscuro effect against a black background, sat up in bed, one finger pointed to her cheek, swathed in bedclothes and nightgown, or with her hands clasped together in a prayer-like rapture, her face and her eyes turned upwards, or with her arms half-outstretched, head lilting to one side, baring her teeth through what might be a smile. Each of these images is labelled and explained: 'Aural Hallucinations', 'Amorous Supplication', 'Ecstasy',[6] simultaneously entering the image into a new psychiatric lexicon and pitifully excusing our gaze now (and, presumably, 'their' gaze then).

Richard Brilliant writes: 'The very fact of the portrait's allusion to an individual human being, actually existing outside the work, defines the function of the art work in the world and constitutes the cause of its coming into being'.[7] This critical act of definition is almost exclusively performed in the context of an exhibition by the (biographical) wall label. Authored by the institution, it is the companion of the portrait as it is displayed in the museum, the correlative of the scientific classification, which turns, ironically, the act of looking into a game of reading as opposed to the reception of an authorised interpretation. In 'Citizens and Kings', this game of reading was underscored by other strategies of display that incorporated it into the theatrical. The gallery's octagonal entrance hall was painted deep red with gilt cornices to present images of majesty majesterially, portraits of sovereigns and heads of state. In the room titled 'The Status Portrait' medium-scale paintings of full-length figures were hung on a line that gave the uncanny visual impression of each person depicted being stood upon the same level ground, the same stage. And what should be found in this exhibition's real *pièce de théâtre* but David's *Death of Marat*, hung centrally in an otherwise monochrome room of white marble busts, a stunning (stunningly theatrical) graphic visual symphony of objects-as-*mise en scène*, a set, a stage upon which the viewer also trod. The work of art's other 'coming into being', here, a game of reading made theatre.

Of course, the *Iconographie photographique de la Salpêtrière* does not declare itself as a collection or an exhibition of portraits. Unlike their symptoms, the sitters are only named in retrospective commentary, but the drive to do so is testament to what these images have in common

94

with the portrait and how we might understand them now. Reading and theatre are precisely the analytical question and the circumstance of these photographs that Georges Didi-Huberman unravels in his seminal book *Invention of Hysteria: Charcot and the Photographic Iconography of the Salpêtrière* – a work that significantly informs my own text. In it Didi-Huberman corrects the contemporaneous conspiracy of silence around these 'silent' women, realigning medical observation as a process of complicity on a number of related levels. He also removes the act of taking these images from the realm of medical observation to relocate it in that of artifice. Hypnosis is the apotheosis of both instances and Charcot's definitive (damning) experiment.

Didi-Huberman quotes Charcot's contradictory position and points to his photographic images as corrupt texts: 'Behold the truth... I am nothing more than a photographer; I inscribe what I see...'[8] The 'truth' of the image lies not in observation but in the conflict between taking a photograph and (thereby) inscribing the image, writing-into it even by excluding its means of construction from the frame. This is not only an illicit manipulation. There is a symbiotic relationship between the photographic document and the way in which the symptoms it illuminates are displayed by Charcot's subjects. Didi-Huberman systematically describes situations in which these subjects become – through strategies of co-dependence, wilful display, involuntary response and survival mechanisms – as active in the construction of their image as the theatrical set of the photographic studio was in recording it. Augustine is described by Didi-Huberman as a co-incidental actress, caught in a complex psychological response to her own incarceration at Salpêtrière: 'With moist lips, she knew that science had lost its ancient conscience beneath a bed, and demonstrated this through a hundred gestures!... what a stroke of luck for psychiatric knowledge spurred on, as it was, by its dramaturgical passion'.[9] The sequential, physical revealing of symptoms that Augustine performed made her the ideal photographic subject, an actress in the still frames of a (silent) film.

Her gestures might be compared to those of the famous actress Mrs Siddons, painted by Sir Joshua Reynolds in 1789. Sat upright on a chair, eyes turned heavenwards, *Mrs Siddons as Tragic Muse* shows

95

her with her right arm outstretched and her left arm raised, the shadowy figures of Pity and Terror over her shoulders. Mrs Siddons's own account of sitting for Reynolds reinscribes the image between the real and the artificial: 'I walkd [sic] up the steps & seated myself instantly in the attitude in which She now appears'.[10] To act, to be a good actress, to perform and repeat reliably was to be also entirely 'natural'.

As if to literalise such associations, under hypnosis, amongst the other tortures of demonstration to which they were afflicted, the Salpêtrière hysterics were trained to theatrically display 'surprises, pouts, disdain, tears, threats, ecstasies'.[11] Hypnosis made every susceptible woman an ideal Augustine, literally, physically manipulable, a person made sexual, dramatic, medical mannequin (made image) and physically presented by Charcot at his Tuesday Lectures. In extraordinary scenes subjects-patients-hysterics – what should we call them now, these living 'dead'? – were displayed under hypnosis to a public audience to '"reproduce" hysterical contractures of all kinds – painful or not...'[12] That Charcot's sales pitch for the Tuesday Lecture disturbingly competes with that of another nineteenth-century entrepreneur, Étienne-Gaspard Robertson's for his 'moving' image spectral slide show, the Fantasmagorie, is surely no coincidence. Charcot: 'No sign will treat you to the interior spectacle, for there is now no painter able to give even its sad shadow. I bring you, living (and preserved through the years by sovereign science) a Woman of bygone days... her hair, folds with the grace of cloth around a face illuminated by the bloody nudity of her lips' etc.[13] Robertson: 'Citizens and Gentlemen... It is... a useful spectacle for a man to discover the bizarre effects of the imagination when it combines force and disorder; I wish to speak of the terror which shadows, symbols, spells, the occult works of magic inspire... I have promised that I will raise the dead and I will raise them'.[14]

'Hypnosis', writes Didi-Huberman, 'was in reality and above all *a recipe for hysteria*':[15]

> Charcot intensely modified his 'subjects.' He transfigured them, body and soul. He failed, of course, in his desire to theorize this transformation.... But he excelled, to the contrary, in describing and *drawing* practical consequences from the hypnotic instrument.[16] (Emphasis mine.)

96

In the final analysis, what this 'instrument' actually reveals is not a set of symptoms that evidence hysteria, but that *'Mimesis* is the hysterical symptom par excellence'.[17] It is the symptom that Charcot's project exploits to the extent that it becomes the condition, a mental state not observed but radically constructed by its recording. Like Tussaud's head of Marat, the real entirely fabricated. Silent films are like pornography.

1. Richard Brilliant, *Portraiture* (London: Reaktion Books, 1991).
2. Ibid., p.7.
3. *Citizens and Kings: Portraits in the Age of Revolution 1760–1830*, exhibition catalogue (Paris: Galeries nationales du Grand Palais; London: Royal Academy of Arts, 2007), p.15.
4. The camera obscura is described, alongside other pre-cinematic devices, in Laurent Mannoni, *The Great Art of Light and Shadow: Archaeology of the Cinema* (Exeter: University of Exeter Press, 2000), pp.3–6.
5. Marina Warner, *Phantasmagoria* (Oxford: Oxford University Press, 2006), pp.36–40.
6. These descriptions are based on the reproductions included in Georges Didi-Huberman, *Invention of Hysteria: Charcot and the Photographic Iconography of the Salpêtrière* (Cambridge, MA and London: MIT Press, 2003), pp.143–47.
7. Brilliant, *Portraiture*, op. cit., p.8.
8. G. Didi-Huberman, *Invention of Hysteria*, op. cit., p.29.
9. Ibid., p.137.
10. *Citizens and Kings*, op. cit., p.375.
11. Didi-Huberman, *Invention of Hysteria*, op. cit., p.227.
12. Ibid., p.192.
13. Didi-Huberman, *Invention of Hysteria*, op. cit., p.237.
14. Warner, *Phantasmagoria*, op. cit., p.149.
15. Ibid., p.185.
16. Ibid., p.186.
17. Ibid., p.164.

Intervention: Stuart Marshall

In *Screen* ('Video: Technology and Practice', vol.20, no.1, Spring 1979) Stuart Marshall points to the lack of a 'legitimising history' for the then nascent practice of video art, while making video art himself and generously attempting to document the work of others. To write about his work is as much to write about the state of video art then. It is ultimately a caustic irony and an ironic testament to his project that his videos, like his sound, installation and live works, have nonetheless shamefully remained outside of an authoritative international canon.

Marshall's article maps an evolving practice, from Nam June Paik's first use of the Sony Portapak in 1965 to video's intersection with the Women's Movement (in works by Lynda Benglis, Joan Jonas and Hermine Freed on sexual difference). Just as notably, the article describes its limited British economy. In 1979 there was no commercial gallery infrastructure for video works in the UK, commercial distribution was unsustainable and broadcast was in the exclusive grip of a closed 'duopoly' between the institutions of BBC and ITV. My proposal is that this latter – television – became Marshall's particular and specific culturally reflective concern, one that found its apotheosis in his 1984 broadcast *Bright Eyes*. It was a concern to which he was theoretically and practically bound, and that accounts for his work as a special kind of intervention, distinct from artists' film in the late 1960s and 1970s and politically challenging to the visual arts in general. In his own words, the televisual offered 'the greatest potential as a critical avant-garde'.[1]

99

First published as 'Stuart Marshall' (2007) on the website *Luxonline*, <http://www.luxonline.org.uk/artists/stuart_marshall/ essay(printversion).html> [last accessed on 10 January 2016].

Still from Stuart Marshall's *Bright Eyes*, 1984.

This is but one line of enquiry running through a body of work that also included multi-monitor installations and environments that performed important examinations of perception, time and space, in other still-developing media forms that were – and are – themselves as equally uncharted and as much in need, still, of a more significant historical reassessment than the one standard art history currently provides.

Rosalind Krauss's essay 'Video: The Aesthetics of Narcissism' was published three years before Marshall's article in *Screen*, in the American journal *October*. Krauss focusses on video works that utilise (feature, figure) the body of the artist or incorporate the body of the spectator, combined with some kind of actual or implied feedback mechanism (aural, visual or temporal, actual in real time or re-presented). She replaces what in modernist criticism would be the self-reflexive, physical characteristics of the art object (such as paint on a canvas for example) with those of a (self-reflexive) psychological situation, such that narcissism becomes the medium of video, over and above any material characteristics of production or exhibition apparatus.

In certain works of Vito Acconci, Richard Serra, Bruce Nauman, Lynda Benglis, Joan Jonas and Peter Campus, Krauss describes the monitor screen as various kinds of mirrors, reflecting the artist or the spectator into the feedback loops that they variously exploit, 'the very terms of which are to withdraw attention from an external object – an Other – and invest it in the Self'.[2] At one point Krauss connects this instant-replay mechanism to the art world's general Pop-art inherited excitement at communication via the mass media, or 'between the institution of a self formed by a video feedback and the real situation that exists in the *art world* from which the makers of video come' (emphases in this and the following quotations are mine).[3] Regardless of how the art world had, according to Krauss been so 'disastrously affected by its relation to mass media', video art was implicitly *like* the mass medium television and this kind of television was uniquely, perfectly related to the cultural and economic climate of the (predominantly New York) art world in America in the 1970s.[4]

Without denying his own significant interest in psychoanalysis, Stuart Marshall proposed a different response to different works (notably by artists that have not since been canonised in/by the art world) based more upon contradiction than theoretical cohesion. In 'Video: From Art to Independence – A Short History of a New Technology', Marshall accedes video (art)'s initial need to be understood within the modernist tradition. It had to not only claim a place within the visual arts generally, but would, by 'being recognised in its specificity' strategically 'guarantee the survival of the current means of production [that in the UK was primarily within educational institutions] and the future support of the *state* funding bodies'.[5]

What disrupted the relationship between video and modernism for Marshall is what serves its psychological situation for Krauss:

> The video image only comes into being at the moment of playback.
> As a stored image its materiality consists of a complex pattern
> of invisible electromagnetic charges on a reel of magnetic tape.
> Modernist work in film involved a direct working upon the image/
> acetate surface.[6]

However interested video artists were with exposing the technology they were using, according to Marshall they were snared in a vicious circle of only ever re-presenting its (visual) effects, rather than its (invisible) physical material: 'there was an inevitable and constant confrontation with illusionism and representation'.[7] And representation for Marshall was precisely the stuff of television. In Marshall's notes on 'Video: Technology and Practice', television is 'the site of production of representations – as both an industry and a signifying practice'.[8] Remarkably different from the language of art, television is the medium from which the language of video derives (for both makers and viewers): '[all] televisual "literacy" was established and is controlled by the television industry'.[9] To make images from the effects of its technology, video art inevitably challenged television's 'dominant modes of representation'. Marshall embraced this radical contradiction if not as the medium of video then as a reassessment of video's relationship to modernism, 'At the heart of [which] lay the seeds of a new *oppositional* practice'.[10]

Video art is oppositional. It frustrates modernism and in so doing opposes many things including Krauss's 'art world'. Marshall's early video works *Go Through the Motions* (1975) and *Arcanum* (1976) *look* like they might adhere to Krauss's medium. Each features the close-up of a mouth. Respectively, the mouth is in- and out-of-synch, with a man's voice heard on the soundtrack repeating the self-reflexive pun (and pun on self-reflexivity), 'go through the motions of saying one thing and meaning another'; the mouth is entirely out-of-synch with an initial heard sentence and gradually revealed as being in-synch with a second sentence that is increasingly intercut until we only hear this second sentence and the order of things is restored. What these works reveal is not a psychoanalytic situation *per se*, but the televisual construction of authority through the otherwise direct, synchronised relationship between what we hear and the lips that we assume speak it.

Moreover, the organisation that Marshall co-founded in 1976, London Video Arts (a 'pressure group' for distribution, exhibition and production), took its precedents from collective and co-operative structures, including the London Filmmakers' Co-op amongst others, while remaining separate from it. Marshall located his (history of) video art alongside counter-cultural activism, of groups such as Radical Software in New York or TVX, based at the Arts Lab in London

102

in 1968, and others exhibiting in alternative London gallery spaces such as Acme or AIR. Given such an alternative social-political context, video art's relationship to the art world seems simultaneously to be the sum and the least of Marshall's concerns.

There are two aspects of television in Britain during the 1970s to note in relation to Stuart Marshall's work: that broadcast remained impenetrably terrestrial, closed to artists, disinterested in experiment, effectively authoritarian; and that it was also preparing for imminent, significant change determined by a unique combination of the demand for diversity and (eventually) the machinations of the free market that we inherit in the form of Channel 4. The first and only British pirate television station NeTWork 21 did not make their short- range broadcasts once a week from undisclosed locations in south London until 1986. Before then intervention by artists was rather cultural and critical, performed not within broadcast schedules but by extracting material from them, making a 'reading' of it into a video work and representing it to expose its prejudices, its formal construction, the illusions of its authority. The system itself could then be re-read, the intervention as much about literacy as any actual insertion into the medium. In *Screen* in 1979, Marshall cites Tamara Krikorian's *Vanitas* (1977) that combines images of seventeenth-century paintings with television news reports as an example. It antecedes the explicitly political, alternative 'news' services of what came to be known as Scratch Video in the mid 1980s in works by the Duvet Brothers and Gorilla Tapes. But my point is that this idea of intervention as literacy is key to Marshall's own works.

Distinct, The Streets of... and the three parts of *The Love Show* (all 1979) are like skeletons of the television genres that they critique. Each is divided into a series of sections that omit entertainment, and often deliberately refute visual pleasure by turning a spare analysis of television into content. The works' elliptical scripts are meta-conversations – commentaries – on the production conditions and visual and economic regulations that ordinarily define industrial television. They reveal constructed sets and fake news, standardised procedures and frustrated creative expression that makes them comparable to the work

103

of filmmaker Owen Land, or David Lamelas's *The Desert People* (1974), which exposes the prejudice of televisual pseudo-anthropological documentary (albeit with a pastiche Hollywood ending). What is uniquely difficult in these three works by Marshall is that their means are also their content – they are televisual assays on the televisual. The more thorough they are in their deconstruction of this experience the less experience we are left with.

Still from Stuart Marshall's Distinct, 1979.

As such, the relationship of *Distinct, The Streets of...* or *The Love Show* to the viewer mirrors the quandary of the subject in ideology, incapable of speaking or operating outside of it, a subject represented by the staged frustrations of Marshall's characters/ciphers in the sitcom-specific *Distinct* on their self-referential, futile quest to work out what there is to say. Marshall's engagement with ideology might share its source – the highly influential writings of Louis Althusser – with another filmmaker, Peter Gidal, but his answer to what there is to say is entirely different. Gidal denounces *all* sexual representation because he finds it inevitably ideological. Marshall, to the contrary, chose to make work in the field of representation, specifically about sexual representation, *because* he found it inevitably ideological, directly aligning his practice with a feminist strategy where 'a cultural politics... would demand interventions *at the ideological level* in order to deconstruct the fictional worlds constructed by dominant modes of representation'.[11]

Raymond Williams's momentous book *Television: Technology and Cultural Form* was published in 1974, in the midst of the cultural petitioning that marked television's transition from its 'first phase' in the UK, from the 1940s to the 1970s, into its 'second' and the introduction of Channel 4 in 1982. Stuart Marshall includes a reading of it in 'Video: From Art to Independence'. Williams attacks prevalent assumptions about the social effects of television by revising the prevalent theory of 'technological determinism', in which technological development is recast from being simplistically asocial and self-generating, negatively impacting society with its results, into a process that is indivisibly connected to and driven by social and cultural development. For Williams, television does not affect society in morally corrosive ways, but rather social (and/or state) intent, need and desires affect technological change. Marshall's *Bright Eyes* is an insertion into this equation, an intervention that functions on an ideological level through its participation in the construction and radical deployment of representations, i.e. it was made for television, broadcast in Channel 4's *The Eleventh Hour* slot.

The work is a counter-attack against the slew of alarmist prejudice that formed the tabloid press's response to the burgeoning AIDS epidemic – a response that collapsed difference between sexuality and the disease (to which Marshall lost his own life in 1993) – and examines the relationships between illness, homosexuality, persecution and representation. It exploits its medium socially and formally, as a public information film, a cultural history and an experiment in disruption that can be understood through another idea in Williams's work – the concept of 'flow'. Flow is the term Williams uses to describe how stations organised their schedules for viewers to stay tuned, so that individual programmes are read in the context of a larger unit, a whole evening's viewing of one programme after another, a flow into which the (unwitting) viewer is monopolised – hooked and carried along.

105

The peculiar structure of *Bright Eyes*, its juxtapositions and variety of registers, emulates the variety of an evening's viewing while staging its own disjunctions as a brilliant seduction into and activation of the viewing experience. There is no single authorising voice-over in the video, connections are powerfully implicit rather than didactically explained. Its various sections wildly but purposefully range from dramatic reconstructions of an AIDS patient being whisked into hospital along corridors that are cleared because of a (misinformed) fear of contamination, to historical dramatisations of (prejudiced) scientific enquiry into the visual signs of illness. Along with art historical analysis, there are sections concerning the Nazi persecution of sexuality, mock confessionals, interviews, literary extracts and an extraordinary collapse of time in a first-person account by a homosexual concentration camp 'survivor' spoken in the present by an actor whilst being driven along German motorways. Also included are the talking heads of medical professionals, AIDS experts, charity workers (The Terence Higgins Trust), the London gay and lesbian bookshop Gay's the Word, and the video ends with the re-reading of American Michael Callen's epochal anti-AIDS-prejudice speech to Congress, now given from the arboretum at the top of the cruising ground on Hampstead Heath.

Bright Eyes shares some of its material with Marshall's important video installation *A Journal of the Plague Year* (1984), shown in the unprecedented media installation survey 'Signs of the Times' curated by Chrissie Iles at MoMA Oxford in 1990, and it resonates with the defiant, tongue-in-cheek anti-Clause 28 collaborative video *Pedagogue* (1988), made with performing artist Neil Bartlett. While 'Signs of the Times' was aptly enough sponsored by Carlton Television, *Bright Eyes* is not only in and of the televisual (referencing and reconstructing representations), it was literally in and of broadcast television. It continuously evokes and undermines flow as a manifestation of social intent, thus effecting social and cultural reassessment. Its formal endeavour was the resolution of works like *Distinct* with their Spartan aesthetic and decoding-as-content, as well as a political reconstitution of viewing.

106

Four more works for television followed – *Desire* (1989), *Comrades in Arms* (1990), *Over Our Dead Bodies* (1991) and *Blue Boys* (1992) – each equally reassessing (homosexual) social and cultural experience and representation, history and commentary, and each commissioned by Channel 4's pioneering gay and lesbian strand *Out*. Given the importance of the televisual not only as a form that he literally embraced but as a way of understanding Marshall's practice and of reading video art as *counter* to art history, how *we* understand these works in relation to the visual arts might be the sum and the least of our concerns.

1. Stuart Marshall, 'Video: Technology and Practice', *Screen*, vol.20, no.1 (Spring 1979), p.117.
2. Rosalind Krauss, 'Video: The Aesthetics of Narcissism', *October*, vol.1 (Spring 1976), p.57.
3. Ibid., p.59.
4. Ibid.
5. Marshall, 'Video: From Art to Independence – A Short History of a New Technology', *Screen*, vol.26, no.2 (March–April 1985), p.59; available at http://www.luxonline.org.uk/articles/Video_From_ Art_to_Independenc(1).html [last accessed on 10 January 2016].
6. Ibid.
7. Ibid.
8. Marshall, 'Video: Technology and Practice,' *Screen*, op. cit., p.110.
9. Ibid., p.69.
10. Ibid.
11. Marshall, 'Video: From Art to Independence', op cit., p.70.

Feelings Are Facts: A Life, *by Yvonne Rainer*

Yvonne Rainer was a key figure in New York throughout the extraordinary cultural re-evaluations that occurred during the 1960s, experimenting actively within the new paradigms of minimalism and conceptual art as a dancer, choreographer and filmmaker. She was one of the founders of Judson Dance Theater in 1962, a revolutionary forum for a loose association of radicals who took their cue from Merce Cunningham and John Cage, attempting to develop an unprecedented postmodern aesthetic. Rainer's work has invariably been about a radical exploration of the 'everyday' in art, evident in her incorporation of quotidian movement and her complex use of diary material. Along these same lines, *Feelings Are Facts: A Life* (2006) is Rainer's attempt to rewrite her life as a memoir, albeit in a similarly experimental, exploratory way.

Feelings Are Facts in part extends from an essay Rainer was asked to write by Pacific Film Archive on her formative influences as a Bay Area filmmaker. The book incorporates her life up until 1972 in great detail, but from that point on her narrative is abbreviated into an 'Epilogue (as Prologue)' at the end of the book. Like her film and dance practice, it is shaped by her highly developed and formidable use of montage ('mosaic', in her words), coupled with a lack of narrative sentimentalism. Third- and first-person description, diary entries, extracts from

109

First published on the *Afterall* website in 2007,
<http://www.afterall.org/online/feelings.are.facts.a.life.by.yvonne.rainer#.
VpGFjza9FE4> [last accessed on 10 January 2016].

screenplays, letters written by herself and by others to her, credited anecdotes and cross-questionings figure liberally. Rainer is generous in her acknowledgements, and makes this diversity of source material visually apparent, each register having its own heterogeneous graphic identity within the book.

Rainer does not begin her story with the usual biographical details of her immigrant upbringing or the vicissitudes of her turbulent adolescence, all of which she details later in the book. Instead, it opens with the casual admission to a series of teenage sexual partners and of dropping out of Berkeley in 1952, aged eighteen. It is an audacious precedent to set while avoiding salaciousness. Rainer's sex life was apparently quite full and the details of her (mostly heterosexual) relationships during the period the book the covers figure prominently throughout *Feelings Are Facts* in various articulations. Rainer experiments liberally with the text, juxtaposing events and terms, elliptically sifting through memories, while constantly in search for a vocabulary: one of her early sexual partners, Wilbur Bullis, 'nearly got in'; another, Frank Trieste, was the man she trusted to 'deflower' her (this peculiar word, 'deflower', used only once, here, rang through my mind throughout the rest of the book); a quoted diary entry describes making love to Jack Warn as 'It is all him-me-the-world'. Rainer constructs a literary prism, describing around and deferring to other accounts than those made from a normalising perspective of history, somehow managing information by telling it.

Rainer's presentation of fragments is both extensive and revealing. For example, instead of a retrospective eulogy or nostalgic account of her arrival in New York in 1956 (marking a period of profound engagement with a radical and burgeoning network of artists – Merce Cunningham, Robert Rauschenberg, Yoko Ono, La Monte Young, John Cage and Robert Morris), Rainer defers to a 4,000-word letter to her brother dated 25 August 1961. Of it she says, 'Its irreverence and details offer a far more trenchant account than were I to reconstruct the period from memory.'[1]

The letter shifts from her relationship with her mother to early dance classes, working with chance procedures, dancing with Jimmy

110

Waring, the Berlin Wall, the nuclear bomb and Simone Forti. After reprinting it in full, Rainer adds a further deferral: 'The New York cultural events in the following years have been amply documented in the writings of Jill Johnston, Michael Kirby, dance historian Sally Banes, and others...'[2] It is a similar, cursory pragmatism that echoes in her self-criticisms. In another letter to Ivan in 1953, Rainer describes her job in a factory, in which she worked with an increasingly politicised group of black women. Commenting on the letter, she displays an angry reaction to a co-worker's suggestion that she joined a group for racial equality, and castigates her own reactions as those of an 'unreconstructed anarchist individualist'.[3]

The narrative deflections and ellipses of *Feelings Are Facts* play like multiple attempts to crystallise the truth of something – some notion of historical accuracy – thrown into tension with (and through) the construction of a present, emotional truth. It is this combination of stylisation and subjectivity that Rainer's first feature film, *Lives of Performers* (1972), definitively makes manifest. But this is not the reason that Rainer decided to stop her memoir right after the film was made. In part, she flips the decision back onto the conjunction of life, art and melodrama that make the film so remarkable: 'More and more of my private life went into my films, such transposition, though fictionalized, reduced my need to reconfigure it elsewhere';[4] and, '*Sturm und Drang* makes a better read than a stable life'.[5] We might understand this '*Sturm und Drang*', so bluntly acknowledged, as containing an indication of the multiple factors surrounding Rainer's suicide attempt in 1971. This is the book's other climax and perhaps the determining factor in its formal derivation of a language.

Rainer's thorough, formal descriptions of her dance practice in the book complicate and reconfigure the theoretical-political readings through which it has been commonly understood. By her own account, this was not a practice derived from an explicit political position or agenda, but rather the enactment of one body thinking and feeling in time and space – a body that developed, in this way, a radical activist politics. The subtle occlusion of this construction is important, and this could be what informs the desire for (and absence of) another

111

explanation, a clearer indication of her decision in the 1980s 'not to enter into any more ill-fated heterosexual adventures'.

With much of the same localising impact, *Feelings Are Facts* prescribes its own reading. It is difficult to escape the awareness of the act of reading, because of a composition that is as visually signified as it is cogently played out. If feelings *are* facts, then what this book also argues is that the fact of a feeling is inextricable from its means of expression; the fact of these feelings is ultimately the fact of this book.

1. Yvonne Rainer, *Feelings Are Facts: A Life* (Cambridge, MA: MIT Press, 2006), p.199.
2. Ibid., p.219.
3. Ibid., p.124.
4. Ibid., p.433.
5. Ibid., p.436.
6. Ibid., p.437.

One Script for 9 Scripts from a Nation at War

*It does not so much allude to antecedent theories as represent,
in the broadest sense of that concept, the contesting claims of
politics, feminism, morality, psychoanalysis and personal needs,
desires, fears and myths, on an individual perplexed by urgent
decisions about how to live and what to do ... [It] is a dialogue
of dissonant and at times contradictory voices discoursing on
topics like political and psychological domination (and oppres-
sion) and the interrelation of the two ... a species of free-floating
forensics with voices antiphonally adding information and
opinion to a breccia of neighbouring issues.*

And in so doing,

*[It] is the kind of film that makes a space for audience 'participa-
tion'... [where] the participatory style itself operates as a metaphor of value, proposing the spectator as a 'free' agent involved
in the active application of 'judgment' as he or she partakes
in the 'democratic' construction of the film. This theme of participation in the fine structures is, of course, strictly analogous
to the position of the spectator in regard to the gross 'dialectical'
structures where the viewer (or perhaps more aptly, the listener)
weighs counter-vailing arguments, judges them and above
all chooses – not only what is relevant to what, but also a stand
on the issues. 'Choice' like 'participation' is morally charged.[1]*

113

First published in *Afterall*, issue 18 (Summer 2008), pp.100–07.

These words are not a description of *9 Scripts from a Nation at War* (2007), a ten-channel video installation by Andrea Geyer, Sharon Hayes, Ashley Hunt, Katya Sander and David Thorne. Although they could be – almost. Rather, they are Nöel Carroll's description of Yvonne Rainer's equally epic film *Journeys from Berlin/1971* (1980), published as an introduction to Carroll's substantial series of interviews with Rainer in *Millennium Film Journal. Journeys* is a complex, if not unique film that Carroll and Rainer discuss in over thirty pages – *9 Scripts* warrants much the same space and time, which is not possible here. The fact that Carroll's words come so close to a description of this other work, made in 2007 and first exhibited at documenta 12, is an indication of how much can and cannot be contained in my text. In the same introduction, Carroll points at a new 'tendency', a 'direction' away from the dominance of (American) Structural film (such as work by Hollis Frampton or Michael Snow) towards 'The New Talkie', a branding that the passage of time has relegated to one of avant-garde filmmaking's lost labels.[2] Carroll cites other examples of this tendency: *Argument* (Anthony McCall and Andrew Tyndall, 1978), *Sigmund Freud's Dora* (Anthony McCall, Claire Pajaczkowska, Andrew Tyndall and Jane Weinstock, 1979) and *Riddles of the Sphinx* (Laura Mulvey and Peter Wollen, 1977) – works of a certain kind of European-influenced cinema which over the past two years have been looked at again, re-assessed, restored and shown again.[3]

Carroll describes these filmmakers as distancing themselves from the modus operandi of the Structuralist filmmaker, 'the epitome of rarefied intellect', not least 'because the qualities [that their work] mines and projects... cannot, for all sorts of reasons, be regarded as heroic in the way they were in the early 1970s'.[4] These new authors are moving from a high-modernist notion of filmmaking to a filmmaking that begins to critically incorporate the social and political positions adopted by its makers both in relation to their practice and in more general terms. If we allow Rainer to be one of the few exceptions, then this also implies a move away from the single (heroic) author towards co- and multi-authored works, towards collective or more explicitly collaborative practice. My appeal to Carroll's text in relation to

114

9 Scripts is not in order to rehearse an argument about the contemporary relevance (or irrelevance) of Structural filmmaking, or to wonder about the precise reasons for a resurgence of interest in 'The New Talkie'. Rather, it is motivated by an interest in the model of mapping that the correspondence between text and artwork performs, as a way of reading (or thinking into) *9 Scripts* and as an example-in-action of one of *9 Script's* strategies: a radical re/deferral or transference, where the words spoken by one person become a transcript to be read and re-spoken by another.

> The New Talkie emphasises language.... Structural filmmakers
> seem primarily interested in the possibilities of language (e.g.
> the polysemy of words) and its limitations, whereas practitioners
> of The New Talkie are preoccupied with this while at the same
> time with 'saying something'. Undoubtedly, it is the urge 'to say
> something' that accounts for the rise of The New Talkie...[5]

Language is the material of *9 Scripts*. In it, a small 'cast' including men and women of different ethnicities say a great amount of things, to the extent that this act of speaking (speaking as something enacted or embodied, as the position from which a person speaks or is spoken to) is also its material. The centre of the piece is occupied by the matter of the position from which someone speaks, the position from which we receive what is spoken, and the position from which the viewer/listener/reader also looks/hears/speaks. These positions are repeatedly made material by the constellation of dissonant and interrelated voices that have been collected together from a variety of sources and grouped in ten sections: 'Citizen', 'Blogger', 'Correspondent', 'Veteran', 'Student', 'Actor', 'Interviewer', 'Lawyer', 'Detainee' and 'Source' ('Source', rather than one of the 'scripts', just shows the source material included in the work). What brings all these voices together is the condition that what is said relates to the contemporary circumstances of war, be they physical, conceptual, political, legal, personal, governmental, etc. This war is both war in general and, implicitly, the Iraq war – America's current state of war that its government does not admit.

115

From what position do I speak (write)? (And from what position are you reading this?) I did not see *9 Scripts* installed at documenta 12, but watched the nine videos on three preview DVDs on my computer at home. There is a material difference between this linear order and the physical movement necessitated by the work's installation, where the videos were shown on separate, custom-built units arranged in space, to be watched by one or two viewers with headphones, some-times facing other viewers, sometimes not. 'Participation' in this work had a physical manifestation, a piecing together that might occur men-tally but that was also staged in time and space through the physical movement of the viewer's body. It brings to mind another artist exhib-iting in documenta 12, Mary Kelly, whose new work there dealt more directly with transference from a specific time – 1968 – to today, and from one artist to another generation of artists. In a recent interview Kelly described to me her preference for the exhibition space over the cinema auditorium, the former implying a self-reflexivity inherent in moving between one thing and another, the viewer determining the duration of engagement, the direction of movement and its construc-tion of a 'psychological time'. The museum is understood as one of the last sanctuaries for experimental work, where 'the outmoded has some redemptive value'.[6] These things, however, remain imaginary to me, a psychic participation that is nonetheless self-reflexive pre-cisely because of the way in which *9 Scripts* represents various kinds of speakers and listeners (viewers), as well as the way in which these representations are paced and ordered by shot changes or repetitions (as moments – or prompts – in which we might move from one screen to another) – and, finally, how *9 Scripts* encodes and enacts position as content. I am in a different time (and space) but I am still addressed.

The nature of this address looks simple but in fact is multi-faceted. Each category of speaker is constituted by a careful, constructed rela-tionship between what is spoken (transcripts derived from interviews, tribunal recordings, blogs, interviews conducted by the artists), the person speaking (not always their own words), the register of their lan-guage (public, personal, informative, formal, casual rehearsal), repre-sented or implied others (questioners, audiences, imaginary readers),

116

and the composition of the image as a scene that describes the power relations (and their institutional foundations) which underpin this language and these addressees. The camera never moves. Like in 'The New Talkie', where according to Carroll 'language is more important than image', in *9 Scripts* such primacy seems equally present, but is also accompanied by a formal arrangement of colour, furniture and choreographed bodies: speakers wear clothing in block colours; suits match ties and the walls of lecture theatres; bodies are arranged asymmetrically in rooms, the frame divided by classroom desks and rows of chairs; and a mass of New York buildings is the suffocating backdrop to an interview. These are representational codes not without analytical *and* visual pleasure, despite how Spartan this form might otherwise seem.

In 'Blogger' a man sits facing the camera, reading from a sheaf of pages in front of him. We see his face in close-up until the camera eventually jumps to a wide shot, showing an audience of six people sitting opposite the reader, with their backs to the camera. Although he inflects the words he speaks with an actor's timbre, these words are not his own: each page contains an extract from a different blog, adding up to a subtle but thorough range of different re-spoken voices. Some writers identify themselves; others do not. They offer details of life in Iraq from the perspective of inhabitants, coalition soldiers or activists. They include personal responses to the war and reports of air strikes; impassioned, objective, resistant, reflective or urgent meditations on whether self-reflection is ever possible; desires, fears and descriptions. They are like the sentences that the cast of *9 Scripts* take turns to write in chalk (and immediately erase on a blackboard) in 'Citizen', showing real (or fictional?) people's responses to the question of what they will do when 'democracy' comes: 'I will comply'; 'I will understand that someone has to die', 'I will force my demands to centre stage'.

'Blogger' is like an alternative news service read on video by one person but with no fixed centre, no single speaker, no common ground other than the fact that all of these things have been written in or about a particular place or a situation, in the first person, for an unknown reader. And that is the thing. If one of the generative and sustaining tenets of the war on Iraq is actually the war on an invisible (read 'silent') enemy, an abstract 'terror', then this section of *9 Scripts* inverts the equation: the imaginary here is not 'the other', but the viewer, figured as imaginary by the reader of these blogs. Me. I am addressed, but the twice-removed writer does not know who I am. So who am I?

'Do you feel it's possible to tell the story of somebody else without telling your own story?', says one woman to another as the first question in the 'Student' section. The image is split in two screens: one showing a room in which the questioning occurs and one showing its closed door, through which another woman enters and replaces the questioner, who replaces the respondent (who leaves). This round-robin structure continues throughout the section. The concern in 'Student' with the understanding of particular words – such as 'enemy', 'ethical violence' – is mirrored by the legal definition of other (related) terms in 'Lawyer', such as 'unlawful enemy combatant', 'ethical violence' and 'torture'. 'Can you imagine me saying something to provoke you to hit me?' The list of questions in 'Student' is fixed and they are occasionally repeated according to the order the questioner chooses. The response is not scripted, which makes me wonder if that means that the language of the responses is more authentic than that of the questions, a speaking and a thinking through definitions – is this where I place myself?

As the correlations within *9 Scripts* accumulate, audiences (listeners, receivers, us or I) are present or figured in other sections by their absence. In 'Veteran' the transcribed words of a female soldier and a male marine are spoken separately by a woman and a man in uniform from a podium to a massive and spectacular auditorium with no one inside. Their speech is intercut with scenes showing the speakers rehearsing their lines backstage – personal stories publicly declared or pronounced. In 'Actor' members of the cast walk through corridors and enter a lecture theatre, with the camera facing the empty rows of seats. They sit briefly in silence and leave again, repeatedly assembling and dissembling. Some actors wander less purposefully, attempting to remember their lines. In 'Correspondent' first a male, then a female journalist (a news reporter and a newspaper columnist) answer questions about their work (the words they use, objective or opinionated, the positions they assume) that the viewer does not hear. The reported speech of their questioner is spoken by a male and a female actor standing in the side aisle of an empty lecture theatre in 'Interviewer'. The nine scripts of 9 Scripts are discrete and interlaced, explicitly and implicitly participating in each other. If I piece them together in this text across its various sections, it is not to resolve their positions into one, but to reflect the accumulation of positions within language.

While the work's structure refutes narrative form – that is, it circles without a single point of climax – words, as the stuff of narrative, become a dissolute, disseminated, mediated theatre that stands for or becomes the theatre of war and its corollaries, itself encapsulated in another kind of theatre, the tribunal re-played in 'Detainee'. Across three screens an expanded cast re-speak the transcripts of the (non-) trials of Guantanamo detainees. Language here is absolute in the sense that it absolutely determines the form and content of the tribunal that persecutes 'unlawful enemy combatants' and withstands deviation by physically removing anyone contesting its terms, its absolutely inflexible semantics made physical, material. Language here is a spectacular injustice, and this is perhaps what 9 Scripts as a whole addresses, as it addresses me in its multiplication of linguistic registers, its self-reflexive and epic exegesis of complicity, subjectivity, authority and 'individual perplexed by urgent decisions about how to live and what to do'.[7]

Complicity too is participation. It can only be a galling irony that this war is one of the most prolific cultural producers of our time. In the radical overhaul of the nature of these cultural representations (into language) I locate the political imperative – and effectiveness – of 9 Scripts. I am not in a room viewing atrocities happening elsewhere, propagated by a political system that is not mine, supported by people who are not me and who are literally and symbolically elsewhere, being fed the comfort or the fantasy of my non-participation. I am in my room and I am *in* language, writing. In the 'Source' section the screen I look at is a computer screen, as the various transcripts of 9 Scripts are being written up from audio recordings of interviewees.

I quote these transcripts from their re-spoken sources and type them into this text. You are reading. I – actually I mean 'I', whoever occupies that position – am/is the subject of *9 Scripts*.

So what about the other inverted commas that frame words in the quotation that opens this text? 'Participation', 'free', 'judgement', 'democratic', 'dialectical', 'choice' – the generative functions of *Journeys from Berlin/1971*? Carroll used these words in relation to Rainer's film in order to indicate critical certainty as a possible outcome of the work. These words *almost* describe *9 Scripts*, but the outcome is now critical instability or complicity, in which the generative function of language becomes representation and a 'polysemy of words' is contested by contesting itself. The contestation otherwise absolutely excluded from our political establishment's absolute construction of this war.

While planning this text I remembered something that I thought Gregg Bordowitz had written in an article in *Artforum* about another time of extreme crisis and radical, urgent activism – 1980s and the nascent AIDS epidemic. I thought he had written: 'There is no such thing as community, only people coming together in a time of need'. But he did not write that. Describing the revelation that occurred to him after visiting the Lesbian and Gay Community Services Center in New York ('the only hospitable place to go' in the face of mass media hysteria, misinformation and prejudice about the disease), he wrote: 'Community is the space claimed and defended by people who need one another.'[8] If that is true, *9 Scripts* is community.

120

1. Nöel Carroll, 'Interview with a Woman Who', *Millenium Film Journal*, nos.7–9 (Fall 1980/Winter 1981), reprinted in Yvonne Rainer, *A Woman Who...: Essays, Interviews, Scripts* (Baltimore: The John Hopkins University Press, 1999), pp.170 and 174.
2. Ibid., p.169.
3. [White programmed all three of these films, as well as Rainer's *Journeys from Berlin/1971* during his time as adjunct curator of film at Whitechapel Gallery, (2001–11). He had a particularly sustained engagement with McCall and Tyndall's *Argument*, which became a kind of touchstone for his ideas around how thinking politically about film required forging relationships between a film's content and an audience's collective experience of it. Having helped to organise *Argument*'s first screening in more than two decades in 2002, as part of the 'nocinema' collective in London, White built a season around it at Whitechapel in 2006, and subsequently also presented the film in a number of other contexts including programmes at the Office for Contemporary Art, Oslo in 2007 and CCA, Glasgow in 2012.]
4. Carroll, 'Interview with a Woman Who...', op. cit, p.169.
5. Ibid., p.170.
6. See 'The Body Politic: Mary Kelly interviewed by Ian White', *frieze* (May 2007), pp.130–35.
7. Carroll, 'Interview with a Woman Who...', op. cit, p.170.
8. Gregg Bordowitz, 'My '80s: My Postmodernism', *Artforum* (March 2003), p.227.

Art on Television

The preface to John Wyver's *Vision On: Film, Television and The Arts in Britain* states that 'the archive begat this book'. The archive in question is 'a complete database of the Arts Council film collection' – the Arts on Film Archive – now fully digitised, viewable and searchable online so long as the viewer is looking at the site from a domain name that ends in 'ac.uk' – i.e. an academic institution based in the UK. The question of who is more or less likely to exploit copyright laws is by the by. But, with the archive protected in this way from the dangerous other public that might once have legitimately watched some of these television programmes, wider questions could have been asked: what kind of a relationship might there be between the archive and the book? Or between the archive of the museum collection, the history of dance or architecture, and their mediation via television? *Vision On* does not so much answer these questions as highlight the peculiarities of its subject and the ambiguity of its own status as the survey of a database. That it nonetheless stimulates such questions is not without value.

Wyver has been at the forefront of making television programmes on art and artists in the UK since the launch of Channel 4 in 1982, when he founded, with Geoff Dunlop, the production company Illuminations, responsible for important series such as *Tx.* (for BBC2, 1994–99) and Channel 4's headline-grabbing live coverage of the Turner Prize (1993–2005). Wyver acknowledges his involvement in the field throughout his painstaking descriptions of changes in funding bodies and broadcasting policy. But implicit in this position of

123

First published as a review of John Wyver's book *Vision On: Film, Television and the Arts in Britain* (London: Wallflower Press, 2007) in *Art Monthly*, no.319 (September 2008), p.36.

undoubted authority is the perpetuation of television as an unquestioned medium-as-institution. *Vision On* is not a history of art, but a history of this history re-presented on television without questioning what might be peculiar to this endeavour, why artists might otherwise want access to television (see the work of Stuart Marshall for such an example), or why or how the institutions of art – or the arts, or government – might fight for such access. It is an ideological situation described without the mention of ideological intention: one list as a book derived from the other list of the online database.

Its five approximately chronological chapters are intercut with 'sidebars' that describe individual films from the collection in more detail. Disavowing nostalgia for any golden ages, Wyver peppers his account with personal anecdotes amid selected details of the most prominent arts strands on terrestrial television (*Monitor, Tempo, Omnibus, Arena, The Late Show*, etc.), the jostling for responsibility between the Arts Council and the British Film Institute, negotiations between these and television channels, and the impact of 'independence' on production opportunities. He does so with such fine detail – annual budgets, their fluctuations, facilitation and limitations – that much of *Vision On* reads like another statistic-laden Arts Council report.

Needless to say there was no single rationale guiding production, which was prey to the flux and flow of varying emphases on audience numbers versus cultural responsibility, giving the public 'what they want' and challenging the status quo, a pedagogic impetus and an onus on entertainment, and the Arts Council's continuous reassessment and restructuring. The Arts on Film archive inevitably reflects an esoteric, unresolved dovetailing of policy and political and social concern. Wyver lists without critique, as if the structures that determine these things are happy givens, and only implicitly indicates that they are not.

The intentions and strategising of museums, like that of artists, are mainly omitted in this history until the very end, when Wyver comments on projects such as the National Gallery's production of films in the 80s and 90s and more recently Tate Media – 'a digital broadband arts channel'. Museums have been remarkably active in using film to exploit their collections and to amplify influence since the early

124

twentieth century, in the form of touring film shows (not television), much like the early Arts Council film tours that were initially so successful. Haidee Wasson's recent book *Museum Movies* details this, albeit with regard specifically to American museums. Alternative (deinstitutionalised) television is also disappointingly omitted. Surely the underground broadcasts of NeTWork 21 in summer 1986 warrant some comment? And what about the precedent of Gerry Schum's Fernsehgalerie Schum in Germany in the late 60s?

All this said, *Vision On* is at its most insightful in the brief, excited description of feminist, anti-racist and other marginalised voices coming to the small screen in the 1980s. Towards its end, Wyver expands on his categorisation of arts documentaries into three tropes: the Lecture (Kenneth Clark's *Civilisation*, 1969, radicalised without precedent by John Berger's *Ways of Seeing*, 1972); the Encounter (John Read's *Henry Moore*, 1951); and the Drama (Ken Russell's *Elgar*, 1962). It is here where Wyver really gives some grist to his lists, and some indications of the criticality that television might have been – might still be – against Melvyn Bragg's lamentable 1982 defense of *The South Bank Show*'s benign promotional profiling: 'Lack of space tends to inhibit the employment of a critical approach.' For anyone wanting to claim or reclaim television as a potentially critical vehicle in relation to the arts: read this book backwards.

Kinomuseum

*The extraordinary fact is that we live in a world in which virtually
anything may be exhibited in a museum, and in which virtually
anything can be made to function as a museum...*

Donald Preziosi and Claire Farago, 'General Introduction: What are Museums *For?*',
Grasping the World: The Idea of the Museum

*Through reproductive technology postmodernist art dispenses with
the aura. The fiction of the creating subject gives way to the frank
confiscation, quotation, excerptation, accumulation and repetition
of already existing images. Notions of originality, authenticity
and presence, essential to the ordered discourse of the museum,
are undermined.*

Douglas Crimp, 'On the Museum's Ruins'

'Kinomuseum' is a project that occurs at the intersection of these two
statements, between the museum's seemingly unlimited ability to
reproduce itself and the threat that reproduction poses to the art museum's primary function as the keeper of unique objects. Ultimately,
'Kinomuseum' is a proposal for considering a particular kind of cinema as a unique kind of museum: one where 'originality, authenticity
and presence' are not undermined by reproduction, but where reproduction either turns these qualities into a new set of questions for the
museum, almost physically disrupting it, or, perversely, where film
and video as potentially infinitely reproducible objects make these
same terms manifest in moving images considered as works of art.

127

First published in *Kinomuseum: Towards an artists' cinema*, ed. Mike Sperlinger and
Ian White (Cologne: Walther König, 2008), pp.13–27. More information about the
'Kinomuseum' project as a whole is contained in that volume. An earlier version of
the text appeared in the catalogue for the 2007 Short Film Festival Oberhausen, as an
introduction to the original series of screenings referred to here; the title of the screening in which each film was included appears in brackets after its first mention.

It leads to a differentiated cinema, a museum based on the principles of impermanence, immediacy, the temporal and the temporary, manifested in the minds of an audience who experience it in the space and time of the auditorium that is the museum's permutating exhibition hall, and who are its active, defining agent.

This essay is an extended version of that which was printed in the catalogue of the Oberhausen Short Film Festival. The first half reflects a pattern of reading that informed the project as a whole, that guided conversations with artists whose work is included in the programmes and with the five guest curators – Achim Borchardt-Hume, AA Bronson, Mark Leckey, Mary Kelly, Emily Pethick – as well as being inflected by them. Concerned with the museum, it is also its own collection of texts and thoughts. The second half of the essay discusses different ways in which cinema and the museum have more in common than would appear at first glance. Throughout, retrospectively now, I draw on particular examples from both individual works shown in the screening series, as well as some of the guest curators' propositions; not to account for every work shown, or to turn artists' works or my own curatorial process into the demonstration of a thesis (when the thesis itself was about the plurality of questions), but to illuminate a specific point when it is useful to do so. (When an individual work shown as part of a programme is quoted it is followed by the title of that programme.) Equally I do not attempt to fully translate the specific experience of watching these works in the cinema in Oberhausen other than to draw from them further illumination. Perversely, in this discussion of reproducibility and the existence of a differentiated cinema, that experience was particular and is unrepeatable.

To echo the question that the American artists Allan Kaprow and Robert Smithson discuss in their 1967 essay: 'What is a museum?'[1] So, many things: temple, tomb, grotto, void, theatre; conservative/radical, establishing authority/continuously unravelling.

In her essay collected in Preziosi and Farago's anthology, Paula Findlen traces the etymology of the word 'museum' in the Renaissance where it signified 'the place where Muses dwell'[2] – an almost-mythological any-place without spatial or temporal dimensions.

128

'What is a Museum? A Dialogue between Allan Kaprow and Robert Smithson,'
Arts Yearbook ('The Museum World', 1967). Photo: Ian White.
In their conversation Kaprow and Smithson discuss the museum and some
metaphoric or comparative structures. The article is accompanied by a series
of photographs that further illustrate these associations and that incorporate:
war memorials, industrial design and manufacture on domestic and corporate
scales, mausolea, a discotheque, fashionable interior decoration, oil-storage
tanks and the Burial Mounds of the Bahrain Islands.

Its nexus of meanings, coalescing as private activity and the private collection became increasingly public (a drive that erupts in the nineteenth century's near-obsession with establishing museums), comes to situate it also between the intellectual and the social, inseparable from the society in whose image it is constructed. Preziosi and Farago name the Louvre as the first state museum, born from the French Revolution.

By contrast, in the late twentieth century, the implications of the by-now innumerable state museums and their otherwise anti-revolutionary, reformist or civilising functions are in part the content of the work of another American artist, Andrea Fraser. In *Museum Highlights: A Gallery Talk* (1989) and *Welcome to the Wadsworth* (1991), for example, Fraser exposes these functions by assuming the role of a gallery docent and delivering political, yet often ambiguously innocuous public tours of the museum. In 'A Letter to the Wadsworth Atheneum', written as a private letter to America's 'oldest continuously operating public art museum' in Hartford, Connecticut as a result of the artist's research for her performance at the same place, Fraser admits this museum – its displays and its architecture – to be a unique, superficially seamless discourse of untroubled, homogenised culture.[3] Which is precisely her critique: it reflects the image of an equally, wilfully homogenised local society. In the nineteenth century when the museum was founded, 'at least in its cultural institutions, social conflict in Hartford is not recognised, not represented – even as a by-product of an attempt to repress it'.[4] The omission of local, social and historical difference or opposition is extraordinarily successful.

The museum is a political place. As an artist, Fraser is not alone in taking the museum itself as her subject. Marcel Duchamp's *Box in a Valise* (1935–41) is an artwork and a transportable collection that contains reproductions of the artist's 'other' artworks. It is the revolutionary impulse of 1968 that Benjamin Buchloh discusses in relation to Marcel Broodthaers's construction of imaginary museum-as-artwork in his essay 'The Museum Fictions of Marcel Broodthaers'.[5] Broodthaers's project, according to Buchloh, was to interrogate the museum's strategy of power by creating 'museum fiction', actual and imaginary 'museums' that simultaneously conceptualised and realised (instituted) the

130

institution. Duchamp and Broodthaers share the fact that they construct both a museum (a museological frame) and the work (their own work/s) that it contains. These 'authors' are also the authorising institution. As such, they exploit or deviate from the definitively museological business of removing something from one place in order to re-situate it in another: the museum expresses its political, social and cultural agendas by establishing and maintaining a collection.

Mark Leckey's *CINEMA-in-the-ROUND* (2006–8) is delivered as a lecture to an audience in the cinema auditorium. It doubly exploits cinema's capacity to yoke together wildly diverse content (like the images of objects in a book) in order to wrestle with (name, institute) the moving images it gathers together – their description of tangible mass, tangibility itself – as its perverse yet cohesive collection: Philip Guston paintings, videos by Gilbert & George and Fischli and Weiss, George Baselitz's sculptures, a pop promo, Popeye, Garfield, Homer Simpson, television adverts, an ancient Egyptian cat, Hollis Frampton's film *Lemon* (1971). Images of objects in this double play become objects themselves: because they are collected and described as such, and because of a reading of their content that is itself a belligerent disavowal of two dimensions. Leckey, the artist, poses as curator, simultaneously presenting a lecture about, and an actual guided tour through, his collection. If this is an assault on the paradigms of art history, it also reveals a paradigm of cinema in which the ultimate object, Leckey's star exhibit, is a spectacular nothing: over the seven minutes of Hollis Frampton's *Lemon*, a light moves slowly around the luxurious fruit, describing it as defiantly three-dimensional, touchable almost, until the light is entirely behind it, the fruit made into a perfect silhouette, three dimensions irreducibly made two, a flat shape that is nothing but a shadow of itself, a space of no light on the screen.

Preziosi and Farago describe the museum as a construct, re-presenting things in order to make sense of them. And it is this – to reiterate – the removal of a thing from one place and its re-situation in another place, which forms a continuous thread through the various cultural readings of the museum. It is the pivot upon which turns Theodor W. Adorno's essay 'Valéry Proust Museum', as it compares the two French

poets' positions, and links institutional responsibility to personal experience, and pleasure. The culturally conservative Paul Valéry experiences
almost an act of violence in the curatorial frame of the Louvre: 'Neither
a hedonistic nor a rationalistic civilisation could have constructed
a house of such disparities'.[6] On the other hand, Adorno quotes Marcel
Proust: 'the masterpiece observed during dinner no longer produces in
us the exhilarating happiness that can be had only in a museum...'[7]

If Valéry's disdain and Proust's exhilaration are the provocation
and the sum of Mark Leckey's lecture, then the mordant phonetics
of the opening of Adorno's essay – where he connects 'museum' to
'mausoleum' – are otherwise played out across a number of works in
'Kinomuseum' as a whole, such that they also define this other institution of the auditorium. Megan Fraser's film of the Pathology Museum
at the London Hospital (*Untitled*, 2007, '7 Guided Tours') shows its
collection of pickled babies being packed away as the museum closes;
Morgan Fisher discusses death through an examination of point-of-
view shots in his lecture '*Screening Room* and Death'. Originally
a museum installation – shown at the Museum of Modern Art, Oxford as
a sculptural arrangement of a monitor – Marina Abramović's *Cleaning
the Mirror* (1995, 'Screening Room'), becomes, projected in the auditorium, another metaphor for this cinematic image. The on-screen 'character' is the image of death as the artist washes a skeleton that we see
increasingly in close-up. The otherwise fixed camera closes in on the
skeleton, in stages synchronised with the sound of Abramović's audible
breathing, this breathing that simultaneously becomes the pattern of
the audience's breathing and ironically reveals the separation, between
the living audience and the (doubly not-living) projected image. In the
short film *Mounting Buffalo* (1920, 'Toute la mémoire du monde') from
the archive of the American Museum of Natural History, a buffalo is
systematically dismembered, its organs replaced by plaster, its body
remade as entirely artificial, its skin draped 'naturally' over its new
(typical) form. Cinema, like the museum, effects a memorialisation.

Adorno's own position in relation to his poet-protagonists is significantly ambiguous: 'When discontent with museums is strong
enough to provoke the attempt to exhibit paintings in their original

132

'What is a Museum?' Photo: Ian White.

surroundings... the result is even more distressing than when the works are wrenched from their original surroundings and then brought together.'[8] His equivocal dissatisfaction signifies what Daniel J. Sherman in an essay, 'Quatremère/Benjamin/Marx: Art Museums, Aura, and Commodity Fetishism', describes as Adorno's 'remedy' to Walter Benjamin's work on how, when a unique work is reproduced, its aura diminishes. Instead of this consummate 'disappearance' of the original work of art in favour of the many reproductions that come to stand in for it, Adorno proposes, according to Sherman, 'more dialectics, at the site of artistic production of all kinds'.[9]

Sherman cites Antoine-Chrysostome Quatremère de Quincy as 'the first full-fledged critic of art museums'.[10] Writing contemporaneously with the very construction of museums as we know them today (principally the establishment of the Louvre), Quatremère, unlike Proust, has nothing but disdain for the removal of an object from its original context in order to re-place it in an alien one. Sherman maps a genealogy of this position to question the separation of the museum from the (art) market that might otherwise supply it. The commodification of an artwork by the market (where 'use' value is subsumed by economic value) and its collection by the museum function in analogous ways. The museum is ideological and finds precedent in the market: 'By both reproducing and implicitly endorsing the decontextualizing strategies of the marketplace, museums rob art of life'.[11]

※

What has all this to do with cinema? Generically, an undifferentiated cinema, defined by its industrial model that is both symbolised by and dependent upon the theatrical auditorium, functions in a strikingly different way from the art museum's collection of objects (the art museum which Daniel J. Sherman suggests Adorno regarded as, 'the most elaborately articulated instance of decontextualisation as a strategy of power'[12]). The principle of distribution, dependent on film as an infinitely reproducible medium, is to show the same work to the maximum number of people, the maximum number of times.

134

Cinema audiences exert a collective ownership over the work which each member pays a small amount of money to watch, and the same work might be watched simultaneously in different cities and different countries. This is a comprehensive and continuous *re*contextualisation by a market, upon which we might argue the form – and meaning – of this work is contingent. The art museum, by contrast, collects and preserves unique objects, at great expense, and their exhibition is strictly controlled. Anyone wanting to see an exhibit must travel to the one location in which it is on display. The fixed start times and fixed seating of the auditorium are different from the perambulatory space of the gallery.

Of course, this is an over-simplification. Emma Hart's *Skin Film* (*Skin Film 3*, 2006, 'The American Wing') is a work that stands on and for the void at the centre of the distinction between cinema and the museum, and asks an equal, critical question of both. It is a unique object, made by Sellotaping the artist's skin to clear film. There are no prints of this 'film', no processing, no copies, just actual tape and skin travelling through the projector (the sound of which material becomes the soundtrack). It disintegrates a little every time it is projected until it is unprojectable, making it a disappearing, uncollectible, unique object that Hart has remade three times (but might not remake again). It is a film without a fixed duration, that varies according to the artist's body shape at the time of its (re)making. It is not a distributable film and it is not a museum object, while being both simultaneously – a set of 'nots' that stands for, perhaps, the tenets of a differentiated cinema or a 'Kinomuseum'.

Pierre Bismuth's *Following the Right Hand of Humphrey Bogart and Ingrid Bergman in Casablanca* (2007) is the imaginary museum proposed by Achim Borchardt-Hume. After the (animated) opening credits of Michael Curtiz's 1942 feature film play on screen, the image suddenly cuts – before any image of actual places or actual people appears – to the scribble drawing derived from the process described by the work's title. Taken from the television screen, this drawing was made into a loop of 35 mm film shown continuously for the duration of the feature film as the soundtrack of the original plays in its entirety. This happens in the cinema auditorium, as if the feature film itself were being presented, once only, at a fixed start time. It is a feature film made into a 'static' image – an image that does not change but that is experienced for the length of the film that it also elliptically describes. Combined with the audible soundtrack, Bismuth's work turns the action that we hear into a metaphor of our situation: *Casablanca*'s themes of entrapment and escape, its romance, come in this unique situation to describe the conditions of the audience's virtual entrapment in the auditorium, the romance of their discipline and the discipline of cinema.

Specific examples aside, we don't have to look very far at the world around us to discover the boundaries between the disciplines of the cinema and the museum starting to erode. The art museum has had to incorporate (industrial) cinema into its strategies of display. Contemporary artists such as Daria Martin or Nick Relph and Oliver Payne show their work in the museum *in the manner of* the cinema: single-channel works shown in dark rooms, with some fixed seating and sometimes fixed start times. But these films and videos also enter into the museum collection – following the principal of unique objects – by virtue of being editioned, and they are controlled rather than distributed. As with Robert Rauschenberg's montages (contrary to the revolutionary status that Douglas Crimp affords them in 'On the Museum's Ruins'), their acquisition does not provoke an actual collapse of the museum even though it might suggest a conceptual one.

Conversely, at Anthology Film Archives in New York in 1968 a committee led by the artist filmmaker Jonas Mekas formed their own collection of works, ostensibly for distribution but also as a means of enshrining the films it would contain along museological lines. As a model it differs, for example, from the London Filmmakers' Co-op (founded in 1966), where membership entitled a filmmaker to deposit their work for preservation and distribution. But then this other model was abandoned as unsustainable, in terms of rising cost, infinite space requirements and a limited distribution circuit (income), with the effective dissolution of the Co-op, its merging with London Electronic Arts and their rebranding as LUX – opening a new set of problems and renegotiations as to the status of the specialist distributor-exhibitor

'What is a Museum?' Photo: Ian White.

Towards the end of their conversation Smithson replies to Kaprow's comments about the institution's pervasive ability to categorise and contain: 'I think to try to make some kind of point right away stops any kind of possibility. I think the more points the better, you know, just an endless amount of points of view' (p.51). His words echo those of Dorothy Richardson, writing in her column 'Continuous Performance' for the modernist magazine *Close Up*: 'It is ... comforting to reflect that so far the cinema is not a government monopoly. It is a medium ... [that] can, at need, assist Radio in tuning the world into a vast council-chamber ...' ('Continuous Performance: The Film Gone Male', *Close Up*, vol.9, no.1, March 1932)

in the twenty-first century that continue to be unravelled in the new organisation's business today, and continuously place it, almost to the point of definition (again), *between* the museum and industrial cinema.

But perhaps the museum is like the cinema not only in terms of the display of moving image work. Like cinema (and often commensurate with it), the museum is no stranger to the entrance fee. Blockbuster exhibitions frequently 'sell out' (the museum finds its capacity) and at this point of ultimate 'success', entrance to the show is regimented into fixed time periods. Moreover, Preziosi and Farago describe the museum itself as 'a *representation*, an artefact as "natural" as the "spec-imens" it preserves'.[13] And, 'museum objects are *staged* or *framed* to be "read" in a variety of ways...'[14] (my emphasis); and, 'museums serve as *theatre*, encyclopedia, and laboratory...'[15] (my emphasis); and, finally, 'museums are "performances"...'[16] Are they also describing the condi-tions of cinema?

The insistence on a work's status as a unique (or almost unique) art object is a recent validation that the museum and the artist have deployed to legitimise the acquisition of some film and video. It is not the only model. At the Centre Georges Pompidou in Paris, for example, industrial cinema (feature films) and artists' films – both potentially infinitely reproducible, the former definitely uneditioned – are con-tained within a film collection, the acquisition process for which is the same as for the museum's other departments.

The appearance of the cinema auditorium itself – today as often curated as programmed – as a common feature of the modern art museum is not unrelated to another alternative, a founding problem if you like: the Film Library established by the Museum of Modern Art, New York in 1935.

In many respects, Haidee Wasson's book *Museum Movies: The Museum of Modern Art and the Birth of Art Cinema*, which articu-lates the institution of the film library, was one of the starting points for 'Kinomuseum' as a project, and partly why my archival research began with major American museums, the precedents and contexts that the Film Library was established amongst. Wasson describes how this unique collection not only instituted cinema through its catholic remit, collecting Hollywood feature films as well as artists' film, but also extended museological practices to radically affect the film industry, introducing a system of dating and attributing authorship to films for the first time and, by introducing the principal of conservation, establishing the new economy of repertory cinema. Prints previously regarded as depleted of any value after the film had been released once were instead kept to be shown again.

The MoMA Film Library and its 'exhibition' in the museum's cinema also had an important social influence. Audiences used to verbally and physically expressing themselves as they watched popular feature films were expected to behave differently in the Museum of Modern Art's own auditorium, to the extent that Iris Barry, the Film Library's champion and first curator, 'had a slide projector permanently installed in the museum's auditorium, equipped with a slide that read: "If the disturbance in the auditorium does not cease, the showing of this film will be discontinued"'.[17] Wasson situates the Film Library as one among a number of tactics employed by MoMA as a critical mediation and implicit extension of itself. Touring film programmes served ideally to 'civilise' provincial Americans, as well as to entertain and inform.[18] The unique status of film as an auxiliary to the museum('s collection) that could be safely distributed (i.e. was replaceable, reproducible), and as an educational tool loaded with institutional authority, turns cinema into a vital annex for the museum's social (and political) agenda. In representing the museum that Preziosi and Farago describe as already being a representation itself, the Film Library – cinema – *becomes* the museum.

David Lamelas's *A Study of Relationships Between Inner and Outer Space* (1969, 'Inner and Outer Space') could be read as taking this formula to its absurd-yet-rigorous conceptual conclusion with political intent. It begins by documenting the dimensions of Camden Arts Centre in London (which commissioned and exhibited it), progressively expanding its frames of reference to the city's transport infrastructure and its media, and ending with street interviews with members of the public about their responses to recent reports of man landing on the moon. An examination of the gallery's interior is yoked

139

to a social and cultural exterior, revealing what it lacks. But there is no clearer example than the film produced by the Metropolitan Museum of Art's Office of Cinema Works, *The American Wing* (1935, 'The American Wing'). This is not so much a work of cinema as film effecting museological categorisation. It chronologically documents the reconstructed period rooms of the museum's American Wing and, in a final, virtuosic ten minutes, depicts individual silverware objects. The methodical camera shows a fixed view of each room, slowly pans from left to right and stops. Each object is displayed on a black velvet turntable against a black velvet ground, is stationary, rotates once, and is stationary again. Each shot is introduced by an intertitle that authorises – gives an historical account of – each room, its furniture, notable details. The occasional dissonance between what is written and what is photographed is in itself an unwitting essay on the museum's illusion of authority: some shots seem to show an actual exterior to these rooms, as if they have been photographed not in the form of their museum reconstruction but actually in situ; some edits suggest the film is a composite rather than an authored sequence. That these questions remain unanswered by the film's apparently uncharted provenance not only testifies to its ambiguous status as an extraordinary work in the archive of the Metropolitan Museum's education department, but also points to that other set of questions that we might have about the museum itself, as a collection of reconstructions which are here indivisible from both aspects of their representation, in the museum and on film.

✳

In an essay written for *Kurz und Klein: 50 Jahre Internationale Kurzfilmtage Oberhausen*, I discuss the ways in which artists' film and video occupies a critical position in relation to both industrial cinema and the museum.[19] In particular through the establishment of the film co-operatives in the late 1960s, and themselves conscious of other legacies than those institutionally received, practitioners were aesthetically and physically operating in a space between the auditorium and the art gallery, employing both or neither – not just as a necessity for getting work shown, but often as an inseparable, political or theoretical constituent of the work itself.

'Kinomuseum' similarly attempts to make content of criticality by locating the museum in and as the cinema auditorium, rather than deploying cinema as the museum's ideological annex. There is a physicality to the proposition, as expressed by Mary Kelly's programme 'Fallout': three epochal works, from three different decades, were shown in three auditoria of the Lichtburg cinema. They were not looped, like film and video in a gallery room that the audience enters and leaves at will, but timed sequentially, one after the other, so that the audience had to physically move from one auditorium to the next at the end of each work. The perambulatory space of the gallery collapsed onto the organising architecture and institution of cinema. The difficulty of such movement through spaces that otherwise control or curtail it (cinemas are more like airports than art galleries in this respect), this peculiar arrangement, was the limit of cinema made physically manifest.

So 'Kinomuseum' is a project equally about finding limits, the inadequacies of industrial cinema in a cultural field, and the radical proposal that a differentiated cinema replaces both this and the museum. It takes its lead (if not the entirety of its contents) from the legacy of artists' film and video, and some precedents from artists whose work has performed similar investigations (some conducted and shown as part of the project, documented in this essay or this book, and others that are not). 'Kinomuseum' as a definite, realised project in the context of the International Short Film Festival Oberhausen attempted two things. One was through cinema to institute a new museum of questions, to explore and represent the museum – not to edify it as an institution, but to replace the institution itself with its own exploration. The museum *becomes* a cinema of multiple points of view, its content the very nexus of its meanings. The other, through the guest-selected programmes, was to make this transference more explicit by 'constructing' *imaginary* museums that are more dependent on the collective imagination of the cinema audience than the authority of any one

141

tangible collection or the architecture of any one particular edifice. 'Kinomuseum', as an idea that remains in this essay largely in the present tense, collects everything and nothing and is one place made many places. To finally admit André Malraux into our equation: 'the museum *was* an affirmation, the museum without walls *is* an interrogation'[20] (emphasis mine).

1. 'What is a Museum?: A Dialogue between Allan Kaprow and Robert Smithson', in *Robert Smithson: The Collected Writings*, ed. Jack Flamm (Berkeley: University of California Press, 1996), pp.43–51.
2. Paula Findlen, 'The Museum: Its Classical Etymology and Renaissance Genealogy', in *Grasping the World: The Idea of the Museum*, ed. Donald Preziosi and Claire Farago, (Aldershot: Ashgate Publishing Limited, 2004), p.159.
3. Fraser, 'Welcome to the Wadsworth', in *Museum Highlights: The Writings of Andrea Fraser*, ed. Alexander Alberro (Cambridge, MA: MIT Press, 2005), p.123.
4. Andrea Fraser, 'A Letter to the Wadsworth Atheneum', in *Museum Highlights*, op. cit., p.116.
5. Benjamin H. D. Buchloh, 'The Museum Fictions of Marcel Broodthaers', in *Museums by Artists*, ed. A A Bronson and Peggy Gale (Toronto: Art Metropole, 1983), pp.46–56.
6. Theodor W. Adorno, 'Valéry Proust Museum', *Prisms*, trans. Samuel and Shierry Weber (Cambridge, MA: MIT Press, 1967), p.176–77.
7. Ibid., p.179
8. Ibid., p.175.
9. Daniel J. Sherman, 'Quatremère/Benjamin/Marx: Art Museums, Aura, and Commodity Fetishism', in *Museum Culture: Histories, Discourses, Spectacles*, ed. Daniel J. Sherman and Irit Rogoff (London: Routledge, 1994), p.138.
10. Ibid., p.123.
11. Ibid., p.134.
12. Ibid., p.123.
13. Preziosi and Farago, 'General Introduction: What are Museums For?', in *Grasping the World*, op. cit., p.2.
14. Ibid., p.4.
15. Ibid., p.5.
16. Ibid.
17. Haidee Wasson, *Museum Movies: The Museum of Modern Art and the Birth of Art Cinema* (Berkeley: University of California Press, 2005), p.2.
18. According to Sherman, Quatremère advocates the distribution of copies, specifically 'sculptural casts', as a means to prevent a country's treasures from being removed from their original settings.
19. [See 'The Projected Object', earlier in this volume.]
20. Andre Malraux, *Essais de psychologie de l'art, vol.1: Museum Without Walls*, trans. Stuart Gilbert and Francis Price (London: Secker & Warburg, 1967), p.162.

History is Written for Historical Reasons

History. What is it? Whose is it? 'If you go into an academic bookshop and look over the shelves occupied by texts on philosophy, you will find a vast array of works wherein the problem of the foundations and limits of what can be known and what can be done "philosoph-ically" are the staple diet.... If you then wander over to the shelves on literature, you will find a separate section on literary theory.... But then continue over to the history area. Here it is almost certain that there will be no section on history theory...'[1] Such was my experience described in a book that I found on a semi-hidden shelf of Foyles bookshop in London. The walls were lined with histories *of*... many things: of London, the British Empire, the World, Warfare, Uniforms, the Military, World War I, World War II, the Vietnam War, etc. I'd gone there after meeting Lis Rhodes, from whose 1979 text this series of screenings borrows its title and which it is based around.[2] Lis had asked me a question that shot through our discussion: 'What are you reading that is history?'... No answer. So I went to find it, to read it, and instead found this search already written in the pages of a book that told me simply I would not find it here, like a closed loop.

Like the closed loop presented by one of Gabi Teichert's co-teachers in Alexander Kluge's *Die Patriotin* (*The Patriot*, or, *The* Female *Patriot*, 1979) as her lesson plans are debated: 'History is written in a certain way for historical reasons.' His fury is that her teaching flagrantly

145

First published in *Festivalkatalog 54. Internationale Kurzfilmtage Oberhausen* (Oberhausen: Karl Maria Laufen, 2008), pp.115–17. This text was written as an introduction to a series of screenings White had programmed inspired, as he writes, by Lis Rhodes's 1979 essay 'Whose History?'

disregards the curriculum, its authorised history disconnected from personal experience. He hopes that there is no way out of this absurd loop. Gabi Teichert's (and her students') relationship to such a history might be described in 'Whose History?' as, 'a reconstruction of events, that I had no part in, causes that I didn't cause and effects that testify to my sense of exclusion. This is the history that defines the present...'[3] Is it this history that Tony Blair meant when he said, 'Let the day-to-day judgments come and go: be prepared to be judged by history' (*The Guardian*, 1 March 2003)? Which history exactly is Blair referring to? Whose history? Breaking the loop is political.

I asked around. Mike Sperlinger suggested I read Friedrich Nietzsche's 'On the Uses and Disadvantages of History for Life' (1873): 'We want to serve history only to the extent that history serves life.'[4] Lis Rhodes's text advocates the subjective over the authoritarian and Nietzsche argues against a blinkered allegiance to history over lived experience, about impossible objectivity and history as a mask for needless wars: 'The oversaturation of an age with history... leads an age to imagine that it possesses the rarest of virtues, justice...'[5]

He identifies three historical modes and advocates a balance between them: the monumental ('great' things unquestioningly revered), the antiquarian (concerned with collecting, preservation, tending the historical object), and the critical (questioning past events, their motives, their recording). Maneuvering between the three is a delicate business. One must also live 'unhistorically', that is, forget in order to take action or to make anything new. At the same time, things in the past venerated 'now' as history are not necessarily fated, but not necessarily more than 'brute truth... an incorrigible stupidity, a blunt "thus it is" in opposition to morality's "it ought to be thus"'.[6] So much for 'history be my judge'.

Nietzsche's essay is nonetheless highly problematic and 'Whose History?' diverges from it radically. It might unravel the double blind of this word 'history' but it does so not to undo government (ideology, authoritarianism) into a necessary condition of critical instability, even if it defines the word as and of the positions we take in relation to the past. Quite the opposite. It is a clarion call for a renewed strength

146

and national (nationalist, German) unity. That he writes, 'The masses seem to me to deserve notice in three respects only: first as faded copies of great men produced on poor paper with worn-out plates, then as a force of resistance to great men, finally as instruments in the hands of great men',[7] reads to me as worse than dangerous, far from the 'crumpled heap' of history that Lis Rhodes's 'Whose History?' otherwise petitions.[8] Her unequivocal, political imperative is that history itself is individuated, a monolithic structure radically re-gendered into one experienced by *everyone*, to radical effect.

✳

What does all this have to do with us?

Tim Griffin's editorial in the February 2008 issue of *Artforum*, 'Personal Histories': 'Art history... is perpetually at risk of adhering to a certain decorous orthodoxy – an idea of what is recognised as *proper* – and this often comes at the cost of any sense of history as a volatile field, the stuff of lives lived'.[9] In explaining his decision to print unaltered the previously unpublished transcript of a 1973 conversation between Lucy R. Lippard, Nancy Holt and Robert Smithson about Eva Hesse, Griffin by default defines how art history ordinarily functions. How it is ordinarily about, in this magazine and in general, 'molding... conversation into a polished document, reorganizing and placing clear emphasis on what we today might deem its most significant thematic parts...' The unedited transcript is the exception that proves art history is not 'thought as process', that it does not risk 'embarrassment and disclosure', that it is not speculative.

This art history is the one replayed perhaps in all histories, but in particular in the histories of artists' film and video that emulate it as a validating discipline. I read it in *A History of Experimental Film and Video* by A. L. Rees, or most recently *A History of Artists' Film and Video in Britain* by David Curtis.[10] The more I think about these texts the more ridiculous such a history project becomes – at this point in time, and as a general practice in relation to a subject that otherwise asks radical questions of the power structures and institutions which inform such (alien) storytelling. Lis Rhodes wrote 'Whose History?' for the catalogue of the 1979 exhibition 'Film As Film' (Hayward Gallery, London). It contests the representation and participation of women in this particular exhibition, the show's self-defining, self-validating emphasis on formalism and the underlying (ideological) structure, the cultural, social and political misalignments-as-exhibition-making that permit these omissions.

This series of programmes was developed through conversation with many people, not least with Lis Rhodes herself. In some ways it is a pendant to 2007's 'Kinomuseum', with which it shares some concerns. The five programmes [comprising the 'Whose History?' programme at the Oberhausen festival] are linked, unusually, to a profile screening of Lis Rhodes's work, which is integral to the series. They circle around a particular point almost to the extent that their titles are interchangeable and some works would sit as easily in one programme as another. They return, again and again, to a period of activity loosely between the late 1960s and 1970s to ask these questions: What is a historical moment? What is a portrait? Can film (or video) be history? How do we construct history? Not how might we write a book (I do not want to write one of these books), but how do we, watching these works in the cinema, constitute history?

As the programmes came together I realised two things. First, the works I was drawn to confound and exploit history not only as a reference found in a variety of forms, but as an homogenising discipline, projecting the past into experience. Rather than supporting an orthodox chronology they are achronological. Individual works often contain multiple directions: a looking back to something past, a projection of this into a present and an implied future. They enact a complex equation of history-making from which the writing of their own history (a history of artists' film and video) might take its lead, or which indeed writes their own history as we watch them. Of course each work in a programme is seen consecutively, but there are ways of reading across programmes, specifically regarding works from the Cinenova collection (which appear in four of the programmes) and in the four works of Alexander Kluge, included in three separate programmes. My second realisation was that the question these works share is one about their status as documents, which quite directly relates to the precise question that Lis Rhodes's work raises: what do we see? What can we be sure we are seeing? So I chose not to describe the works in their catalogue entries but to replace their description with a found text, to site them in and as an interplay of documents, not to document them, but for them to be seen.[11]

1. Keith Jenkins, *Re-thinking History* (London and New York: Routledge, 2003), p.2.
2. See Lis Rhodes, 'Whose History?' (1979), *Film as Film: Formal Experiment in Film, 1910–1975*, exhibition catalogue ed. Deke Dusinberre and A. L. Rees, (London: Hayward Gallery, 1979), pp.119–20.
3. Ibid., p.119.
4. Friedrich Nietzsche, 'On the Uses and Disadvantages of History for Life' (1873), *Untimely Meditations*, trans. R. J. Hollingdale (Cambridge: Cambridge University Press, 1997), p.59.
5. Ibid., p.83.
6. Ibid., p.106.
7. Ibid., p.113.
8. Rhodes, 'Whose History?', op. cit., p.120.
9. Tim Griffin, 'Personal Histories', *Artforum* (February 2008), p.63.
10. [See also White's review of the exhibition 'On General Release: Avant-garde and Artists' Films in Britain 1968–72', co-curated by David Curtis, in *Art Monthly*, no.263 (February 2003), pp.36–37.]
11. [For details of all the works included in the original programme, and the texts used in place of their descriptions, see *Festivalkatalog 54. Internationale Kurzfilmtage Oberhausen*. A PDF of the catalogue is available to download from the festival's website at the time of writing.]

Recording and Performing:
Cinema as a Live Art/Becoming Object

This text – that I am writing in 2008 – is an extended version of a magazine article written in 2003 that was based on a would-be argument I gave during a ten-minute contribution to a panel discussion at the Whitechapel Gallery, London in 2002.[1] As such it has a peculiar relationship to the thing that it speculates upon: the relationship between the inconclusive media of live art and the moving image, and the relationship of both of these to the museum as an ultimate repository (or a cultural conclusion). It is a text that itself (or the writing of which) is a reperformance. Its original form migrated from the ephemeral to the edified through a kind of repetition. Its ideas have shifted in their reiteration like a series of interpretations, an accumulation that is more formally permanent but no less speculative than those originally expressed.

In 2002 at Whitechapel it was a question about the reperformability of live art works that initiated the discussion: the relationship between a live work and its documents, or how we come to know it without (originally) witnessing it, how it assumes its place as artwork defined as something collectable. It accompanied the first instalment

151

Originally commissioned in 2008 for a proposed issue of *Cinemamatograph*, the journal of the San Francisco Cinematheque, on the subject of 'live cinema' to be edited by Thomas Beard; the issue was ultimately never published.

of the gallery's ongoing series 'A Short History of Performance' that saw the restaging of historical works (works that happened in the past which we would otherwise receive through their documentation in books, or sometimes on film). The series presented specific works by Carolee Schneeman (*Meat Joy*, originally 1964), Bruce Maclean (*There's a Sculpture on My Shoulder* and *Pose Work for Plinths*, originally 1970), and Jannis Kounellis (*Untitled (Twelve Horses)*, originally 1969) amongst others.

'A Short History of Performance' was an experiment: it asked whether, like a film rented from a distributor many years after its pre-miere, a live work could be performed outside of the physical, social, now-historical context that it initially occurred within. The (almost literal) location of meaning became a game of physical and conceptual constructs, with failure as a valid outcome. A game in which meaning might be lost, but equally in which something particular might be discovered about the role of circumstance and instance, or a prob-lem solved/exposed about history and commodification, art and its institution. The ambitious means of exploring this was to re-witness historical works as live, rather than their document as record.

What I spoke in 2002 or wrote in 2003, described as a would-be argument, remains as such in 2008 even as those spoken or written words are both here and not here, obscured by this extension. They were/are a speculation that seeks to go beyond the binary distinction of action and its document, via what – after these years have passed – I prefer to call artists' film and video, and its counterpart – something I hadn't differentiated previously – an artists' cinema. As a speculation it is intended more to confuse the binary between action and document, not to replicate this structure by means of an oppositional argument, but to propose an arrangement/problem-in-progress of production, exhibition and acquisition that artists' film and video might share with live art. It realigns their challenge to the standardising hierar-chies of cultural production (making, showing, collecting) specifically in relation to artists' film and video (and live art) and tries to replace the question about where the meaning of a performative artwork might be located by reconstituting this 'location' as the question itself.

I think now that it is this challenge that is the 'something particular' which 'might be discovered'.

What I proposed in 2002, on this panel about live art and its documents, was the possibility of inverting the equation between the act and its relics; a way of thinking about artists' film and video and (a differentiated) cinema that would implicate the (reperformed, or, projected) document as an equally primary act. I'm not sure now whether this 'equally primary act' was an overly optimistic declaration, but this argument was mapped through two separate lines of enquiry. Firstly through a suspicion that live art and artists' film and video are described by parallel histories – broadly considered as oppositional (materially and institutionally), challenging to dominant culture, exposing ideology, developed most prolifically (though not without precedent) during the 1960s and 70s. Secondly by looking at examples where the live act, reconfigured into the space-time of the moving image (or into a form that exceeds 'merely' its registration) effectively replaces what we understand as the document with a process of translation-made-form, or made visible, or, better, process conceptually (re)enacted by the act of looking. The question I didn't ask, but which I think I was trying to answer was whether film/video as a medium

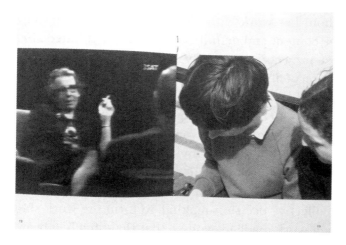

Emma Hedditch, spread from exhibition pamphlet
'A Political Feeling, I Hope So', 2004.

153

could be understood as performative – not simply by considering artists' works that incorporated live action, but also by a consideration of what an artists' cinema is, how this functions. If this wasn't answered then, then it is asked now, with more examples.

Then I was thinking about the work of Emma Hedditch, Carolee Schneemann, Kurt Kren, Vito Acconci, Mike Kelley and Paul McCarthy, Yoko Ono, Kira O'Reilly and Emma E. Wilson. Each of these artists, often in very different ways, I understood to be making (or using) film or video and confusing the distinction between something live and something recorded, something only known in the instance of its happening and something repeatable.

Emma Hedditch's work re-presents the systems of control or organisation that it also examines as content, with political intent. Her work is not medium specific, but rather a process of organisation or reorganisation, and it is this process that becomes the thing experienced like a challenge posed not only to a viewer, but also to her co-organisers or the system of organisation that shapes what is experienced in ways by which engagement with the work on any level becomes mutually implicating. By doing so it not only investigates but actively intends to instigate structural change. To who we are as viewers, or organisers, to the system that makes 'work' visible. In 2002 I was writing about her work with video where a social strategy becomes equally the content and definition of what is 'exhibited'. In particular about those projects where she would respond to invitations to make a presentation of film or video works made by women (in the past) that she turned instead into video-making processes (in the present), producing the work to be shown in and of the town she had been invited to present works in: a shot list would be posted in advance of the event that was effectively an open invitation for local people to come to the screening venue with their own videos derived from this shot list. The separate videos would then be put together, through discussion and collective decision-making, to form the work shown at this screening of work made by women that Hedditch had been invited to present, that might be accompanied by a live voice-over, a text written by one or more of her collaborators and read by them or by her.

154

This is one brief example of a complex and actually delicate practice that extends increasingly to text-based works (interviews, publications) and event-based presentations of work made by others, collectively organised and presented (such as her 'exhibition' – her project – at Cubitt, London in 2004, 'A Political Feeling, I Hope So') that warrants really an essay in itself. This work is indivisible from the relationships to its range of, effectively, co-authors, institutions, subjects; women-only organisations (Lambeth Women's Project, the London-based distributor Cinenova which Hedditch runs in an unpaid position, her own alternative distribution project 'and i will do'), community groups, other artists, schools and progressive collectives such as the Copenhagen Free University, as well as those who work in the system that makes this project visible. In short, the politics of this process are not commodifiable gallery or cinema products, but the direct engagement of a radical, re-gendered political consciousness foregrounded in a radically re-experienced relationship (politically complicit) between viewer and 'screen', audience and artist that simultaneously challenges these divisions.

Other examples drew upon film and video, which in and of themselves have a more complex relation to the actions they document than that of the secondary to the primary. Carolee Schneemann's film *In Quest of Meat Joy* (1968–69) is a record of her orgiastic performance *Meat Joy*. It is a record that references (with deliberate irreverence) Kurt Kren's extraordinary (silent) documentations of performances by the Viennese Actionists. Schneemann translates Kren's meticulously mathematical editing structures into a pop-soundtracked parody, employing these referential aesthetics to accrue meaning specifically through and as a filmic reading.

Vito Acconci recorded 'performance' to re-articulate it in and for film-space/time. *Conversions* (1971) is a long film, that describes a meditative, transformative space, that plays upon concerted efforts of looking and thinking, which over its duration correlates to the acts of *trompe l'oeil* sex-change that he performs. Mike Kelley and Paul McCarthy respond to other Acconci performances in fantastically ironic, filmic terms in *Fresh Acconci* (1995), where porn stars replace

155

performers who mirror Acconci's original actions, translating them into the setting of a luxurious Hollywood mansion, the generic set of a sex film. Kelley and McCarthy's explicitly indulgent response to Acconci is equally a comment on the look and our desire, making clear something other than conceptualist engagement which might occur when we view Acconci's own naked actions.

Yoko Ono's *Cut Piece* (where Ono sat on a stage and allowed members of the audience to approach her with a pair of scissors and cut away at her clothing), first performed and documented in Tokyo, 1965, was re-staged and re-filmed by Lynn Hershman in 1992. The radicalism of this, like that of Ono's instruction pieces, simultaneously liberates the intended action from the actual body of the performer and integrates this with the production of a new document.

And then there were some other contemporary examples: Kira O'Reilly replacing an advertised performance of *Wet Cup* (2000) for one made privately for the camera, when the local council refused to allow her to perform the work because of 'health and safety regulations'. This censorship of a carefully controlled performance where the artist as subject re-enacts the medical technique of wet-cupping (hot glass bowls placed directly onto the skin) was subverted by means of its document that replaced it. Emma E. Wilson's *Swelling* (1998) was also made for the camera. As in O'Reilly's *Wet Cup*, the intensity of the video is extraordinary: moving, profound, affective. Wearing only a pair of modest pants, the artist was bound into a long, transparent plastic corset (a process we hear via non-synch sound, as measured as breathing). This corset is the inner core of a transparent, inflatable globe that slowly rises around her with a quiet hiss, eventually so large as to cover half her face, her arms extended above her head. This is a deeply personal demonstration of image and self-image, desire and despair, the intensity of which is both facilitated by its private recording and emphatically re-experienced in its public screenings.

Reading these examples again I realise that they do not make a category other than one of things I saw or experienced, recalled as questions about the relation between the live and its document. Like the photographs that Roland Barthes presents in his book *Camera Lucida*, that

156

I will discuss, they do not, in and of themselves, form a theory. I would add some more, now, briefly, that continue this chain of experience.

In an undocumented performance of his famous(ly documented) *Performer/Audience/Mirror* as part of an exhibition at Lisson Gallery in 2007, Dan Graham incorporated a description of the camera – the one thing he doesn't point at or name in those early recordings of the work – as part of his commentary on his own actions, the audience's reactions and the situation they are in.[2] So as well as describing a look, the movement of an arm, leg or foot, he also described the audience's heads turning to look at him in the manner of surveillance cameras.

As an opening performance for his exhibition at Cubitt, London in 2008 Jimmy Robert added to the list of *Cut Piece* re-presentations, performing a version of the work where Ono's dress was replaced by small pieces of masking tape covering the artist's otherwise naked torso that the audience were invited to peel off, one by one.[3] This was not a replication but a reference, the historical further mapped onto our present as he intermittently quoted lines from contemporary

Jimmy Robert, *Figure de style*, 2008.

157

reviews of Ono's 1966 London performance of the piece. This text, as in Graham's work, implicated the audience, its descriptions of reactions in 1966 also examining – making complicit – us, the audience, in 2008 as we looked at this other, actually present body and chose when or whether to remove a piece of tape.

Redmond Entwistle's *Paterson-Lodz* (2006) is an impossible film – that is, it is a work to be shown in the auditorium while its installation simultaneously defies the architecture of the space and the logistics of exhibition. Six speakers are installed amongst the rows of seating in the auditorium. A computer, triggered by the projection of a 16mm film randomly selects the work's soundtrack of soundscapes (which are spatially experienced through the positioned speakers) and recorded interviews. Alternating with black screens and fixed shots of glass panels made from ground impressions in Paterson, USA and Lodz, Poland, it describes a complex picture of history, identity and migration through the involvement of the Jewish populations in both towns and two key events: the 1905 revolution in Lodz and the 1913 Paterson Silk Strike. The work enacts a kind of migration and repetition – a random soundtrack that moves around the auditorium and a fixed order of images. There is no live action here but this too is an event-based work.

Guy Sherwin's *Man With Mirror* (1976-) is a performance made by the artist with a hand-held mirror and a super 8 projector. In a pitch-black space the artist makes precisely choreographed movements with the mirror to variously catch and reflect the image thrown by the projector, a film of the artist in a rural idyll making the exact same movements with a mirror that he is making in the space in front of the audience. Its effect is magical, an image floating in free space, a complex optical illusion. But contemporary performances of this work are extraordinary for that which is revealed by the actual face of the considerably older artist in contrast to the younger artist in a sunlit field whose physical movements he mirrors: it is the passage of time not as a problem of original and re-enactment, but as content, an inversion of the relationship between action and document which constitutes meaning.

These examples are specific and testify to what I understand as a continuously opening field against any attempt to fix relations between an

158

Guy Sherwin, *Man With Mirror*, 1976–.

action and the documents by which we come afterwards to know it, or that constitute its continued existence as an artwork. They do not define the media of artists' film and video or live art by the modernist paradigm of what these things are in themselves. Such concerns are the provenance of a system of control that determines (art) history – systems that these works, like a definition in the form of exception, would otherwise contest and whose dominance I think provoked the questions in our first instance, in 2002.

✳

In 2002, this quotation from a text written in 1955 by Hans Richter seemed to be a stepping stone to other ideas:

> The main aesthetic problem in the movies, which were invented
> for reproduction (of movement) is, paradoxically, the overcoming

159

of reproduction. In other words, the question is: to what degree
is the camera (film, colour, sound, etc.) developed and used to
reproduce (any object which appears before the lens) or to produce
(sensations not possible in any other art medium).[4]

All of the examples which Richter cites in defence of this statement
are made by men – Fernand Léger, René Clair, Dalí/Buñuel, Len Lye,
Jean Cocteau, Man Ray – and his proposition alludes to a formalism
from which histories of artists' film and video might still suffer. But
his point remains interesting: to clarify the difference between film as
document (reproduction) and film as medium, reconfiguring space,
producing its own set of circumstances. Richter is writing about aesthetics but critically these terms – reproduction/production – map
onto our own problem of (re)performed live art. By doing so they
extend beyond questions about content, material or montage in early
film to incorporate the auditorium (as a social space) and the instance
of projection (as a 'live' moment). Is there a parallel between the live
act in live art and its physical context and what occurs on the screen
and the place in which we watch? If these things can be commonly
named as the *frame* (the image on screen, the live action in live art)
and the *field* (the auditorium, the location of the live act), then the
dynamic between them is what constitutes something particular
about the exhibition of live art and artists' film and video, about the
two media themselves. This dynamic cannot reproduce. It produces.
And by so doing it is what characterises both practices as an abiding
challenge to the institutions that attempt to exhibit and preserve it.

Artists' film and video, like live art, has consistently posed radical
questions through this relationship between the frame and the field.
The London Filmmakers' Co-op was founded in 1966. I have written elsewhere about the non/anti-institutional nature not only of the
work being made during this time but also of the actual spaces which
this practice and its exhibition occupied, suggesting the two are at
least connected if not inseparable.[5] Formal experimentation (reactions against the dominance of narrative in industrial cinema) took
place in physical locations that were outside the walls of the museum

and theatrical auditorium, such that physical location might also be understood to define a political position or to illuminate the politics of this practice. As forms, experimental film and live art refuted the dominant institution/s with other kinds of public space in ways that I imagine made what was seen to have been indivisible from where it was seen, or make, now, what is seen indivisible from where it is seen. Which is another way of reaching the same point, the problem posed by and at those Whitechapel (re)performances.

Of course this is a generous generalisation – Constance Penley's brilliant feminist critique of the British filmmakers Malcolm Le Grice and Peter Gidal, for example, counters their (very different) meta-psychological theories and practices with the inescapability of the psychological and transcendent in both the act of looking and their films, arguing that they in fact replicate systems to which they would otherwise critique or protest their radical difference.[6] But my point in this generosity remains, even if its anti-institutional description is questionable: that the meaning of an image on the screen is not neces-sarily divided from the audience's experience of it at the site of exhibi-tion, the material conditions under which the screening is performed. This is no less emphasised than by the long legacy of underground and experimental forums that have made visible these works that I now call artists' film and video, from Jean Vigo's politically charged illicit screenings of the early twentieth century to, in London, the form-content-theory engagement of the London Filmmakers' Co-op, the dynamism of the Arts Lab, and contemporary film/video clubs and collectives; kinoKULTURE at The Horse Hospital, and others for whom space is impermanent, where filmshows happen at different locations each time – OMSK, The Exploding Cinema. This is an *event* culture of non-standardisable forms. Even when artists' film and video is shown in the permanent auditorium of an institution it becomes an event, equatable to a live work by its determining material factors: that the screening invariably happens once only, possibly endorsed by the presence of the filmmaker, the print or tape possibly having been imported from abroad and unlikely to be shown again before enough time has passed to re-amplify the rarity value of the occasion.

This cinema of non-standardisable forms is the contrary of industrial cinema – the feature film industry – with its guarantees of quality and quantity. Rather it stakes a claim to differentiate the term, for what I choose now in 2008 to call an artists' cinema.

The museum display of film and video, by contrast, deals in permanence. It does so by various means: works of film transferred to video formats to be affordably exhibited without disintegration. The commercial contemporary art system in 2008 selectively recoups filmmakers (now artists) of the pivotal 1960s and 70s: Morgan Fisher, Jack Goldstein, Paul Sharits, Tony Conrad, Owen Land, Anthony McCall. Museums collect their works and the works of others. Sometimes the arrangement hangs on a (sometimes retrospective) commodification of the works themselves – films or videos editioned into limited series of prints or tapes – to align them with the unique objects that otherwise take up the shelf space of these mausoleums. That is, to remove them from precarious, uncontrollable distribution into collected permanence, with its criteria of controlled access, both because of and to endorse their (cultural, economic) value. Film and video in this context become objects to be housed in the name of preservation. Is it such a copy-becoming-object that the investigation of 'A Short History of Performance' also pulls into focus? How might a live act become an object? We start now to open a discourse about the relationship between live acts and their repetition. That is, about theatre.

No form is actually pure despite (or because of) the 'something particulars' we might decide it possesses, but nonetheless (or because of this) this text fumbles in the darkness of ideals. As a pure form, theatre is predicated on repetition – on actors ideally making the same action at the same time every time the same piece is performed. To quote an anecdote of the American theatre director Robert Wilson on his fascination with Marlene Dietrich, whom he saw perform the same role in the same place seventeen times in 1968: 'She would remove a tear every night – it was always right there at the exact same time'.[7] Repertory theatre companies keep scenery in their stores, productions can be 'revived', the same actions performed again in the same costumes on the same sets. The theatrical production is one flawed model

162

of the object that live art could become – flawed not least because it omits that the place/s in which the live action might have occurred and from which it constitutes meaning are actually never the same place as that of its (museological) re-exhibition. Live art is not repertory theatre.

At the same time, the first projection of a film in a theatrical auditorium by the Lumières is popularly labelled the birth of cinema. Eisenstein regards the late-sixteenth-century invention of the (theatrical) proscenium arch to be 'one of the first manifestations of cinematographic space'.[8] The industrial cinema which these things describe – showing the same work to the maximum number of people the maximum number of times, in a standardised and regulated (seats in rows) environment, an immersive experience in which the screen becomes a window, or our disbelief is suspended – is the sustainable model that experimental film fails to achieve (despite its practical and political relationship to distribution) and from which it is radically differentiated as an artists' cinema (manifested by a practical and political relationship to distribution). This other 'theatrical' – theatrical release, theatrical distribution – is another inadequate model, here of a way in which artists' film and video – like live art – might become an object.

Roland Barthes discusses theatre in *Camera Lucida*, a book that attempts to derive a theory of the photograph (the staple document that stands for the live act after it has occurred) by systematising subjective experience. The photograph is the common denominator between Theatre and Death, of something living made object:

> Yet it is not (it seems to me) by Painting that Photography touches art, but by Theatre... by way of a singular intermediary... by way of Death... the first actors separated themselves from the community by playing the role of the Dead.... Now it is this same relation which I find in the Photograph; however 'lifelike' we strive to make it (and this frenzy to be lifelike can only be our mythic denial of the apprehension of death), Photography is a kind of primitive theatre, a kind of *Tableau Vivant*, a figuration of the motionless and made-up face beneath which we see the dead.[9]

163

What Barthes argues is not that all photography is a disappointing, lifeless representation of that which it depicts, even if this might describe the photograph-in-general and its relationship to theatre, but that some photographs affect him – those from which he derives a formal language to describe these special moments – in ways similar to moving pictures:

> The cinema has a power which at first glance the Photograph does not have: the screen (as Bazin has remarked) is not a frame but a hideout; the man or woman who emerges from it continues living: a 'blind field' constantly doubles our partial vision ... When we define the Photograph as a motionless image, this does not mean only that the figures it represents do not move; it means that they do not *emerge*, do not *leave*: they are anaesthetized and fastened down, like butterflies. Yet once there is a *punctum* [the detail that arrests his gaze, resonates, the 'accident which pricks me (but also bruises me, is poignant to me)'], a blind field is created (is divined): on account of her necklace, the black woman in her Sunday best has had, for me, a whole life external to her portrait.[10]

But what constitutes this *punctum* remains entirely arbitrary, subjectively – mysteriously even – identified. It is, perversely, unclassifiable. Theatre, for a third time, is inadequate. Which is as much to describe another (short) circuit that leads to another peculiarly open field of works without categories and forms without definition.

I wrote, in 2003, that 'this is a speculation that also suggests, in the broadest terms, that the modernist might be replaced by the feminist and by being so might reconnect to something about being alive, now, recovering ways of looking and thinking that have been obscured by the recent self-positioning of artists' film and video within the exclusive boundaries of an art history that it otherwise sought to challenge'; and that, 'the relationship between the work and its site that interests me is one which shifts the (gendered) dominance of the screen that Richter describes, into a discursive (re-gendered) relationship which expands the object into the local space-time of its experiencing'. I would extend this past 'now' into the now of this writing. The challenge of artists' film and video to the institution which we were and still are being asked

164

to wrestle into validating it as a form – because and so that it occupies a place in this category 'art' that defines the business of this institution – is in fact structural. On a simple level we can understand this as the challenge of distribution to the exclusivity of the museum collection. But we might also connect this challenge of distribution to an equation between the peculiar indivisibility between the live act and the place in which it is performed. Live art and artists' film and video refute the institution as a containing system because, *as inconclusive forms*, they do not cohere into a system of collection as easily containable objects, or as strictly repeatable experiences, without breaking the controls upon which this system is dependent into a set of meanderings and questions that constitute their meaning and that constitute this text.

The question cannot be answered. The relation between a live act and its reperformance (where an artists' cinema – artists' film and video – is understood also as live art) – that relation which we hope to resolve to satisfy its classification as an artwork, its passport to the museological system upon which such classification depends – in fact cannot be resolved. The question cannot be answered because it is the form itself.

1. [cf. Ian White, 'Recording and Performing: Cinema as a Live Art', *filmwaves*, 21 (Spring 2003).]
2. 'Imagine Action', curated by Emily Pethick, Lisson Gallery, London, 5 July–22 September 2007.
3. 'Figure de Style', Cubitt, London, 18 January–17 February 2008.
4. Hans Richter, 'The Film as an Original Art Form', *Film Culture* no.1 (1955), reprinted in *Film Culture Reader*, ed. P. Adams Sitney (New York: First Cooper Square Press, 2000), p.15.
5. [See 'The Projected Object', earlier in this volume.]
6. See Constance Penley, *The Future of an Illusion: Film, Feminism and Psychoanalysis* (Minneapolis: University of Minnesota Press, 1989), pp.3–28.
7. Robert Wilson, interview by Horacio Silva, *Pin-Up*, 1 (2007/08), p.18.
8. Philippe-Alain Michaud, *Aby Warburg and the Image in Motion*, trans. Sophie Hawkes (New York: Zone Books, 2004), p.153.
9. Roland Barthes, *Camera Lucida*, trans. Richard Howard (London: Vintage, 2000), pp.31–32.
10. Ibid., pp.55–57.

'As thin as they could be and as strong as they could be': Isa Genzken's Chicago Drive *and* My Grandparents in the Bavarian Forest

Discontinuous, constructed syntactical and temporal disjunction external to the spectator's body; incongruent, contemplative and 'distanced', detaching the viewer from present reality. Such is film according to the opening two sections of Dan Graham's seminal 'Essay on Video, Architecture and Television'.[1] That is film as process and material, as opposed to video, which is a paradigm of immediacy, a technology that can transmit the body of the spectator immediately onto (into) the monitor. Video uniquely facilitates the feedback loop between a thought intention and the witnessing of its action, demonstrated in the video documentation of Graham's equally seminal performance work *Performer/Audience/Mirror* (1977). It is video read as a kind of code that Graham subsequently uses to re-imagine – and predict – the function of modern architecture, the dissolved boundary between public and private (space). Glass in architecture conflates these opposing models of film and video, simultaneously combining the stasis of the Renaissance picture plane that Graham argues is established by all mirrors (in their actual or imaginary frames) and visually revealing the continuous action of the scene from which it separates us. It both effects and is emblematic of a unique collapse between the physical body, the imagined self (say, ego) and the image of that/your body, a collapse that describes the functioning of the corporate, consumer

167

First published in *Isa Genzken: Open, Sesame!*,
exhibition catalogue, ed. Iwona Blazwick (London and Cologne:
Whitechapel Gallery and Museum Ludwig, 2009), pp.108–15.

and civic power that these buildings are constructed to house, or disingenuously mask as the seduction of twentieth-century spectacle.

Isa Genzken's *Chicago Drive* (1992) is a film that might equally be described by Dan Graham's generalisations of the medium: discontinuous, disjunctive, incongruent, contemplative. It is also largely a film of exactly those buildings with which Graham's essay concludes and for which video is his code. Genzken describes it as an 'architectural film'.[2] It is a disjunctive, incongruent visual essay on the relationship between public and private space, between art, (corporate and civic) power and the celebration of a city – a game of scale that pitches bodies against buildings to reveal the collapse inherent in all towers and the dynamic of this collapse as peculiarly also the description or the business of artistic production at the time of the film's making. *Chicago Drive* is a difficult window that is of course no window at all. Through its alliterations with Graham's essay, written thirteen years previously, it also seems to run parallel to earlier discourses of minimal and conceptual practices.

The film opens with the camera circling a mausoleum, which almost by definition is the ultimate public statement of private grief: the testimony of social (public) status, a monumental shell with ornately gated windows and door that protect the (private) space of the tomb/s inside, to which only its owners have access but that others can glimpse. Mausolea address the public in scale and design and by doing so render memorialisation – or grief itself – as spectacle, an activity from which the viewer is excluded but which is nonetheless proven to be taking place in their imaginary. It is an opening sequence that appears like a coda to the rest of the work, a scene to which we do not return, but which invokes – even unwittingly – the opening of Theodor Adorno's essay 'Valéry Proust Museum': 'Museum and mausoleum are connected by more than phonetic association. Museums are the family sepulchres of works of art.'[3] Does this mausoleum deploy relationships between public and private space, between something revealed and something concealed? Does it perform the museum *like* the glass-encased corporate headquarters that Graham describes, where transparent walls imply transparent activity even though actually the public are excluded?

168

What seems to be suggested in *Chicago Drive* is that the ubiquitous and disingenuous openness of such actual separations is an architectural language that art – public art – culture, entertainment, other social spaces and the gallery find themselves amidst. The film cuts from the mausoleum to a lone figure in a room, looking out of a window. The subsequent streetscapes could be a clumsy catalogue taken straight from Graham's essay: glass foyers, mirror-clad buildings, empty streets and unstaffed receptions, walls dissolving beneath multiple reflections, a confusion between surface and depth, the superimposition of light and shadow, a disorientated public, as if bewildered, wandering over marble-clean pavements, a window cleaner and an increasing sense of unreal chiaroscuro, a skyline of jumbled rectangles. A monotone might be heard on the soundtrack and the camera begins to pan; being driven through these streets, it stops a-rythmically and cuts to another look at different buildings.

It is in this camera movement from mid-shot to close-up, in the optical illusion of foreshortening, from a view of the horizon to a surface pattern of regular office windows, that a public is sometimes pictured and at other times other viewers – those watching the film – are instead figured. There is seemingly no logic to the progression of Genzken's cameraman through the city, no descriptive-poetic montage as in Walter Ruttman's genre-defining *Berlin: Symphony of a City* (1927). Instead there are 'syntactical and temporal disjunctions... external to the spectator's body',[4] a compilation of shots accumulated with clunky grace, or elegant asymmetry, that picture bodies in seemingly unreal relations to buildings into which they no longer fit, or which are so large that the body becomes invisible. The radical juxtaposition of shots imagines – figures – the body of the (film's) spectator in equally radical relations to these empty glass cubes; and it renders the skyscraper as a surface pattern without physical shape and, alternately, as a manageably unitary box about which we are – albeit metaphorically – able to move.

Michael Fried describes the role of 'distance' in minimal sculpture in 'Art and Objecthood', his brilliantly unsuccessful denunciation of the movement that defines what it attempts to denigrate. Integral to the 'new genre of theatre' that minimalism constitutes is the physical relation of the sculptural object to the body of the spectator – the art object assumes a stage presence because of the distance from it that the viewer must keep in order to be able to see it in its entirety. *Chicago Drive* precisely negotiates this very position – by which I mean the viewer's position in relation to the buildings that it depicts – in its disjunctions of scale and scope, which occur like oscillations around an ultimately unitary object, reducing buildings to boxes (or almost abstract shapes) about which we are – albeit metaphorically – able to move. It does not do so in order to demonstrate Fried's proposition any more than the film attempts to illustrate Graham's essay. Rather, *Chicago Drive* renders the collapse of power that minimal and conceptual practices endeavoured to effect into a peculiar complex of representation and subversion, in a manner, furthermore, that is not dissimilar to something in the early work, for example, of artists such as Robert Morris.

In his book *Beyond the Dream Syndicate*, Branden W. Joseph summarises and elucidates such dynamics in Morris's early sculptures of the 1960s – plain rectangular boxes, standing, falling, made into identical L-shapes and laid on different sides, their scale roughly corresponding to that of the human body. What is interesting for us is these works' relation to power: 'Morris understood power as a transcendental, autonomous form that operates in an exclusively "sovereign" manner: a mode of repression exerted by a hierarchical authority.... Repression was, for Morris, necessarily a top-down affair, a vertical imposition, a standard, a rule, a "tower".' Joseph goes on: 'The gallery, the museum, the bedroom, the factory, the university, the government, the media: each one is the purview of a despotic, repressive law.'[5] Each one is a tower depicted in *Chicago Drive* collapsing under the formulation of its own stage presence. Collapse is inherent to their form, here.

Morris's work *Column* (1961) was a plywood rectangular tower stood upright onstage for three-and-half minutes, until it was toppled when Morris pulled a string offstage. The pulling of a string might then seem to indicate a simple collapse of (sovereign) power as a function of the artwork-become-gesture. But the arrangement is not as binary as it might appear: 'The era of the late twentieth and early twenty-first century is filled with oppressive, hierarchical structures... Yet power is not, nor was it in the 1960s, univocally or exclusively sovereign, but multiple...'[6] The body is in and of itself subject to (and made a subject by) the vectors of a Foucauldian disciplinary power. Its physical movement and other behaviour is restricted and shaped, performing in any given situation not what we might understand as its freedoms but as its prescribed set of possible actions. So that the collapse of a tower 'was not so much a dialectic of subversion as an oscillation between two distinct but coterminous loci of power: the despotic form [represented by the sculpture] and the disciplined body [of the spectator, looking and moving around]'.[7]

It is in this respect that *Chicago Drive* might be read as paradigmatic of Isa Genzken's work as a whole and in particular offer a possible reading for another film, also made in 1992: *Meine Grosseltern im Bayerischen Wald* (*My Grandparents in the Bavarian Forest*). Here a seemingly idle camera wanders through the rooms and across the furniture of the artists' grandparents' house as they go about their daily lives. There is no authorising voice-over, the narrative arc of traditional documentary collapsed under the pressure of duration and of a sporadic exchange with the cameraperson. Perspective is foreshortened in the small rooms of the house (private space made public by its documenting), activity captured in medium-shot or close-up. *Meine Grosseltern...* is a request for the viewer to enter a kind of space and time that could be characterised as domestic, or lingering with a developing, unique aptitude for productive disengagement.

My proposal is that *Chicago Drive* (like *Meine Grosseltern...*) equally oscillates between the despotic form(s) of vertical structures continuously collapsing and reconstituted, and the relation to these of the body; the represented body, the imagined body of the artist, the body of the spectator – the addressee. Not until a third of the way through *Chicago Drive* do we hear a human voice as the unseen cameraman addresses the (absent) artist: 'OK... hello Isa, we're at the auditorium building...' It is as if she is receiving the filmed image like a postcard from a foreign city, as if the work were made by instruction. A few

171

people singly cross the marble foyer without populating it. This is a city made strange to the bodies that we only occasionally see moving through it and to the artist herself. The cameraman speaks again to introduce the precise location and other details of the city's public sculpture by Picasso: an abstracted bull in flat steel that sits in another empty public space, its stare not quite an accusation nor a welcoming smile, exerting distance but nonetheless dwarfed by its surroundings.

Only once is the viewer addressed indirectly, at the end of the film when two gallerists are talking to whoever is behind the camera about the interior architecture of their new exhibition space: 'You can put weight against these walls and they are like, still very thin... we wanted that elegance: of getting them as thin as they could be and as strong as they could be.' After all these other bodies made strange by the filmed cityscape, their comments seem absurd, on the edge of comprehension, they describe a virtuosity for the new walls that once again makes strange the relation to our body. These gallerists are not building a tower even though they might occupy one. Through their address to camera we are trapped by their giggles like rabbits caught in headlights. Such a sense of paralysis comes as no surprise in a film that figures its viewers in representations of physical alienation, and as the dissolute or invisible bodies that, in a way, we have become.

Chicago Drive is a 'discontinuous, constructed syntactical and temporal disjunction external to the spectator's body'. It employs the 'incongruent, contemplative and "distanced", detaching the viewer from present reality' and proposes this as the city it portrays, as (the) architecture (of film) in the age of video. It tells us that towers are always collapsing and being rebuilt and that we/she are/is in the middle of this.

1. Dan Graham, 'Essay on Video, Architecture and Television', in *Dan Graham: Video/Architecture/Television: Writings on Video and Video Works 1970–1978*, ed. Benjamin H. D. Buchloh (Halifax: The Press of the Nova Scotia College of Art and Design, 1979), pp.62–76.
2. 'Isa Genzken: Excerpts from *Sketches for a Movie*, and Other Writings', *Journal of Contemporary Art*, <www.jca-online.com/genzken.html> [last accessed on 10 January 2016].
3. Theodor W. Adorno, 'Valéry Proust Museum', *Prisms*, trans. Samuel and Shierry Weber (Cambridge, MA: MIT Press, 1967), p.176.
4. Graham, 'Essay on Video, Architecture and Television', op. cit., p.62.
5. Branden W. Joseph, *Beyond the Dream Syndicate: Tony Conrad and the Arts After Cage* (New York: Zone Books, 2008), p.132.
6. Ibid., p.133.
7. Ibid., p.135.

~~Death~~, Life and Art(ifice):
The Films of Sharon Lockhart

... it is not (it seems to me) by Painting that Photography touches art, but by Theatre... by way of a singular intermediary (and perhaps I am the only one who sees it): by way of Death.

Roland Barthes, Camera Lucida

... the real is always a performance...

Peter Gidal, Andy Warhol: Blow Job

Everything we see has at once already happened. In a film if someone raises a glass to their lips and drinks some water, then that person has actually once in the past made that action even if that person is pretending to be somebody that they are not, if they only pretend to drink or were not even thirsty, irrespective of their fictions. What we apprehend of this action – how we understand what we see – is dependent on what we are shown of it, the register that this action takes place within, the actual and mental place from which we see it, what we see before it and then later what we see after it. Everything that we see in a film has at once already happened, but we might not see everything that has actually happened. Someone might have told somebody else to drink some water, but all we see is a person drinking.

The narrative feature film – industrial cinema – the illusion of 'life' – is dependent on maintaining the invisibility of the not-seen ('death'). Making the not-seen visible is an entirely other kind of thing altogether, with entirely different effects and it is this – the excavation or the re-presentation of such a limit – that concerns me. This line of enquiry is in general a pre-digital argument at the intersection of film

175

First published in *Painting Real: Warhol Wool Newman | Screening Real: Conner Lockhart Warhol*, exhibition catalogue, ed. Peter Pakesch (Cologne and Graz: Walter König and Kunsthaus Graz, 2009), pp.149–57.

as an analogue medium, considered in the context of the visual arts as an essentially photographic practice. Briefly it reads in particular Andy Warhol's *Blow Job* (1964) and Bruce Conner's *Report* (1967) – inflected by the ideas in a recent book on *Blow Job* by the British filmmaker and theorist Peter Gidal – as a context for the work of Sharon Lockhart in their linked but very different investments in the not-seen: works with linked but different incorporations of death as acts of resistance that displace an absorption in the cinematic image into a conscious acknowledgment of (*real*) time passing.

Warhol's *Blow Job* and Conner's *Report* are conceivably antagonistic; refusals, interruptive, disruptions. Formally both present a fragment as the on-screen image, a part of something that happened, in ways that mark the limit of their own representations. In *Report*'s use of iconic footage and commentary of President and Mrs Kennedy in their motorcade in Dallas moments before his assassination – a categorical historical moment – repeated over and over, news becomes material, actuality a staccato denial that works against the impulse to see everything that it also feeds. The President is dead (to images of academy leader counting down to zero but never quite getting there) and the film spirals into other images that function metaphorically (matadors killing bulls, Kennedy visiting the Pope, pictures and verbal descriptions of him arriving in Dallas) in a series of verbal-visual associations and self-reflexive puns. But at the point of actual death – the gun shot, the dash to hospital, an operation – there are no images, just a frantic commentator telling us that he does not know exactly what has happened. The screen is blank grey, then a stroboscopic flicker, then black. We do not see it. It is the not-death of Kennedy, a generalised death as John and Jackie become subjects-made-objects, and the film its own object that *involves* its viewers through a division into parts that alludes to narrative while playing desire against itself. We do not witness the death of Kennedy, we witness a film (that is not without poetics, illusion or displaced spectacle).

Blow Job is a single film of a sex act that we do or do not witness. Peter Gidal describes it in his book of the same name.[1] The ten reels of 16mm film that recorded a man's head as he apparently experiences

176

this act (which is offscreen and onscreen at the same time) are placed one after the other – not edited to any industry standard (pornographic or otherwise), but shown complete with flare-ins, flare-outs and other material properties of the medium itself. His experience was/is continuous (we assume). Our perception of his experience is the opposite: not assumed but actual, frustrated and disrupted as a reel of film begins, ends, begins... and we cannot see what is being done to him. Our perception of his experience is discontinuous, but our perception of *the film* is not. One continuous act that determines the length of the film(s) and (because it) gives it its title is represented in a way that produces a radical kind of immediate present. Here, film-as-material is a representation of the not-seen. If the end of *Blow Job* is an orgasm, what he/we are both left with is what in French they call *la petite mort* (the small death). This vacuum that in *Report* is filled with metaphor in an anti-chronological game (against the end) is in *Blow Job* the white light and other visual noise and gaps between reels of the film strip as material fact (as a photographic material): the (usually) not-seen. Which results in an awareness of time passing, running out – our time, watching, against his time recorded – this running out of time figured by the clock counting down on academy leader towards zero, or death defined in this way as an experience of the immediate present (the room you are in, the film strip passing through a projector, what else surrounds you, what has and what will). Death becomes life, of sorts – and this awareness (of material), its anti-ideological function, its refusal of an escape into the imaginary space (and ideological constructions) of any represented plot, character, set, etc. – any representation – is political.

The films of Sharon Lockhart relate to these other works and are different from them. They are documents and they are theatrical – theatre of a very particular kind and a kind of death different but related to Conner's and Warhol's which, in the quotation that prefaces this text, Roland Barthes connects to photography. Primitive theatre, Barthes says, was a form of *tableau vivant* where the living played the dead and by doing so, through make-up, costume, etc., at one and the same time also became an image. Barthes reads this act in every pose for the camera, every framing: every photograph is the inscription of light onto paper of something (or someone) that was there in that time, however long ago or recently it may have been taken, and is the image of this thing, or the time, which is not here now as we view it. In a photograph stasis becomes emergence by way of what we do not see – the 'blind field' of what is beyond the frame that is also the off-screen space in cinema. It is the photograph defined in this way that is also the 'cinema' of Sharon Lockhart's invariably fixed frame or the construction of an image in which we see everything at once and ourselves. Moreover, the theatre that I think Lockhart's work proposes is uniquely linked to and can be traced through a reading now (towards a realisation, the assertion of a complex 'real') of a combination of early critical discourses on experimental film and minimalism in the visual arts.

Lockhart's early films figure theatre as content. In *Goshogaoka* (1997) an all-girl Japanese basketball squad perform a set of choreographed movements (divided into a series of ten-minute sections) against the backdrop of their gymnasium's stage and red theatre curtain. Increasingly intricate and requiring precise timing, the geometrical forms of this performance point both to the physical vocabulary of a virtuosic gymnastics demonstration and the postmodern language of dance exemplified by the work of Yvonne Rainer. In *Teatro Amazonas* (1999) the camera, mounted onstage and facing outwards, frames the full auditorium of the famous opera house in Manaus, Brazil. A choir, hidden in the orchestra pit, sings a commissioned work by American minimalist composer Becky Allen (who Lockhart also collaborated with on the soundtrack for her recent work *Lunch Break*, 2008). It is a single tone that incrementally decreases in volume. The audience have been systematically invited through a pseudo-ethnographic process which the artist consciously employed (and is further exploited in the series of photographs that are also part of this project). They variously react to this music, shifting in their seats, talking to their neighbours. Some leave: an induced but unpredictable unrest. That audience in Manaus are facing the camera and they are facing this audience watching the film. This exchange of looks is a question about who is figuring who, about the two sides of a mirror. This room and that room are different and equivalent. Behaviour (ours and theirs) takes the form of a fixed picture. We are performing incidentally or incidentalities.

'The everyday' is claimed as content as often as the work of Yvonne Rainer and Chantal Akerman are quoted as influences in/on Lockhart's work. It has the air of something casual, ordinary or untheatrical. By definition, the everyday would seem to be something done which is not thought (as in planned). But by definition also it is something that is repeated to an extreme degree – every day, in fact. At the same time we do not see Jeanne Dielmann in life, we see her in Akerman's famous – and famously iconoclastic – film.[2] It is choreography, a precisely theatrical art, that is the model for repetition on whichever level it occurs, however it has come about.

Yvonne Rainer's seminal dance piece *Trio A* (1966) is described as consisting of everyday movement – task or task-like activity – as opposed to the visually, physically virtuosic or psychologically expressive. 'Work' embodied against illusionism, or acting. In *Trio A* the audience is not addressed (looked at) by the performers, a thing (a four- to seven-minute-long phrase – an even stream – of continuous movement without stress or rest) just happens. Of course it does not just happen.[3] Despite (or because of) the fact that in the years immediately after it was performed Rainer dismantled the dance establishment (and the dominance of spectacle) to the degree that anyone who had performed the piece had permission to teach it to others, actually *Trio A* is a set of precise movements (fixed for every part of the body including the direction of the eyes) with a set of precise guidelines for performing them, that make account for the individual body but are nonetheless set. It is now a work inscripted by Labanotation and the teaching of it is the responsibility of trained and practicing custodians. It is an image of work (perhaps strangely *like* the photographic image described by Barthes), the complexities, ironies, critical, political and theatrical resistance of which Catherine Wood elucidates in her book on Rainer's *The Mind is a Muscle* (a longer work of which *Trio A* is one part):

179

On the one hand [Rainer] creates an abstracted indication of the 'labour' that she sees all around her in everyday life, in a manner that she describes as having a 'factual' rather than 'mimetic' quality (i.e., it is a conceptual transposition, not an illustration). At the same time, however... she performatively displaces and reconfigures the premises of the post-War Fordist working culture by representing labour as an aesthetic end in itself, as a form of energy consumption that negates the demands of productivity.[4]

This negation is specific. Rainer's 'work' is a radical affiliation to the (subjected) worker that challenges the imposing political-economic system by which activity (labour – work – production) is otherwise determined, in life and by the ideological, counter-affiliations of spectacle and entertainment. 'Work' is represented not undermined by (being in and of) aesthetics. It becomes an image which *acts*. '[Rainer's] provocation... has a double edge: by staging work as dance, she displaces labour from the context of mundane economic reality into a non-productive consumption of time.'[5] Which is to say one (repetitive) reality – the everyday – is transposed into another: our time spent watching and not escaping, time running (out), this gripping mundanity measured like the serial frames of a film strip running through a projector at a regular speed, an actual, material, (other, equal, more equal) reality.

It is this reading of the image of work (as a spectral impression and figured) that is emblematically and/or literally returned to – and reworked as a map and a meditation of a contemporary condition – in the various subjects of all of Sharon Lockhart's films that follow *Goshogaoka* and *Teatro Amazonas* to the point of compulsion, as sustained interrogation, repeated continuous representation; the costumed workers in *No* (2003) methodically spreading hay across a dark field (across the picture plane), the constructed scenes of children playing or doing 'nothing' in *Pine Flat* (2006), the workers in *Lunch Break* documented by a seamless panning shot along a factory corridor that follows (anti-dramatically) our line of vision, slowed down to one eighth of its actual time.

The image of the worker finds it apotheosis in *Exit* (2008), made, like *Lunch Break*, at the Bath Iron Works in Maine, North East America.

180

This factory is one of the few remaining examples of large-scale mechanical production in America. Part of General Dynamics Marine Systems, it is a 'full service shipyard specializing in the design, building and support of complex surface combatants for the U.S. Navy'.[6] But it is a different work of life and death, as we are reading it here, that *Exit* points to. The film consists of five single fixed-camera shots (taken from the same position on 16mm film and transferred to HD) showing workers leaving at the end of the day, one for each day of the working week nominated by intertitles. It assumes a place in an important lineage of films and artworks of this very same subject – workers leaving the factory – which Harun Farocki catalogues in his research-driven video *Arbeiter verlassen die Fabrik (Workers Leaving the Factory*, 1995), the point of origin for which is one of the first films made for the cinema by the Lumière brothers in 1895.[7]

But there are critical differences. Unlike the Lumières and the works which re-perform their documentation, Lockhart's camera is not positioned outside the factory gates facing the workers (who are nearly all women in the Lumière film) released and hurriedly walking towards us, but inside the factory grounds. The workers (here nearly all men) walk away from the camera, with an air more of resignation than release, if such an interpretation is not my poetic imposition. In any case, they walk away from us, their backs to the camera (like audience members leaving the theatre in *Teatro Amazonas*), along a tarmac road marked with lines that follow its – and their – direction, through an underpass and beyond towards an outside (free – 'free' – time) which we do not see or occupy. Apart from the very few instances when one of them turns around, acknowledges the camera or stops, turned to one side, waits and talks with others, we do not see their faces. Their conversations are only ever distinguishable as snatches amidst a rhythmic but general hum. What is displayed is not the mechanical, repetitive movement of factory work, but a pattern of unrestricted yet prescribed bodily movement, flow (pace, density), the balance between sunlight and shadow, appearance and disappearance (coming and going), minimally varying, a measuring of workers leaving the factory, walking away from this place where we and the camera remain. This place, which is also the position (the room) from which we are looking (through the camera), is one where, by definition, time is regulated and, through work (this (art)work), is also being measured.

The work being done in *Double Tide* (2009) could not be more different or more similar. It is two films of one location (South Bristol, like Bath, in Maine), shot from the same position with a fixed 16 mm camera (transferred to HD) and shown in two separate rooms. A lone figure digs for clams by hand in an estuary, visually – and aesthetically – synthesised in and of the extraordinarily beautiful landscape that surrounds her. Bending her body at regular intervals to reach into the mud which also maps her footprints, she treads a zigzagging path. It seems irregular but we see her do this twice, once in each film, once at dawn and again at sunset. In our minds the paths map onto each other so closely that it is arresting. It is the shock of an almost mechanised activity represented as both in and of the natural world. Actually as both in and of *this particular image* of the natural world: an American sublime slowly and sublimely emerging from the morning fog that was obliterating it and submerged again by nightfall. The doubling in *Double Tide* is an absolute cycle, the contents of which are indivisible from its means and from a certain monumentality that pervades the documentary impulse which part informs Lockhart's project as whole. Metaphorically put, *Double Tide* is the opening and closing of a curtain that is figurative but that is also, contradistinctively, simultaneously perceptual and the product of time passing (film time and sunrise and sunset) and that by being so occurs (actually can *only* occur) in (our) *real* time.

✳

The films of Sharon Lockhart figure a particular kind of theatre (or theatricality) and the particularity of this theatre can be further stated.

When Peter Gidal writes about *Blow Job* and its effects he is also writing about the theatre of Brecht that finds its blueprint in his 1976 essay the 'Theory and Definition of Structural/Materialist Film'. In Gidal's

Still from Sharon Lockhart, *Double Tide*
(Jen Casad, South Bristol, Maine, July 22, 2008, Sunset), 2009

structural *materialist* paradigm, it is not just the representational codes of narrative (industrial) cinema that are exposed and dismantled – this exposition is an anti-ideological counter-attack. The visible materiality of the film itself – the film as material – further exacerbates or disrupts the viewing situation into a set of self-reflexive confrontations in an anti-illusionistic way similar to what we know as Brechtian distantiation: audiences directly addressed by characters, for example, to refute the (invisible) fourth wall of the proscenium arch as a window through which we look at/into another world, insisting instead that we (the audience) are people in the same room as these other people (onstage).

This is not quite what the American critic P. Adams Sitney suggests in his earlier definition-in-progress, 'Structural Film' of 1969, which is a model of theatre different but related to Gidal's, through which the difference and similarities between Sharon Lockhart's films, *Blow Job* and *Report* might be better understood. Rather than by time disrupted, Sitney's structuralism is identified in the works he discusses (by Michael Snow, Hollis Frampton, Tony Conrad, for example) by a simplifying tendency: films that move away from complex forms of multiple parts (that operate through conjunctions or metaphor, exemplified in some of the works by Stan Brakhage, Gregory Markopoulos or Peter Kubelka) towards what he characterises as an indivisibility of shape – 'a cinema of structure wherein the *shape* of the whole film is predetermined and simplified... what content it has is minimal and subsidiary to the outline'[8] (his emphasis). Shape *is* structure, shown as an irrefutable, absolute (indivisible) self-representation irrespective of content.

Sitney is developing a vocabulary at almost the same time as the art critic Michael Fried had defined the threat to art and its institutions posed by what we know now, generally, as minimalism. In Fried's 'Art and Objecthood', this threat is described as the indivisibility of shape seen in the purely regular, unitary, geometrical forms made and named as sculpture by Donald Judd or Robert Morris, for example, on a scale that relates to the human body, but in a way which entirely erases the mark of the artist's hand along with any other indication of craft or its poetics by which a work of art had been traditionally identified.[9] In other words, by the way in which these works of art risk

184

Still from Sharon Lockhart, *Teatro Amazonas*, 1999.

no longer being perceived as such. Their potential to be seen 'simply' as objects Fried denounces as a theatricalisation, an effect of their engagement and incorporation of the situation in which they are experienced, from which they cannot be separated. What Fried denounces we might celebrate as a liberating self-reflexivity: the viewer becomes the activating agent – simultaneously a player and an audience – in a theatre without stage, props, costumes, etc. The meaning of these indivisible shapes is entirely constituted by their equal indivisibility from the room which surrounds them and their relationship to the viewing body which sees – experiences – both these things and itself. This might be the distantiated theatre of Brecht, but it is also its opposite: the pictographic theatre of Greek tragedy read by Aristotle and understood by Racine that was also absolutely defined by another kind of shape as structure. In this neo-classical theatre, the stage should only ever represent one space in which a single line of action (without subplots) is played out over the course of a day. One space, one action, one day: an absolute fourth wall the effect of which is not necessarily also the opposite of Brecht. Peter Gidal quotes Samuel Beckett's instruction for his 1967 production of *Endgame* (*Endspiel*, 1957) at the Schiller theatre in Berlin: 'Play it exactly as if there were a fourth wall there'. An amplification of illusion to alienate absolutely its viewers, 'an unhinging of means and ends' that is also a property of *Blow Job*.[10]

This theatre which is Brecht's played (like Beckett knew how) as if it were Racine's is perhaps the particular theatre of a single shot made by a fixed camera, that records a single action which takes exactly the same amount of time to perform as the length of film on which it is photographed minus flare-ins and flare-outs. This absolute frame of Sharon Lockhart's.

The sun rises and the sun sets.

Encore une journée divine.[11]

186

1. Peter Gidal, *Andy Warhol: Blow Job* (London: Afterall, 2008).
2. *Jeanne Dielman, 23 Quai du Commerce, 1080 Bruxelles* (1975).
3. In 2004 the artist Jimmy Robert and I were taught *Trio A* in New York by Pat Catterson, and performed it at Tate Britain as part of our joint work *6 things we couldn't do, but can do now* later that year. In 2009 Jimmy, Pat and I performed the dance at the Museum of Modern Art, New York. My comments draw upon this personal, physical experience as well as my reading and thinking about it.
4. Catherine Wood, *Yvonne Rainer: The Mind is a Muscle* (London: Afterall, 2007), p.85.
5. Ibid., p.87.
6. From the website of General Dynamics Bath Iron Works, <www.gdbiw.com> [last accessed 10 January 2016].
7. *La Sortie des usines Lumière* (*Workers Leaving The Lumière Factory, or Exiting the Factory*, 1895).
8. P. Adams Sitney, 'Structural Film', *Film Culture*, no.47 (Summer 1969); revised Winter 1969 and reprinted in *Film Culture Reader*, ed. P. Adams Sitney (New York: Cooper Square Press, 2000), p.327.
9. See Michael Fried, 'Art and Objecthood', *Artforum* (June 1967), reprinted in *Art and Objecthood* (Chicago and London: University of Chicago Press, 1998).
10. Gidal, *Andy Warhol: Blow Job*, op. cit., p.25.
11. The first line of Samuel Beckett's play *Happy Days* (1961) translated into French by the author under the title *Oh les beaux jours* in 1962. Its theatrical aplomb is hidden in English – 'Another happy day' – which is why I quote the French.

Hello/Goodbye Jack Smith/Berlin

Other people's insights into their own psychological situation are just as boring as other people's dreams. Nonetheless I have come to realise at the end of this stay in Berlin that while I have a passionate belief in and commitment to the idea (and often the reality) of the public, at the same time I also have an abject aversion to the idea of groups of any kind. I don't want to join them. Thus in part my response to the opening of 'Live Film! Jack Smith! Five Flaming Days in a Rented World', for which there were queues around the block not seen at the Kino Arsenal outside of the Berlinale.

Well OK, not around the block: snaked back upon themselves in the dark grey metal cage that is the unfortunate foyer for this historically important cinema (which is so dimly lit at street level that it hardly looks like it's there, let alone open) and emblematic of the organisation's effective imprisonment in the Sony Centre at Potsdamer Platz – itself the horrible architectural 'triumph' of corporate towers so spitefully angled they seem to slice your body in two every time you pass them by. So much for reunification.

I mean, it should be a great thing that there are this many people wanting to see this work in this place. But at the time the frenzy and the late start (repeated throughout the five days) rather provoked anxiety and difficulty despite the fact that I too sometimes work with Kino Arsenal and the fact that they have been actually incredibly supportive

189

First published as a blog post on the LUX website on 19 November 2009, <http://lux.org.uk/blog/hellogoodbye-jack-smithberlin-artistcurator-ian-whites-latest-blog-berlin> [last accessed on 10 January 2016].

– of experimental ideas, in taking risks and to me personally/professionally in ways that have been invaluable.

So I don't want to write that from the outset there was a separation between this curatorial and artistic project and the large and initially eager audience even though it felt like the project as a whole was something semi-private that the other few hundred of us in attendance had surprised by our presence. They were overwhelmed, we were more simply present. Such a situation perhaps reflects how the event and especially its commissioned work (videos and performances – hosted during the event at the Hebbel Theatre) were developed: through a closed screening in March of all the films by Jack Smith that the Kino Arsenal exclusively hold, attended by the artists invited to make a work in response to them as well as others involved in their restoration and preservation.

I don't understand how any conversation between contemporary practitioners about Jack Smith's work could result – almost across the board – in pieces that failed to effect any kind of critical enquiry or translation of the original work into something more than images of men prancing about in women's clothing (there's a lot of this in Berlin) or bare-breasted women – pretty basic looky-likeys, often appallingly so – but that's what we were consistently offered and by Marie Losier, Guy Maddin and Uzi Parnes and Ela Troyano in particular.

And these new works (frustrating, disappointing tokens) seemed always to occupy the prime programme slots, Smith's films ironically enough marginalised to the first or last screening of the day or shown on the cinema's second screen where you quite literally couldn't get in the door for the people packed into its aisles, and over every inch of floor space.

Mario Montez, superstar (of Jack Smith and Warhol films), with a rekindled excitement for this new limelight, volunteered to be wheeled out every single day of the event to either introduce a screening or appear in conversation – twice with the event's co-curator Marc Siegel and once on a red leatherette sofa wearing a special 1940s-style floor-length gown in black with silver sequins next to a day-glo Tony Conrad in pink and green. His enthusiasm and generosity were in

190

Shop display case on Ku'damm. Photo: Ian White

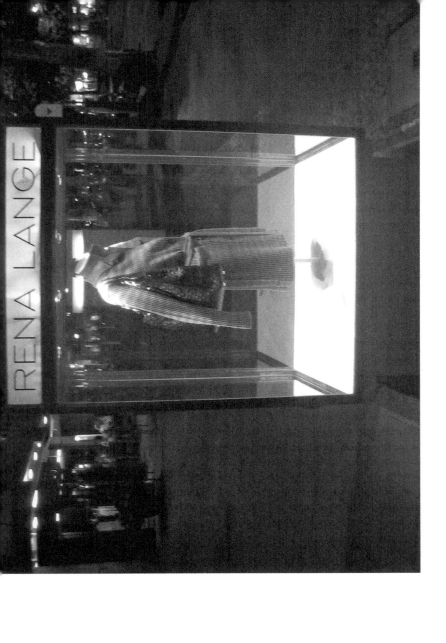

more abundance than his memory of the halcyon days of 1960s abject poverty and radical, underground artistic practice – and not because of the drugs. He only ever once inhaled and didn't like it because hash makes you lose track of time. Mario's line 'Who wants to lose track of time?' was perhaps more apposite than he realised.

In both conversations the very clever and dedicated Marc Siegel was incapable of overcoming the childlike awe to which he was reduced at meeting his hero, sitting with his feet turned inwards and mustering not much more than a pathetic appreciation of Mario's outfits, sighing with drool-like reverence over how beautiful Mario looked in one pose after the next. One became extremely aware of (bored by) the passing of time, of then and now, but also of every minute and second that watching this chat show took – and they were very slow ticks.

Thankfully academia was on hand despite us all in part agreeing with Penny Arcade's denouncement (via what I thought was a confused assault on identity politics) of the relationship between the theoretical reading of Smith's work, her experience of then, and our common (sense) preference for being alive and not fossilised now. The brilliantly thorough Warhol Chief Detective Callie Angell gave an informative account of his collaboration with Smith – the unrestored (labelled but unedited) film reels of *Batman Dracula* verbally identified shot-by-shot. And Douglas Crimp delivered a lecture on the peculiar dancer Paul Swan who shares the stage with Smith in Warhol's *Camp*. Crimp's clarity of thought and excitingly clear line of argument and entertainment was like the blessed relief of clear water, even if both talks suggested that Smith's status now should be confirmed by proximity to the already canonised.

All that said, three highlights:

First, a performance of the play *The Life of Juanita Castro*, in tribute to its writer and Warhol collaborator Ronald Tavel, who tragically died on the plane journey back from Berlin to his home in the Philippines after the project's March meeting. The play stages a photo-call centred around Juanita and her life and times, and what a photo-call this was, consisting of all the project's participants and organisers from Ulrike Ottinger (who delivered a breathtaking impromptu a capella song to accompany Mario/Juanita's final dance) to Tony Conrad via Diedrich Diederichsen (who as Raoul Castro gave it his all in repeatedly snogging Che Guevara with intermittent simulated fucking).

The younger generation involved included Pauline Boudry and Renate Lorenz and Oliver Husain, whose other work I'll show in the film programme at Whitechapel next spring. So of course I'm biased when I write that their videos here – and Husain's especially – were sharper than most, but nonetheless they were. Boudry and Lorenz continue their working relationship with the superlative, captivating performer Antonia Baehr, here delivering Jack Smith quotations from cue cards dressed as an ordinary bloke in a scrubby field who seems to be discovering them – with gusto – for the first time. Comment enough on the others' cross-dressing default position, so the video's cut-aways to Baehr dressed like a Jack Smith dandy at the zoo were not necessary.

Husain's video was a work of expanded cinema. Two neo-drag entities entered the cinema and held a screen in front of the auditorium's red curtain on which a video was shown that consisted entirely of zooming shots of veils revealing more veils, increasingly baroque in nature until a voice-over addressed the audience directly. As we'd been watching these 'reveals', it told us that what we hadn't noticed was the screen itself which was moving slowly closer towards us. At which point we did notice this and the screen kept on coming, its supporters clambering over the cinema's seats and audience's heads, finally laying it down on top of half a dozen of them who had to struggle out of it as the cinema lights came on. A simple but successful deception distinct from the silly drag shows to which we were otherwise subjected. Real time.[1]

Phew. And that was that. Goodbye Berlin. A week later I got on a plane to Kansas City to go and stand on one leg with my trousers round my ankles and walk out of an art gallery as part of the exhibition 'Ecstatic Resistance', for want of anything else to do.

1. [The Husain work is *Purfled Promises* (2009); see also White's essay on Husain's work, 'Wishful Thinking', later in this volume.]

Ecstatic Resistance, Jingle Bells

So to Kansas City. That's Kansas City, Missouri, not Kansas City, Kansas. There's a difference in the skyline (it's bigger) and the alcohol laws (you can buy it on a Sunday), but it loses out on thrift stores, so cross the state line for them. Stay at the Hyatt Regency for Ernie on reception, KC's only revolving skybar, wallpaper that looks like its just about to start to begin to peel and the cagefighting tournament in the ballroom and the cagefighters in the sauna (who swipe the sweat from their flesh with credit cards). Don't walk the streets after 7pm (not that there's ever anyone on the streets at any time, but still you might get shot). Do line dance with lesbians at Tootsie's. And eat, eat, eat... Oh, and there's an art show too...

The kitchen at Grand Arts is as much an engine room as the impressive workshop where they produce artists' projects, its fuel on a par with any in the exhibition spaces. I mean, it was always a great invitation. To go and make a performance as part of an exhibition conceived by the American artist Emily Roysdon – as much the gathering together of a group of people and the extension of a set of ideas that she has been exploring in theory and practice through and as her own work as it was anything like a standard curatorial proposition.

Which is to say as much the relaxation of unlimited breakfast, lunch, dinner and/or room service as the anxiety of making the private public. Ecstatic resistance. The exhibition as a radical queer expression,

195

First published as a blog post on the LUX website on 18 December 2009, http://lux.org.uk/blog/ecstatic-resistance-jingle-bells-artistcurator-ian-whites-latest-blog [last accessed on 10 January 2016].

with the questions, the problems, the risky communication of any project making this kind of trouble, the dissolution of a binary code or the massaging-away of the infliction of a social blueprint into the energy of an oscillation... (toasted muffin/fresh pineapple chunk/muffin/chunk/muffin... etc.). I think that's what it was/is...

I was enjoying my second breakfast in the gallery the morning after the show opened, sat on a staircase next to a wall orgiastically covered in photographs by A. L. Steiner. Here are friends, lovers, sometimes semi-strangers, in various states of expression, undress, abandon – absolutely, incontrovertibly whole, somehow, wonderfully, defiantly present without always knowing it, solid against these fleeting moments. Real sexy and full. Full of love/I love them.

A school party arrives for a guided tour and the gallery assistant begins with Steiner's wall. It is, she says, an artwork against normative values. I like this person but as she describes the work she seems trapped in and by this word – normative, the norm – and repeats it in every sentence like the involuntary blink of a person caught in the headlights of a car on an empty road at a proverbial midnight. And I sat there, within earshot but out of sight, and thought about just how potent and hideously loaded such a description could be understood to be, and how to make sense of my instinctive reaction to it.

It seems to imply that the subjects of these images are absolutely, incontrovertibly from somewhere other than where those viewers were from – socially, psychically, perhaps geographically. That they are at a distance from each other, in other lives, on different planets. Actually what was going on was the construction of these viewers, not these subjects, as coming from somewhere else, by what they were being told about where they are viewing from. That they, the viewers, were being told in this explanation of the work that they were utterly outside of what these images were depicting – an awful, normative otherness inflicted upon these (and by implication all) viewers as the receivers of news which the images carry.

Nothing could be further from the truth of Steiner's images presented in this way (and I use that word 'truth' consciously, with every problem it invokes and everything that it suggests about something to

196

Paris Opera ceiling. Photo: Ian White

believe in). To me they are the rich and valued evidence of the life that we are in and its unadulterated mess, for which read 'joy'. They are not news of somewhere else, they establish pictorially a situation which we are already in, in and of life – life as opposed to the constructed, adulterated, tortured and manipulated, obliterating representations that otherwise occupy the everyday constituency of, let's say, the mediasphere from which they'd like to imagine we are indivisible. It is there, not here, where I see the other to be jabbed at with a pointed finger. We are not it.

Which was much the same point that I came to at the end of the Rameau's Baroque opera *Platée*, which Jimmy Robert and I happened to stumble upon and actually get tickets to see as we wandered past the Galeries Lafayette to the Opera Garnier, while we were in Paris together a couple of weeks later to perform our work *Marriage à la Mode et Cor Anglais* for the last time in a while.

This opera – a play-within-a-play devised to 'correct the faults of humans' – like this opera house is excessive perhaps beyond Versailles, dripping in ornament and dazzling to such an extent that there you (we) could only ever feel like jaw-dropped day-trippers in dirty jeans. Apart from the fact that everyone in the auditorium was figured on stage by the chorus who were dressed and positioned to represent us, The Audience, figuring and encoding our act of watching as they respond to and comment upon the play-within-the-play.

Composed for the marriage of the French Dauphin to the Spanish Infanta and scandalously premiered in 1745, in short *Platée* tells the story of a trick played by the gods on Plataea, the ugly queen of frogs, a ridiculous water nymph performed by a man. They tell her that Jupiter wants to marry her. She is ebullient with unabashed, naïve delight. The gods play out the preparations for her marriage in the form of grotesque burlesque vignettes with much hysterical-awful dancing and she can barely contain herself with excitement. Finally Mercury conspires to rumble Jupiter's plans by alerting his wife Juno, who catches up with him, by design and to his relief, just before he says 'I do'. Juno tears the veil from Plataea's head and bursts out laughing at her ugliness, seeing the marriage was obviously an elaborate joke

198

at Plataea's expense, a creature such as Jupiter was only ever going to torture and never marry. Jupiter and Juno run off together laughing at the game. Utterly humiliated and destroyed, in abject misery Plataea is simply left alone and in this production disappeared in a silent, shocking flash into a black hole through a trap door in the floor of the stage. And this is played like a pantomime.

For nearly three hours we've watched a game (of love) in the name of raucous, riotous entertainment and bravura spectacle. There's a lot to say about this, but for now I'm affected by the device of this production that figures the chorus as the audience. Because how I think it functions is to suggest a radical inversion of affiliation.

That for the whole way through the opera we think we are affiliated with the gods, we share their jokes, their knowing position, wit and intelligence. But by the end the sustained celebration that we've been complicit in is revealed as nothing other than sustained sadism. We have been watching ourselves, watching the opera. Its entertainment becomes the nasty infliction of a hetero-determined spiteful institution that affects (here, tortures) all of us in different ways and forms, for different reasons as we inflict it upon others for our own amusement.

It is the horrible game of marriage and everything that its associated expectations imply that I will not play (cannot/am not playing?). At the same time as realising I have been watching myself I recognise that actually I really have been watching myself. There I am, in no royal court but in the brilliant, beautiful, rancid swamp of frogs, jabbing with a pointed finger that I hope I can laugh at too, centred and happy, disappearing into whatever black holes there are to fall down. And I do not think I am the only one.

On Yvonne Rainer

I've just finished giving a seminar series called *6 or more kinds of theatre* at no.w.here.[1] At the beginning 'why theatre?' was an unanswered question. I don't know that it's answered now, but nothing that we talked about put me off. In fact I've started thinking in particular about the auditorium as a vehicle, architecture, channel of communication in a much more explicit way than before. This is one of its key pleasures and critical functions, for me, as an artist who makes performances and a curator working predominantly in cinema. Could theatre be a site of production, rather than of reproduction? In the instance. I know these things need more explaining...

Just over halfway through the seminars, Tramway in Glasgow presented two evenings of performances by Yvonne Rainer. Something of a coup. It's no secret that I've been a fan, learning her 1966 dance *Trio A* with Jimmy Robert in 2004, which was performed by us as the end section of the first work we made together. And loving her films (which were also all shown and will be again soon at the BFI Southbank). But I had thought I was getting over it. Well forget that. What happened in Glasgow flattened me with its deluge of direct intelligence, generosity, integrity, coherence, departure, challenge, love (new love) and slapstick. I don't know that I've been at an event with such a momentous sense of cultural significance and I like many others there – maybe everyone there – remain fuelled by it.

All the works were performed by the same four dancers – women of different ages, physicalities, sensibilities; Pat Catterson, Emily Coates, Patricia Hoffbauer, Sally Silver, saluted. *Where's the Passion?*

201

First published as a blog post on the LUX website on 12 November 2010, <http://www.lux.org.uk/blog/artistcurator-ian-whites-latest-blog-yvonne-rainer> [last accessed on 10 January 2016].

Where's the Politics? or How I Became Interested in Impersonating, Approximating, and End Running Around My Selves and Others', and Where Do I Look When You're Looking At Me? was a lecture delivered by Rainer herself from a lectern at the front of a bare stage as *Trio A* was performed in a number of different variations – forwards, backwards, balletic, 'facing' (with Rainer replaced at the lectern by two of her dancers as she ran around one of the others who was performing the dance and attempted continuously to look into her eyes). What was spoken covered subjectivities, the direction of the performers' and audiences' gazes, the situation as a conundrum to be productively broken in and by – or even against – its assertion. It described while addressing the instance of our own witnessing. Word and movement had the air of a demonstration positioned as the work itself, a kind of undercutting of its own moment for the sake of this moment now, and as such become more deeply affective than spectacle ever really facilitates.

I'd never been in an audience watching *Trio A* before. What I realised there was that the performer's consistently diverted gaze, which is never directed at the audience, is an act that we might watch and that it is an act of generosity: it gives you back your own position, I'd say yourself if anything so identifiable existed, but here at least your own present, in that situation, watching but also within yourself. 'You go about your business and I'll go about mine', to quote Rainer. It's an incredibly deep thing to be given, this radical emotional sense, and something I could not have articulated from reading the volume of discourse around *Trio A*, or even from having performed it.[2]

The jubilant, defiantly, hysterically simple *Chair-Pillow* closed the first evening – a dance for a person with a chair and a pillow to Ike and Tina Turner's 'River Deep, Mountain High': 'When I was a little girl I had a rag doll...' Yeah right. More like 'When I was a little girl I ate my rag doll for breakfast and tore down all the walls of your houses in the same way that I now gleefully destroy all assumptions about gender, virtuosity, patriarchy, dispossession because they were all bullshit, while smiling inwardly and saying, "Look mum, no hands!" and now we're free, and so are you, and isn't that pleasurable, thank you very much.' Bravo bravo.

202

The writer at home in Berlin. Photo: Ian White.

Two recent works on the second night – *RoS Indexical* (2007), based on Stravinsky's *Rite of Spring* (well, the soundtrack from the BBC's docu-drama reconstruction of the ballet's iconoclastic first performance) and *Spiralling Down* (2008). What they share in part is something to do with the facticity of the body, its limits, awkwardnesses, jerks. Small movements not grand gestures, precise clumsiness that is of course meticulously choreographed. Over half of *Spiralling Down* is performed to Ravel's *Bolero*, the music's cheesy slow sweeps never more romantic than when four women in a loose huddle repeat, in an order they decide, such a set of movements; almost frenetically, against the pace, legs jab, arms half extend, hands flex at the side, modest display. It's a political, social position this describes, a brilliant illustration not of tragic love and a final collapse onto the ice à la Torvill and Dean, but the radical fissures of living, not consuming. And at the end two of the dancers slip into the final movement of *Trio A* that has now become a breaking-out into pure line, exquisite form, sheer, relaxed stretch and the height of elegance.

Compared, say, to the dances of Trisha Brown – which were presented at Tate Modern two weeks later – where the body is figured as pure (pure balance, yogic concentration, all-white outfits, meditative connections), Rainer rather posits the body as an order of impure mess that can and must be seen. It's the mess for which I'm grateful.

I could go on. This was invaluable work – the work seen being done, the work of seeing itself – impressive, influential, inspiring. More than unforgettable, it is the absolute fuel of practice. Stand, cry, applaud.

I stole the handwritten sign from Rainer's seat in the audience on the second night and thought about wearing it taped over my face for the whole of my current performances at the Kunsthaus in Bregenz,[3] until I realised you can't ride a Segway while bumping into a funerary urn on a trolley and read out notices of local deaths as all the lights are switched off one by one, shutters come down and curtains close automatically without being able to see, much as that blindness would have been apt. So I took a photo of it instead to indicate the debt and a state of permanent albeit metaphorical affiliation, by which I mean that I am still wearing it, like stupid truth. Thank *you*.

1. [no.w.here is an artist-run project and production space
   for film in East London.]
2. [White performed *Trio A* with the artist Jimmy Robert several
   times, including at the Museum of Modern Art, New York
   in March 2009.]
3. [White is referring to his performance work *Hinterhof feat.
   James Richards Untitled Merchandise (Trade Urn), 2008.*]

The hole's the thing...

Artworks are objects. This is the foundation for everything we come to know about art, how we come to know it and for all of its institutions. But artworks are not simply objects. Rather, let's say, they are specific objects that are made by an act, if not always of making, then possibly of naming and certainly of framing, of showing and collecting, by virtue of the will for them to remain while life goes on or passes by. The idea that they might be *simply* objects, considered in an ever-expanding, equally material context, or even not objects at all (experiences over time, for example) is what has defined the threat to the institution since the late 1960s: a somewhat tautological and often illusory battle against art's own institutions aims to attack dominant ideologies, economies and our subjection to them. We might understand such a situation not as one based upon the real promise of any actual kind of triumph, but at the very least as one in which a reversal of terms – from certainty to its opposite – produces instead a kind of generative, productive crisis. It is just this situation that the work of Gerard Byrne re-presents, examines, extends and participates in to the point of a peculiar kind of stasis. And it does so particularly by its continuous representation, examination, extension of and participation in one seminal text of the crisis's originating moment: Michael Fried's 'Art and Objecthood'.

207

First published in *Gerard Byrne: Images or Shadows*,
exhibition catalogue, ed. Pablo Lafuente (Dublin: Irish Museum
of Modern Art, 2011), pp.199–210.

Fried's essay, first published in *Artforum* in June 1967, is an influence that Byrne has long acknowledged, and his installation *A thing is a hole in a thing it is not* (2010) explicitly deploys the essay's arguments into five videos to an exemplary or pedagogic degree. In one of them, Robert Morris's famous *Column* (1961) falls over in Judson Church, tugged by an invisible thread, the art object made subject to gesture; in another, a live recording of a radio conversation between Dan Flavin, Donald Judd and Frank Stella is set to a video of the reconstructed studio in which it first took place, although we only see what surrounds the speakers and never their faces; in the third, the definitive anecdote of Tony Smith's drive along an unfinished turnpike is re-enacted, the turnpike – or the experience of it (here represented) – proposed as the ultimate work of art; in the fourth video iconic Minimalist works of art are shown on display in a museum, being looked at, presented, installed/dismantled, occupying time more than space. Finally, the fifth one enacts the composition of a letter by Hollis Frampton on Carl Andre addressed to Enno Develing at the Van Abbemuseum.

But Fried's text provides not just scenes-in-waiting, or straightforward source material; it also contributes seemingly inexhaustible blueprints for Byrne's work, almost to the extent that it is conjured by it as a crucial and crucially absent object (as but the first and equal absence) by an act of the very theatre that in 1967 Fried was so brilliantly, incisively afraid of.

No irony should be lost on the fact that it is Fried's objection to the new work he saw being made around him – what we now file under Minimalism – that actually provides a set of terms that have since stimulated a radicalised engagement with, and analysis if not a championing of, the very works and their function he was attempting to dismiss. In short, for Fried, Minimalism was theatre and theatre is the enemy of art.[1] Generally, and in particular in relation to sculpture, it becomes so first by a consideration of its simple forms – indivisible, geometric shapes – that, second, have a relationship to the human body not only in terms of scale but also by the way they occupy the exhibition space, prescribing a distance between them and the viewer. The experience of this distance becomes a material part of the work itself, which confronts the viewer in a kind of drama played out between the act of looking, the object, and the negotiation of these things via physical movement, the body around the art work, over time. The artwork is no longer a discrete object of meditation or consideration. It threatens in fact to be an any-object and/or indeed a situation, in and of 'life' itself. Thus it threatens the institution. This double threat is the one that Gerard Byrne remakes as theoretical and material content in his work.

Forms of theatre pervade Byrne's practice, often explicitly; acting and re-enacting (*Subject*, 2009), stage props (*In repertory*, 2004–06), found texts as scripts (*Why it's time for Imperial, again*, 1998–2002; *New Sexual Lifestyles*, 2003; *Hommes à Femmes (Michel Debrane)*, 2004; *1984 and Beyond*, 2005–07), historical live recordings set to images (the 'Radio Waves' section of *A thing is a hole...*), the exhibition space as a stage set, the theatre a location (**ZAN-T185 r.1: (Interview) v.1, no.4–v.2, no.6, (1969–Feb. 1972): (Andy Warhol's (interview) v.2, no.21 – v.3 no.9*, 2007), art objects removed, replaced, made subject exclusively of/to experience (*'68 Mica and Glass*, 2008; *A thing is a hole...*), etc. Often using video and occasionally film, theatre here is a function of the moving image, itself the very definition of a demate-rialised artwork (the image/work is but light), which also makes it, as a medium, the obvious affiliate to Fried's antithesis of art. Byrne's the-atre has specific characteristics, established by the process and effect of a practice of *re*-staging, of collapsing into a new unit the recent past – defined perhaps as being between the publishing of Fried's essay and now – and the 'present', via sources mined as much from popular culture as from literature and from the visual codes of television as much as the techniques of experimental film or video. The implica-tions of such a theatre are conceptual and political.

Many of these works – especially *New Sexual Lifestyles*, *1984 and beyond*, *Why it's time for Imperial, again*, *Hommes à Femmes*, but also the 'Radio Waves' section of *A thing is a hole...*, *Subject*, **ZAN...* – re-imagine (enact) the live situation that originally generated the texts transcribed in publications, and from which Byrne receives them, while simultaneously disintegrating its live characteristics. The recon-structed situations become videos (and installations) that dissimulate the improvisatory nature of conversation into its seamless opposite – and by doing so are emblematic of Byrne's project read through Fried.

For example, *New Sexual Lifestyles* takes as its script a group conversation between libertarians, movers and players published in the September 1973 issue of *Playboy*. In it contributors candidly discuss aspects of their own sexual experiences, permissiveness and limits, contemporary mores, theories and alternatives to the nuclear model, at a particular post-1960s moment. Byrne replaces the interlocutors with actors, and situates the conversation in the Goulding Summerhouse – an exemplary modernist glass box suspended above a stream by iron girders in an idyllic spot of stunning forest, in Enniskerry, County Wicklow, Ireland. It is a building that, by virtue of being so hermetically sealed, is deeply sympathetic to nature, effecting a perfect symbiosis of inside and outside. In the gallery, the three resulting videos are shown on three separate, freestanding plasma screens, each with two sets of headphones. They are surrounded by seven photographs of the house. Its glass walls, the lush foliage outside and its shadows cast by sunlight onto the interior's floor are framed by the rest of its architecture, as if each image were a hall of mirrors or a window from the gallery onto an inaccessible but visualised exterior.

Sections of the re-recorded conversation are spread across the three screens. Some parts, shot from different angles, repeat on more than one screen. The viewer, moving from one to the other, is bound in a disconcerting loop, our own hall of mirrors. The camera sometimes plays with its subjects, focussing on details – hands clutching a cushion, framing posture and gesture in relation to what is being spoken – in such a way as to almost subliminally indicate that this is a staged scene, not reportage or the simple means to the magazine's ends; rather, an enactment, after the fact, with more information, now sealed. There is no mess of life here; it is not the miracle of video that wowed Andy Warhol with the possibility of instant playback,[2] nor the instant broadcast by which Dan Graham defined the medium.[3] Nor is it the radical splitting of text, sound and image that occurs in Anthony McCall and Andrew Tyndall's ripping critique of *The New York Times Magazine* (and ideology too) in their seminal film *Argument*, from 1978.

The scene, instead, is posed to point rather to a kind of classicism, a relief, hyper-synched, as something like a post-live.

Such camera work is consistent across Byrne's video-making. Everything it features is immaculate – spaces, objects, equipment, period. The camera peruses them all with smooth strokes in a wealth of equal detail and surface. Time does not mark with use the image or anything it features. The immediate past is an always brand-new image that stands like a brick wall against historical perspective, itself further confused by the semi-recognitions and half-distances between us and the ideas and values participants express, that arise because we live in the immediate aftermath of these conversations – an aftermath manifested as a vacuum. The live is cast, the viewer in the gallery becomes a theatrical subject, projecting on both the illusion of independence but ultimately denying them any actual agency in the scene – a position/effect exemplified (paradigmatically so) in another work of Byrne's, *In repertory*.

In repertory is a location-specific installation in two acts, with an interval. For the first act the gallery/stage is set with 'borrowed' (remade) props from canonical theatrical productions, including the tree designed by Alberto Giacometti for Samuel Beckett's *Waiting for Godot* at the Odéon Theatre in Paris in 1961, a backdrop from Richard Rodgers and Oscar Hammerstein's *Oklahoma!* from the 1943 production at St James Theatre in New York, and the cart of Bertolt Brecht's eponymous *Mother Courage* from its 1963 representation in Broadway – the three of them emblems of existential emptiness, artificiality, alienation. The visitors/cast to/of the exhibition are recorded on video moving around these copied props as if they were artworks (maybe they are). The scene changes for the second act, in which the props are stacked to one side and replaced by a screen, onto which the earlier recording is projected. The viewers of the work now see previous viewers looking at what was then the artwork (even though it wasn't, or not entirely) and that is now absent, or at least replaced. The work proper is neither the now of the second act nor the then of the first. In act two, the subjects' acts of looking from act one are simultaneously content and redundant (they could not see the artwork because they themselves subsequently figure it) in a space now 'empty'. A double evacuation occurs exactly as it does in another of Byrne's works, *'68 Mica and Glass* – a 16mm film of two museum conservators constructing and dismantling Robert Smithson's 1968 work *Untitled (Mica and Glass)*, projected onto the side of a plinth, only activated by the viewer's physical presence. Or exactly as it does in *A thing is a hole...*, when the moving images of artworks being installed, removed or surveyed replace those artworks as new, evacuated objects, or the images by which evacuation is made material. The hole's the thing...

In these new (art)works –'new' because they are predicated on the replacement of what was actually or imagined as there before (other artworks, interview transcripts, physical presence) – we do not see ourselves, but experience this evacuation as a portrait of the immediate present and almost as a call to arms in relation to it. Context, in the form of space, distance and perspective – the most feared by Fried of all uncontainables, the very disintegration of art (the art object) – becomes content. And it does so by works that are also acts, of at once a drawing-in, or attraction, and also, by the very same means, of exclusion, or evacuation with a specific purpose: an incitement to extend our own act of looking and to position these works not only by default within the rooms that situate them but beyond this. The thing-as-a-hole is like an anti-gravitational force, or an amplified threat. What remains when we are faced with this very particular nothing is something like the context of context, that is, not what is there (nothing is there), but everything else that is passing by, life itself, outside. Art is cast as its own enemy-by-necessity: necessary because by these means it is constituted entirely by an act of engagement and as functioning *against* subjection, an experience of and over time. Fried's resistance is pushed to a pristine, extreme conclusion, and under such pressure (as both scrutiny and form) it flips into its opposite: present/absent, theory made content. Itself, now, in and of the very things it is not.

1. 'Theatre and theatricality are at war today, not simply with modernist painting (or modernist painting and sculpture), but with art as such.' Michael Fried, 'Art and Objecthood', *Artforum* (June 1967), pp.12–23, reprinted in *Art and Objecthood* (Chicago and London: The University of Chicago Press, 1998), p.163.
2. 'Friday, 30 July 1965: Andy Warhol was an hour into audio taping his superstar Ondine when a large package arrived at the Factory. Warhol was attempting to capture Ondine non-stop for 24 hours so he could transcribe the tapes into a book that would record a day in the life of the Factory's most flamboyant star. The box held a videotape recording system, one of the earliest designed.... Paul Morrissey arrived at the Factory and gave Warhol the low-down on his new machine:

    Morrissey: [This is] the tape recorder, right? You... aim... this microphone at people. You aim the... lens at the people.
    Warhol: Oh.
    Morrissey: And the picture goes onto the tape and then you [play] the tape... just like you play back your tape recorder and the tape plays through a television set.
    Warhol: Oh, man, you get a picture too?
    Morrissey: Yes, immediately.
    Warhol: Oh, wow.

    In his typically deadpan way, Warhol hit the nail on the head: "Oh, wow." For Warhol the "Oh wow" of video was the fact that you got a picture immediately, that the moving image was represented in real time and instant replay.' William Kaizen, 'Live on Tape, Video: Liveness and the Immediate', in *Art and the Moving Image*, ed. Tanya Leighton (London: Tate Publishing and Afterall, 2008), p.258.
3. 'Video is a present time medium. Its image can be simultaneous with its perception by/of its audience (it can be the image of its audience perceiving). The space/time it presents is continuous, unbroken, and congruent with that of the real time which is the shared time of its perceivers.' Dan Graham, 'Essay on Video, Architecture, and Television', in *Two-Way Mirror Power*, ed. Alexander Alberro (Cambridge, MA and London: MIT Press, 1999), p.52.

213

Foyer

The word used in English for copies of a film distributed to cinemas is 'print'. A film print. Like screenprint or newsprint, that from which the print is made has no value or no use value in the way that the printed item does. The mass-produced is primary. There are objects; there is not *an* object. In German, the word used for a film print is *Kopie*, which also straightforwardly translates into English as 'copy'. In cinema, then, an industry and economy are built on reproduction, and spectators are fashioned by it, delimited. We do not contest that film is a distributable media. We might though question what is ordinarily a clear assumption about the implications of this, or if/how distribution is used. The assumptions and implications are less clear, or at least muddied, or repressed by at least one industry and economy that reproduction sustains and by one that it might threaten. Vested interests are muddy waters to be splashed around in (not drunk). Might such pressures be relieved? Made into content? Exploited for other means? A differentiated cinema...

First: I am always writing about the need to calibrate this category 'cinema' – a process of differentiation that would begin by separating off, or pointing to, industrial cinema and everything that it has been/is responsible for (the auditorium as we receive it, multiplexes, mass-distribution circuits, hierarchical organisation of labour from

215

First published in *Poor Man's Expression: Technology, Experimental Film, Conceptual Art – A Compendium in Texts and Images*, ed. Martin Ebner and Florian Zeyfang (Berlin: Sternberg Press, 2011), pp.97–98.

production to exhibition) as just one form of cinema rather than *the* form. Industrial cinema only defines itself, being the subsection of a category that might also be occupied by other subsections, none of which exactly regulates the others, even if it might also – quite appropriately and in part – reproduce them. Like experimental film, or artists' film and video, etc. Once this calibration begins, we very quickly find ourselves in a field of copies, where the original has no value or no use value, or cannot even necessarily be identified. A potentially uncontainable sea of reproduction that is not about one form of cinema borrowing from or reproducing aspects of other kinds of cinema, but more broadly one that also extends from the film print (copy) to the situation(s) of its public display – an amorphous mass that has no origin, no point of origin within it, does not point to an origin outside of itself. There are no originals although such a liberation should at the same time be interrogated and invites license, regulation and definition, while also potentially threatening already established systems of knowledge, power and authority that otherwise depend on them.

Second: By means of this invitation in some hands we can imagine that 'things' could start to collapse. The film or video considered (whether as a work of art, a unique object and/or as a distributable infinite number in whatever form) is inevitably immaterial. Look at a reel of film, a tape, a hard drive and you cannot see with the eye alone the information it carries, as its purpose would have you see it. The projector is (just!) a machine. You cannot touch a projected image and feel anything other than a screen or wall.

Second (a): Though it might only be imaginary, what (other) 'things' collapse? I mean what things collapse other than/as well as/because of what can happen to unique objects in this situation? The collapse of: political regimes, private ownership, 'passive' reception (being told), narrative, hierarchical order, the Institution, exclusion, lies. There is (or was) this much at stake. The film co-op movement in America and Europe pinned much on such promises. In 1971, what the first Forum at the Berlinale[1] shared with contemporary Conceptual art practices

216

was not necessarily anything entire or even coherent, but was an ethos predicated on the critical (new) intersection of cinema (auditorium), media and communication. A kind of cinema-as-vehicle. Perhaps, as the early columnist Dorothy Richardson had already optimistically described in one of her columns for the modernist periodical *Close Up* in 1932, this is/was cinema as 'a medium... at the disposal of all parties' that is/was 'turning the world into a vast council-chamber'.[2] A dissolution of political and geographical boundaries (or at least a reordering). A giving-voice-to as content, or as the criteria that determined the works' selection. A connection between making, representation, and the erosion of traditional authorship immediately understood, if this is/was a project.

Second (b): Douglas Crimp has famously theorised this collapse in his essay 'On the Museum's Ruins', which is another talisman to which I return and return in thinking and working among all of this. I point at it often in things I write (and still it still doesn't bore me). It's an essay ostensibly about the works of Robert Rauschenberg. In particular, about the way in which Rauschenberg's use of silkscreened photographic *reproductions* transforms the picture plane into that of a flatbed printing press, while at same time making a peculiar museum of the canvas – like an extension/derivation of André Malraux's museum without walls, which is after all the description of a book – with revolutionary implications. 'This flatbed picture plane is an altogether new kind of picture surface, one that effects, according to Leo Steinberg's 1968 essay 'Other Criteria', "the most radical shift in the subject matter of art, the shift from nature to culture."'[3] But as for the picture plane, so as for the institution and its accumulation and ordering of knowledge. This *re*ordering of 'the tables on which knowledge is tabulated',[4] is a disintegration and interdependent reconstitution of the institution: the museum, ruined. (Jump to *Fourth*)

Second (c): Which is how I still regard the potential threat of reproduction to the tables on which knowledge is tabulated now: it is the threat (read: potential) of distribution (as a definitive attribute of

217

the legacy/history of the moving image, read through the co-operatives and their collections, which are, as they always have been, continuously still falling apart, rightly so). If the meaning of a work is at least
in part contingent upon its distribution – a work disseminated not as
a unique object, but as many (immaterial) objects viewable everywhere, simultaneously – it is also a medium that works against the
very foundations of the museum that persists in spite of Crimp and
Steinberg. Institutional responsibility in this schema would not be to
protect an object by limiting access, but to present it by doing the
opposite. To undo and be undone.

(Or)

Third: *'Things' could start to collapse* and (in even the same or some
others' hands) positions could be constructed, or even actual buildings
– careers, definitions, collections, archives, restricted zones, police
patrols. Is it that fiefdoms are built in the name of definition (of industry and economy)? Utopia: control, exclusion, limited access. The film
co-op movement in America and Europe constructed canons, collections. And where they did not, we do now. Jonas Mekas's Essential
Cinema collection was a deliberate establishing of a canon for pedagogic and associated cultural purposes, a power structure the effect of
which remains current. The collection of the Freunde der Deutschen
Kinemathek in Berlin, absolutely tied to the Berlinale, to a mission
centred on access (*Second [a]*), can nonetheless still be experienced
as a secret society, databased against access, inaccessible to anyone
who does not know what a name/title they've never heard of might
indicate about anything in a language they do not necessarily speak.[5]
When every member of the London Filmmakers' Co-op had the right
to deposit their own work there as available for distribution, what was
established was an ideal that was limited then by the number of artists
active in this area; now, it is limited by the impossibility of sustaining such a model, because there is hardly an artist who has not made
a moving-image work, and who would not want this work to be available. The moving image enters the museum as an object, not a medium.

218

And up until our digital present (which is radical with regard to all these issues), this work might only have been seen by the physical movement of the viewer, sometimes across continents, to place a reel of 16mm on a Steenbeck at a distributor's in New York, London or Paris. Even now, we might only aspire to the digital, and still also resist it. So these collections could be understood to have been effectively open *and* closed (inaccessible, barely catalogued, unnavigable without having already, somehow, somewhere, been navigated). Geography uniquely in tandem with material is re-imposed like borders that it becomes difficult to cross. As difficult as getting a reader's pass for the British Library which houses every book ever published (here, I write from London), by law, if you only have an interest in reading. Insider jobs. (Digital present: China vs Google (or vice versa); America maybe not bothering to distribute DVDs in Spain vs Googlebooks; Ubuweb increases audiences.) Enough. This is hopeless.

Fourth: The auditorium need not be understood as the indivisible sum of the industry and the economy of the cinema, with which it has become synonymous. There are splashes in muddy waters.

Fourth (a): It could, for example, be considered a ruined museum. Such a thought might precipitate others as a plethora of hybrids, and this proliferation might make a differentiation out of such excess. The copy made into theatre. Context and/or the act of reading (anything) made into content, the wrong/right material, a proper inappropriate, productive almost-mess as the only way to describe a reordering without/before knowing what this looks like.

Fourth (b): And by so doing it becomes a situation as well as, or even instead of – a location that is architecturally, culturally or socially determined. A place that slides between positions, potentials, instructions, opennesses, closures. Say, the site of language rather than inscription. Such a site might be imaged as the fixed form of the auditorium-as-industrial cinema transposed, decomposed, ruined, or disintegrated and reconstituted as if it might now more accurately occupy its own foyer – an engine room that is also by necessity otherwise regarded as marginal. That is, the foyer understood as the Antechamber described by Roland Barthes, the arena of Racinian tragedy, if Racine and tragedy could be put to one side in borrowing his thought.

Fifth: So annihilating gender specificity and crossing out 'tragic', imagining a situation in which we are all actors and viewers, equal with a thing presented where:

> The Antechamber (the stage proper) is a medium of transmission;
> it partakes of both interior and exterior, of Power and Event,
> of the concealed and the exposed. Fixed between the world, a place
> of action, and the Chamber, a place of silence, the Antechamber
> is the site of language: it is here that ~~tragic~~ man [*sic*], lost [or found]
> between the letter and the meaning of things, utters his [*sic*]
> reasons. The ~~tragic~~ stage is therefore not strictly secret, it is rather
> a [wonderfully] blind alley, the anxious [as in productive] passage
> from secrecy to effusion, from immediate fear to fear expressed
> [from a being-told to expression]. It is a trap [opened because
> it is] suspected...[6]

Which might be optimistic, but is to say nonetheless that it is where things happen(ed).

220

1. ['Forum' is the International Forum of New Cinema, the strand of the annual Berlinale film festival dedicated to experimental film and video art.]
2. Dorothy Richardson, 'Continuous Performance: The Film Gone Male', *Close Up*, vol.9, no.1 (March 1932), reprinted in *Close Up, 1927–1933 Cinema and Modernism*, ed. James Donald, Anne Friedberg and Laura Marcus (London: Cassell, 1998), p.207.
3. Douglas Crimp, 'On the Museum's Ruins', *October*, no.13 (Summer 1980): reprinted in *Postmodern Culture*, ed. Hal Foster (London and Sydney: Pluto Press, 1983), p.44.
4. Ibid., p.45.
5. [The database was still in development when this text was first published, but can now be found at <https://www.deutsche-kinemathek.de> last accessed on 16 July 2016.]
6. Roland Barthes, *On Racine*, trans. Richard Howard (Berkeley and Los Angeles: University of California Press, 1992), p.4.

A Life, and Time:
Alfred Leslie's letter to Frank O'Hara
+ Roland Barthes on Racine

The notion behind this film is quite simple and direct. At the same time though it is cinematically complex, both in structure and editing. From the point of view of shooting and 'drama' it is terribly simple.

We will shoot for two SEPARATE LEVELS on the film. One is the VISUAL, the other the HEARD. Unlike most films the sound track of this picture will be a SEPARATE continuity. It will relate of course and be part of the VISUAL circumstances but at the same time the spectator will be in TWO places or more SIMULTANEOUSLY. NOT AS MEMORY BUT AT THE SAME MOMENT. PARALLELISM! MULTIPLE POINTS OF VIEW! From all points this is a powerful and never used cinematic idea, which also presents the possibility for reducing the number of shooting scenes because they can be developed through the EAR at the same time... You would have then three sound tracks working at once with at least two VISUAL tracks. Essentially the problem of keeping control over the whole thing would be to always make sure that the HEARD track was always well established as a PLACE before you could start manipulation or cross cutting.

223

First presented as a performance/reading on 11 May 2011 at Kino Arsenal, Berlin before a screening of *The Last Clean Shirt* (1964) by Alfred Leslie and Frank O'Hara, as part of a series of events called *Poor Man's Expression*. The audience sat in the cinema space in the darkness as White read, his voice relayed over the cinema's sound system, whilst he moved from the left exit to the right exit, crossing in front of the (empty) screen. Finally he closed both exit doors, leaving the space in complete darkness.

The PLACE must be established and the TIME... and the TIME MUST ALWAYS BE IN THE PRESENT. The opening scene will be the key to the technique of the film. The WHOLE procedure depends on these first few moments. The following scene may be considered a sample... and should not be thought of as fully developed....

On the image of a dark screen...

... geography sustains a special relation between the house and its exterior, between the Racinian palace and its hinterland. Although there is only one setting, according to the rules, one might say that there are three tragic sites. There is first of all the Chamber: vestige of the mythic cave, it is the invisible and dreadful place where Power lurks... It is both the abode of Power and its essence, for Power is only a secret; its form exhausts its function, it kills by being invisible.

The Chamber is contiguous to the second tragic site, the Antechamber, the eternal space of all subjections, since it is here that one *waits*. The Antechamber (the stage proper) is a medium of transmission; it partakes of both interior and exterior, of Power and Event, of the concealed and the exposed. Fixed between the world, a place of action, and the Chamber, a place of silence, the Antechamber is the site of language: it is here that the tragic character, lost between the letter and the meaning of things, utters their reasons. The tragic stage is therefore a blind alley, the anxious passage from secrecy to effusion, from immediate fear to fear expressed. It is a trap suspected, which is why the posture the tragic character must adopt within it is always of an extreme mobility.

Between the Chamber and the Antechamber stands a tragic object which menacingly expresses both contiguity and exchange, the tangency of hunter and prey: the Door. Here one waits, one trembles; to enter it is a temptation and a transgression...

The third tragic site is the Exterior. Between Antechamber and Exterior, there is no transition. The palace walls plunge down into the sea, the stairs lead to the ships ready to sail, the ramparts are a balcony above the battle itself, and if there are hidden passages they no longer constitute part of the tragedy, they are already Flight. The line that separates tragedy from its negation is thin, almost abstract; what is involved is a limit, in the ritual sense of the word: the tragedy is simultaneously prison and protection against impurity, against all that is not itself.

Hinterhof

I was not there.
I did not know him.
I don't have any evidence. I did not witness anything.
How do I come to know this work?

By the means that we come to know it now: by a cultural and
economic system that a fantasised affiliation to this work
makes us also naïvely believe might also itself be a fantasy.
A system we might try to pretend does not exist, or could be
transgressed, one to which we are not subject, supporters,
within which we are not – all of us – workers – or do not
want to be. And yet here we are.

We might think about what is adequate and what is
inadequate in the way we come to know this work now?
Is there anything live here?
We are sat in a room inside a room. And someone is
always speaking at a pace we all agree on, because this
is a situation that has a form, which we know, that we
receive.
This whole season, the very reason why we are all here is
because we think we are able, we are able, now, to know
that we have been or will be watching works that we
think or they think we can guarantee will be the same
whenever a projectionist presses 'play'.

227

First presented at a Jack Smith symposium at the
Institute of Contemporary Arts, London, 9 September 2011.

Why might we not want it to exist?

Because it has very little to do with being alive and very
much more to do with itself. In fact it is the very product
of somebody's death, of product as death, even if not our
own. Product over process. We are not living here, but
elsewhere...

The way somebody breathes is inimitable. I wonder if the diaphragm is
the membrane between life and work. Our desire to imitate the inimitable is precisely that same construction of desire that Jack Smith's
work occupies to rail against, or revolutionise, as it flips the escape of
otherwise doing so onto/into a surface that is a mess of not-seeing,
falling, failing, flailing, nearly-doing. All of which this situation here
and now – a situation for seeing and hearing clearly, attempts to
work against. Seeing and hearing in this instance are self-defeating.
I wonder whether they can explain anything that needs to be explained.
We shouldn't be. Yet we are.

Desire like this does not need to be reinscribed by me or anyone
else although perhaps a kind of re-occupation of it *is* possible, which
would be a different thing. The means of this occupation are different
kinds of not-seeing, not-doing, not-hearing, in other words a deliberate mess, excess, the site of exchange, precisely that which is figured
perceptually in these films, performances, photographs of Jack Smith
that we do *not* know, that *I* do not know.

Inevitably Making Sense

(with Martin Gustavsson)

This text is derived from a set of questions and answers between the author and the artist [Martin Gustavsson], *that constituted a live performance at Maria Stenfors gallery, London on 12 November 2010, during* In No Particular Order's *exhibition there. Ten questions and more answers were written separately in advance by the author and the artist respectively, neither knowing what the other's were. The questions derived from a series of intense studio visits and private conversations between the two during the development of the work. The answers take the form of carefully selected quotations from a diverse range of sources that variously (pre)occupy the artist. During the performance, questions and answers were drawn at random, one pair at a time, in the order that they appear below. Their conjunction was pure chance (or something else), emulating or enacting structural and interpretive characteristics of the work exhibited, representing the kind of communication that might occur within a friendship.*

Here these questions and answers have been used by the author to produce a further set of thoughts (which could in turn produce more); an ever-expanding open web of hypotheses, conjecture and poetics that also proposes emulation and enactment as communication and this also as the means by which the work might be described.

229

First published in *Martin Gustavsson: In No Particular Order*, exhibition catalogue (Gothemburg: Gothemburg Museum of Art, 2011), pp.10–51. *In No Particular Order* is the title of a body of paintings by Gustavsson.

Ian White (left) and Martin Gustavsson (right) performing *In Particular Order, No?* in front of Gustavsson's paintings, Eastside Projects, Birmingham, June 2012

To what extent is the understanding of this project helped by its exhibition – within an architecture, an institution – and to what extent does it work against that architecture and institution?

Dark and wrinkled like a violet carnation,
It breathes, humbly lurking in moss
Still moist from love following the sweet flight
Of white Buttocks to its rim's heart

These canvases are framed only by
the room they occupy when exhibited (unconventionally stacked) and
this room then becomes them, as
in it is also the work. Space becomes
material, a terrain plunged into by
the viewer, that same strange ravine
between at least two ideas of flesh
that the viewer occupies in an act of
looking. This work becomes by virtue of being there, in a room etc. that
it works against, a crack, where a
wall meets the floor, or canvases butt
the ceiling, there if it is anywhere,
of many parts and also indivisible.
Thought. Almost a fresco, but split.

232

Is painting the expression of desire, even of an obsessive desire? To own, to make flesh if you like, a kind of transubstantiation of the depicted, image-paint-flesh?

Outside what used to be a massive General Motors car plant in Dayton, Ohio, I stand with two women who used to work there. It's closed now, a victim of recession and globalisation. Road signs and overhead traffic lights swing in the wind. The only sign of life inside the derelict factory, which stretches as far as you can see, is a security guard who eyes us warily through the perimeter fence.

Otherwise defunct production continuing in the mind's eye is here made manifest, enough to be understood as a practice that is also work, the ongoing production or reproduction of images, a production line proposed by the imaginary projection of their number into the kind of endlessness that these paintings and their organisation suggests. Personal relations are written in but more often written out, even dismembered, and this is a coldness to be contended with, seen. Conveyor belt emotion, horror, the modern gay corporation. Happy Days.

In this context is it ever possible to make the wrong decision? What could a wrong decision be?

I felt very unwell.
Woke up with a proverb that seemed very profound at the time: 'Only when dogs are fierce will the inhabitants be loyal.'

So there it is. Only we are amongst
a set of rules that cannot be read
outside of an experience that it
also determines, like how habit is,
when there is every reason and no
reason. Obedience to what? Loyalty
to whom? Nothing and no one.
No wonder you feel unwell because
everything is connecting within one,
single, enveloping rupture, but gen-
tly like a seasickness of the emotions
still to emerge.

234

Some of these images are explicitly religious and some explicitly sexual. The sexual images are erotic because of what they exclude. The religious canvases make me feel uncomfortable because of what they suggest. Why is that?

What the painting freezes is the terrible stillness of looking at a body that is neither living nor dead, neither Christ nor the artist's model, an insatiable looking that is the living eye's search for the image (the still image) of its own death. Since we are emphatically not redeemed, we call this body paint. We revere it and love it and look at it again and again because, unlike God, painting has and is a body we can touch.

Roland Barthes writes of Robert Mapplethorpe's *Self-Portrait* (1975) in these terms – that it is erotic because of what it conceals, not pornographic for what it reveals. And yet in the photograph he refers to we still see Mapplethorpe's face, his outstretched arm approximately Christlike. In *In No Particular Order* there are no faces as such. No image-mirror-paint-flesh in that sense. And we cannot touch even though somebody – you? – might have touched that which is depicted twice, in person and in paint. Is looking touching? Is painting, like desire, that absence? Light moves but I still wonder who they are. And then there is this other body pictured – and I know who it is meaning to be mainly by its wounds. He does not have a face here either. He is not unknown to me as the anyman of a sexual encounter, but rather as religious iconography, which is to say that like these other bodies he is somebody else's.

Self-Portrait, 1975
© Robert Mapplethorpe
Foundation

Are we looking at a map?

'The division seems rather unfair', I remarked. 'You have done all the work in this business. I get a wife out of it, Jones gets the credit, pray what remains for you?' 'For me', said Sherlock Holmes, 'there still remains the cocaine-bottle.' And he stretched his long white hand up for it.

Land and the self might both be divided – into countries, constituencies, property, a grid of rectangular images, public/private, consciousness/oblivion etc. The map can be read contingent upon how visible or invisible the reasons for its divisions are, and it can give rise to material goods, a body or mysteries.

Is this the work or is that the work? Like, will there always be a performative aspect to this project? And how?

He looked, he stopped, he pondered before some object, dismissed it ironically, passed on to another. The same thing happened before a stall poorer then the others – if it could be called a stall. In fact, all the wares were spread on the ground, on the bare dust. Behind them, grazed by the feet of the crowd that walked along past the open doors of the shops, were the sellers; three young men between fifteen and thirty, whom the excitement and the night spent in the open (sleeping on the ground, just where they were now) had reduced to silence: an extraordinarily expressive silence, however.

The presence of the artist's body is more often than not used in contemporary culture as a currency facilitator, as if it is evidence, proof or validation of the work made – or at the very least a supporting structure on which the visibility of the work made is dependent, or mediated as entertainment, even as the artist browses. At the same time there is an institutional conspiracy of silence around this functioning, as if this body might be but grazed by the feet of art history as it passes by. For to do otherwise would acknowledge an instability that the institution cannot contain, as in, it cannot be owned. It is in this way – when the body or its idea becomes the work in whichever way – that all performative structures offer the potential of resistance to a dominant culture and its means, bodies may be sat on dust but also be themselves sand underfoot.

237

How do you make the decision about what to paint when? i.e. is there a connection that you make in your process or progress from one canvas to the next that remains invisible – or is deliberately obscured – by the way in which the work is shaped by this method of display?

The key incentive in his measures was that 'work should always pay and that you should be better off in work than out of work'.

Back to the line. Narrative is an inevitability – one thing always happens after another, even if this is just the passing of time rather than events, words on a page, or images in rows. This linearity almost always intimates causality. We look for it and insist upon it compulsively as a condition of the act of reading so familiar as to be subconscious. Here, though, a new line of chance supercedes the chronological order in which the individual canvases were made while at the same time suggesting it as something to be thought about. Narrative does not go away but in the combination of choice and chance, a/the line is broken and remade continuously, an endless game of sorts, just the suggestion of an unaccountable economy.

Across the individual canvasses here there is a flatness and a dismem-
berment and the two seem to have a relationship to each other – pattern,
an almost photo-realism (broken by a blob of paint straight from the
tube), a leg, a bum, a trunk. What's the nature of that relationship?

The difference between illusions and delusions – so far as comedy,
tragedy and tragicomedy are concerned – is that delusions are
best gotten rid of, whereas illusions are never abandoned without
some risk.

The form of these illusions – these
formal illusions – reveal delusions
which would otherwise have been
ours. The hand is definitely but
only intermittently visible as a
brushstroke. In the flesh – the flesh –
images hang between what is sometimes a near-photographic surface
(grapes, plums) and the depth of
a painterly materiality (drips, blobs,
unfinished finished-ness). Both
situations might be read in the way
we read a truncated body, like stop-
points to the imagination, the refusal
of a *mise en scène*, disbelief not
suspended, against romance. Of the
personal but things in themselves.

Is it inevitable that we – as in you and I and all viewers of this work – will always make sense of how the canvasses are ordered and presented? A certain inherent narrativising that we can't avoid?

Orange and hazelnut go wonderfully well together. They offer a good balance of freshness and earthiness and the flavours are subtle enough to complement the beans without overpowering them.

Narrative does not go away. Passages appeal to taste (or distaste), which itself becomes the thing seen, while always understood within an irrepressible act of individuated reading – one that does not succeed through the conditions of collective agreement by which meaning is usually established, but rather threads separate, sub-rational stories that are most times silent.

240

How do you understand the balance between the personal and the formal in this work?

Saturday's New Moon brings both very personal issues to a head and, equally, shakes up existing arrangements. You're overwhelmed. Therefore, withdraw and allow what must happen to take place without attempting to influence events. This may be out of character. But you'll soon realise things are far less fixed than you imagined. Plus you can make any necessary changes over the coming weeks.

Februari/February,
Les Tres Riches Heures du Duc
de Berry, c.1450

241

Time/Form(s)/Friendship

(with Jimmy Robert)

Perhaps time does shape friendship, the same way one forms an opinion, or sees it changing over time; it has taken us time... from one work to be able to think about beginning the next (three years, each time), to see them with a different inflection than when we were working on them, or to unravel our experiences afterwards into... our own practice.

Now, *6 things we couldn't do, but can do now* (2004) and *Marriage à la Mode et Cor Anglais* (2007/09) communicate with one another even though the latter was always considered a direct response to the former. The first investigated the act of spending time together, part of which meant shifting a relationship between an artist and a curator (we'd come to know each other through some mutual friends and a screening of Jimmy's films curated by Ian at the former Lux Cinema on Hoxton Square in London) to one between collaborating artists. The latter occupied theatre, a deliberate artificiality, and formally introduced elements that the other didn't prioritise: speech, image-making, a stricter choreography. The structures we've assumed as a working process – a sustained serial coming-together over many months for *6 things...*, two shorter, fixed working periods for *Marriage...* – have always been a kind of generative reflection of the final forms and themes of the resulting performances. In our new work, *Lemon Rose*, we move back to the cinema auditorium. A place where we first met. We have approached the exchange that follows as part of our – and this new work's – process: a risk, or a line of thought, argued.

243

First published in *Jimmy Robert: Vis-à-vis*, exhibition catalogue (Chicago: Museum of Contemporary Art, 2012), pp.61–74. White had a long and important working relationship with Jimmy Robert, and *6 things...*, *Marriage à la Mode* and *Lemon Rose* (2012) were all performances they made collaboratively.

has always been material, both a problem and content as it is here and now.
Whatever else there was, was something
spent by the occasion; props, clothing,
choreography... all these things that
were fixed in the work were actually
transitory, spent by/in the work, *of*
time. So time, then, remains (it is material in this way) because actually it is the
framework upon which (other) things
hang and because *we* are in and of it
now. Are these works present or past?
I'm uncomfortable with reminiscence,
which is only making stories about
things that are not here, and we are
being overheard.

In *6 things we couldn't do, but can
do now* this problem is most explicit.
Let's say the performance itself was an
instance that crystallised the passing of
time into a series of actions, almost-
abstractions drawn from our spending
time together... then that they established
an imaginary grid-like structure as
a mechanism to measure the time spent
with others during the performance, like
a transfer or a channel, actions becoming a kind of clock. The acting of this, the
sense in which the work was marking
shared time, during the process and in
the moment, was deeply emotional. That
perhaps was a surprise. There were not
six things, there were more, or *none* –
no matter, being the point. The title still
points at content specifically to remove
the work's relationship to anything like
actual objects or even tasks. There were

244

A slow, and solitary confrontation with
change: learning.

This slow confrontation with change
is not just the times we are living in,
although there are particularly extraordinary and necessary shifts in perspective, but isn't this a constant?

As non-dancers it took us two trips to
New York and intense rehearsals to
learn Yvonne Rainer's *Trio A*. We spent
even more time in and out of studios
to work out a language that became our
own that would allow us to articulate
our position within the tasks we set for
ourselves; which resulted in an almost
silent 50 minute piece. Finding our
weight through a set of gestures dissect-
ing our perceptions.

One is less vulnerable when in company
and perhaps learns more about one's
limits. An experience allowing idio-
syncrasies, validating one in their own
body, encouraging the occupation of
time and space.

Through various theatres *Marriage*...
introduced repetition; the non-event,
most Performance Art runs away from
the Theatre, we embraced it, folie
à deux. The time is the duration of
a studio portrait, its pause/pose against
mortality.

objects and also tasks, or what we came to realise was an illusory task-like-ness, images of tasks. The title insists the work is spoken about because it sounds like it's describing what happened only it isn't and by being spoken about, as it has to be, it again only exists in and of time (it was also the beginning of a vocabulary).

If *6 things...* was an instance then *Marriage à la Mode et Cor Anglais* was much more consciously in and of

form(s)

– a form, or a formalism. That is, a performance for the theatre that could by definition then be repeated, like a dance, or something live that by being fixed became more like an object. Possibly kept. A choreography. Memorised words. Bodies and actions describing graphic images, like photographs (which was where we started from, copying one). Perhaps we made (or spoke) the same work again – isn't that the problem with any vocabulary? – but we wanted to deal with that problem of time, and form, and we could do it again and again. 'To be alert is to be decorative.' On the line was the status of the body-in-performance, via Roland Barthes's ideas about photography (or his attempting a theory of photography while expediting grief), in *Camera Lucida*, that as a form photography is connected to art not by painting, but by theatre, mediated by a kind of death:

form(s)

The intricate pattern of lace everywhere. White t-shirt and jeans as uniform for long and slim improvised one night only gymnasts against the chinoiseries of red silk gowns of statuesque apprentice synchronised swimmers.

On looking at the floor one could notice a grid that is criss-crossed, diagonals, living frescoes.

We are at once images and making images, objects and sculptures; Yvonne Rainer is on a monitor we dance together; in another context we become tableaux vivants, shape-shifters?

We might escape any denomination, run away from stable identities. We are as instable as representation itself.

Speech even became a formal device where meaning was opaque, but the frailty or confidence of the different voices never lied; even against the involuntary iconography of our somewhat similar morphology.

Lace against a pattern, a modern congregate: a suggested way of reading double self-portraits, could venture as far as saying performers against personas.

'It is not through painting that photography touches art, but through theatre', wrote Barthes and alongside this quote

245

the body on stage, dispossessed of what constitutes a person when a body is not on stage, is a form. Colour. Shape. Even if it moves. Or when it is ridiculous. So that at the end when we deliberately exhausted ourselves to the point of formlessness, of no control, by running as fast as we could from one side of the stage to the other for two minutes and twenty-two seconds, well, we had to do that in the dark. This running was the opposite of our static lit pose at the beginning of the work (if my leg hadn't nearly always wobbled). Pitch dark. The sound of breathing because hiding it wasn't a choice. I am dramatising. By this time we were dramatising

friendship.

Which is always a risk – not least to friendship itself, which is private. These two works were made in different ways; they describe different time periods and, by being so, both made this – time – form. Maybe that's why we only work together once every three years. It's not Twitter.

Time now is like a coiled spring. We're calling it *Lemon Rose.* Wound-up one night, released the next. Or vice versa, but I don't think so. Finite. That's how I understand an argument. A rhetorical construction of diminishing options until only one is possible. Once you're at the airport you can only get on the plane. Like transforming gas into solid mass, slipping into limits,

'to be alert is to be decorative' from Frank O'Hara, the two sources we intertwined which became for us at once a reference, a form and consequently an almost abstract dialogue/series of monologues.

friendship.

Once in a documentary about Derek Jarman, I was struck by how Tilda Swinton referred to some of his films and the acting in particular as very much having the feel or quality of school plays, thought it a bad thing initially, but maybe there is something there, as in how over time one processes ideas, through attempts, and repetition and not necessarily always from knowledge as otherwise there wouldn't be anything left to risk, even less authenticity of expression.

It's somehow very much our own theatre that we are constructing, we are speaking with our own voices and bodies, perhaps even it is queer in its appropriation of existing genres; but that never felt as if it were a primary motivation.

Which one is a curse? Which one is worse, knowledge or ignorance? Perhaps that is not the question that matters, as one should focus more on how one generates one's own means of addressing a plethora of issues while remaining open to transformation and

a person into a passenger. That's how the image of an object can become an object; how an object can become a colour, not the colour of the image or the object, but a word; language, space and time, architecture; architecture argument. Parabolic. Something is being said.
I mean made.

None of this is messy enough. Shit.

Love,

experience through the clarity of their essences rather than the accuracy of their chosen forms.

The dichotomy identity/subjectivity springs to mind. Who are we? What do we feel? *Feelings Are Facts* is the title of Yvonne Rainer's autobiography which itself takes its title from John Schimel, her psychotherapist in the early 60s: 'while we aspired to the lofty and cerebral plane of a quotidian materiality, our unconscious lives unravelled with intensity and melodrama that inversely matched their absence in the boxes, beams, jogging, and standing still of our austere sculptural and choreographic creations', which to me underlines the fact that whatever we think we might be doing at the end of the day it is always about our relation to one another, one person to another person, materialised and made manifest through various forms, time, and our friendship.

I have learned to love and accept differences, to develop a language through time without fear, as some form of defiance against adversity, a slow but no longer so solitary confrontation with change.

Jimmy Robert and Ian White, *Marriage à la mode et cor Anglais*,
STUK, Leuven, 2007. Photo: L. Bernaerts.

Wishful Thinking:
Morgan Fisher at the Ziegfeld Follies, or,
Oliver Husain and the Potential of Theatrical Excess

To invoke the work of a West Coast American structuralist in the title of an essay on a queer German fantasist may seem like wishful thinking. But then wishful thinking is Oliver Husain's modus operandi – the blueprint of a radically whimsical, sharply experienced politics and the re-imagination of normative orders effected by a contemporary repurposing of the suspension of disbelief – so just such a coupling might also be completely appropriate. More specifically, my aim is to read Husain's *Purfled Promises* (2009) in relation to Morgan Fisher's *Screening Room* (1968-) (no two works might be more different and yet as similar) and through their differences and similarities to establish the co-ordinates of a proposition that figures in Husain's body of work as motif, content and structure: the political imperative of theatricality, of theatre, of cinema read as theatre for the sake of new social formations.

Fisher's *Screening Room* might be thought of as a kind of instruction work in the conceptual idiom (with the political resonances of such), although it is only made known as such by and in its materialisation. It is a unique work. Or rather, it is one film that consists of a potentially infinite number of unique works, each of which is materially inseparable from the auditorium in which it is shown. Which is to say that the film is made exclusively for and featuring the auditorium in which it is shown and its immediate vicinity, the streets

251

First published in *Oliver Husain: Spoiler Alert*, ed. Emelie Chhangur (Toronto: Art Gallery of York University, 2012), pp.34–40.

by which it is approached, and each print produced cannot be shown anywhere else, although it may be shown in the same venue no matter how many years ago it was shot.

On screen the audience sees a point of view shot, that of the person behind the camera approaching the cinema by the same route they would most likely have just taken themselves. The camera (person) enters the cinema through whichever passageways the viewers will also probably just have walked and into the (empty) auditorium, coming to rest on the empty white screen. Slowly the camera zooms closer and closer to the empty white screen until the empty white screen fills the actual screen of the auditorium – filling it with its own, empty, image. The light of the filmed white screen projected onto the actual screen lights the room. It is a kind of collapse the effect of which, amongst other things, is an awareness of the immediate present in a potentially Brechtian sense: illusion is broken by/into the actual space/time of the viewer's own present, a kind of crushing.

Oliver Husain's *Purfled Promises* is a single-channel video for the auditorium that is also a live work. The audience is seated. A screen is carried into the room by two people costumed to excess as hybrid post-drag almost-aliens. The video is projected onto this portable screen, held in front of the permanent one. Silent for its first seven minutes, we are mesmerised by a series of curtains – or veils – supported by a frame not unlike the one that supports the temporary screen itself. The camera slowly zooms into each curtain to an extreme close-up, at which point the curtain is drawn to reveal a new one immediately behind. The pace at which this continuous zooming or moving through occurs gradually increases. We begin to see the (painted, gloved, bejewelled) hands that pull the curtains' strings. They play with/for us. The materials from which the curtains are made (and the means by which they reveal) begin to vary, from different fabrics to increasingly wild, baroque variations on the theme summarily evocative of Hollywood's Golden Age: a progress – or descent – into artifice. From green crushed velvet to white petals, studded wooden cabinet doors, billowing silk, an outsized black book redolent of the magical entry to the Ziegfeld Follies, opened to reveal an empty box that becomes a frame, women's

252

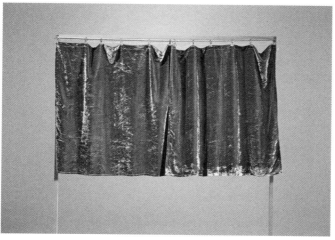

Stills from Oliver Husain, *Purfled Promises*, 2009.

dresses directly referencing those of Kenneth Anger's mother in *Puce Moment* (1949), helium balloons, umbrellas, peacock feathers, a comedy keyhole, black feathers, an ad hoc lens, a cocktail glass, a sparkling venetian blind, strings of beads that are *cut* to finally reveal a plain and empty screen, like the image of that on which we are watching the work. At this point, for the first time, we hear a male voice, redolent

253

of the simple awe, mystery, drama, and doom of bygone cinema, with a torrid soundtrack to match. What this ominous voice explains is that, without our noticing, the screen on which we've been watching this work has been incrementally moving slowly towards us, actually, physically. In fact it is almost on top of us – and it is. The two people carrying the screen are climbing into and over the first row of the auditorium, then more, gradually lowering the screen onto the heads of those seated there. The voice-over describes the theatre now as a decadent ruin through the rubble of which we try to clamber (we're not, but we're imagining we are because the immersion is physical *and* metaphorical) and as we do so – stop! – somebody TOUCHES US,

Still from Oliver Husain, *Purfled Promises*, 2009.

finally reaching the exit only to find that it is an entrance, '*an entrance to another entrance*': the outside world collapsed now onto/into the one inside, inside there – the auditorium – and one affected (changed forever) through a now-altered perception.

The trajectories of *Screening Room* and *Purfled Promises* map onto each other: imagistic familiarity, uncanny self-reflexivity, optical illusion, material collapse (that is also structural), the immediate present. The former might in this light be reconsidered as a theatricalising

254

(camp) gesture and the latter a work of structural reconfiguration. But the terms of their immediate present are different. *Screening Room* eschews illusionistic narrative. Even though its denouement is the product of optical effect, it is a cold light. *Purfled Promises* over-saturates the situation of its own screening with the effects of illu-sionistic narrative such that its proposal is rather a transformation as opposed to a reveal – the materialisation of a series of veils that in fact constitute the frames through which material reality might be mutually-exclusively experienced.

These curtains that the camera continuously passes through in *Purfled Promises*, only to reveal another set, are those of the theatrical auditorium itself. In the auditorium they function as a division between the audience and that which is presented to them, like a promise. No matter what is revealed when they part, they frame it and they promise that we, the audience, are as separate from it as life is from an image or three dimensions are from two. And that they will close again. At the same time they broker the invitation to an audience to enter into a shared world that extends from the stage to peculiarly occupy the auditorium as well, the model of a new world order. This is the power of theatre, its political and social significance, and its impor-tance as a form: this ability to define the model of a new world order that we occupy, which, however temporary, has a utopian potential. Theatre as political threat. Reactions to this situation – and there are many – could be said to inform the entire history of twentieth-century theatre *and* much of the debates that have circulated around artists' film and video since the late 1960s. And yet mostly they remain, these curtains. Opening and closing. Only for Husain they actually never close. Rather, their functions (frame, window, membrane) become those of the screen itself, itself an invitation into a new world order (an inversion of familiar relations), played out in his work as a whole where in equal measure the screen is an object, motif and metaphor with transformative potential.

It is a relation otherwise expressed, for example, in *Green Dolphin* (2008), where the life story of a Filipino woman blurs unnotice-ably into and out of the fiction of the 1947 Lana Turner vehicle from

255

which the video takes its title. The moral of the work might be that appearances should not be trusted (location, identity, history might all be suspect), but this is not because they represent 'fake' as opposed to 'true'. Rather, it is because in and through the work they have become material, porous, true and false: a new truth located neither in the hand-wringing of a documentary confessional nor in the total absorption of a Hollywood fantasy, but rather in the act of viewing-as-experience. Similarly, in *Mount Shasta* (2008) we are given two versions of the pitch for a film yet to be made – a written account and an ethereal, surreal puppet show with its own internal logic. The first almost falls into the second and both together defy the formal constraints that introduce them, the bureaucratic administration of a business that the viewer is nevertheless moved beyond, that we cannot help but forget or simply give up for something akin to reverie.

These are not superfluous strategies – they have a gravitas beyond (and actually because of) the seeming superficiality and playfulness of their ingredients. Something of a companion work to *Purfled Promises*, in *Leona Alone* (2009) a series of stained-glass windows, constructed on a similar, free-standing frame to that which supports the former's curtains etc., are seen in various, incongruous suburban situations, slightly absurd, seemingly abandoned, just standing there. They are windows, screens, veils and membranes simultaneously and by association or accumulation with these other works, at some times seen as objects and at others filling the screen on which the video is projected. Their designs are abstract, not exemplary religious allegory; curved, geometrical patterns, with an art deco bent. Excess, or, art for art's sake, let's say. At first they make little sense, displaced in this way. Gradually though they are drawn into increasingly material relationships with their surroundings. Some act as filters, recolouring the mundane scene beyond. On some a pane might be missing but the panel is positioned and shot precisely so that the remaining glass frames the ordinary (a busy road, a pocket of social-housing scrubland, the shadows on a brick wall) to near-hallucinogenic degrees. The lead dividing lines of a panel's design become synchronous with the mirrored skin of a bland office block, they perfectly outline the neon

Stills from Oliver Husain's *Leona Alone*, 2009.

graphics of a local gym, the signage of a shopping centre. It is as if they are not objects in space but agents of change – that is, by shifting our perception, the material world, inseparable from it, melded to these coloured lenses, might also shift. In the final section of the video introduced by the intertitle 'maybe, potentially...' (taken from the magically random words spoken by a passerby into her telephone) there are no stained-glass screens. So these final shots, of similar no-places-in-particular (as in, places passed through all the time, places that somehow define life) become propositions, or invitations. It is as if, based on the examples given, the viewer is in a position independently to perform the same operations here. And these places stand for an any-here – an anywhere that you want to transform by these means which might now have been given like an internalised tool kit.

Leona Alone and *Purfled Promises* both have a specific genesis that underlines a social/cultural function to which neither work is limited but which reveals something of Husain's project described by me up until now as the product of an act of reading/looking. The former was commissioned by The Leona Drive Project – a Toronto-based collective attempting to address the problems of gentrification in Willowdale, a northern suburb of that city. *Purfled Promises* was commissioned by Kino Arsenal, Berlin, as part of a five-day screening event around the work of the inimitable American artist, filmmaker and performer Jack Smith. In a 1978 interview Smith proposes a model for a re-imagined society, one reorganised by intellectual activity generated through the free exchange of that which we no longer need:

> I can think of billions of ways for the world to be completely different... I can think of other types of societies... Like in the middle of the city should be a repository of objects that people don't want anymore... That would form an organization, a way that the city would be organised... this centre of unused objects and unwanted objects would become a centre of intellectual activity. Things would grow up around it.[1]

Smith's 'unused' and 'unwanted' figure in Husain's work as other cultural outcasts. And not only in his videos but also in installations such as *Rushes for Five Hats* (2007) (spectacular grey baroque-constructivist hats, designed to be worn for a screening where they will deliberately disrupt the projected image) and the exhibition 'Hovering Proxies' at the Art Gallery of York University, Toronto, where an installation of party balloons, metal poles, and feathers effects a garden in Jakarta and is mirrored in a film, *Hovering Proxies*, both of which 'spaces' we enter at the same time as each other by the magic of perspective and a wind machine. The whimsical and the incidental and romantic fictions are carefully, delicately heaped together. They occupy a reinvented centre that might also be described by that image conjured at the end of *Purfled Promises*: a deliberately refined and wrecked auditorium, a situation of collapse, an audience crushed by a screen where that which separates us from it has become the thing itself, now a semi-porous membrane in/through the mind and a physical reorganisation of space and bodies has occurred, an endless series of exits that are entrances. Cinema, actually, remodelled, almost without us noticing, into a model for a new society. Nice.

1. Jack Smith in conversation with Sylvère Lotringer, *Semiotext(e)*, vol.3, no.2 (1978).

Performer, Audience, Mirror:
Cinema, Theatre and the Idea of the Live[1]

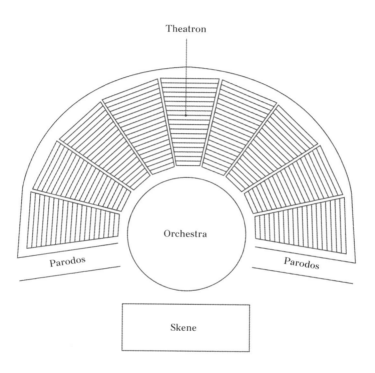

First published in *The Sensible Stage*, ed. Bridget Crone
(Bristol: Picture This, 2012), pp.30–43.

The body is a false promise. To be lifelike is not to live. Or, live-ness (liveness) is not life*like*ness. Just because somebody is actually there, a body on a stage is no more of a guarantee that what we are seeing is categorically live than an emotion portrayed by an actor on the screen is an indication that something was actually felt, even though we might think they are these things. Cinema is not live by definition. The same 'film' is played every time. A theatre play might require bodies but the actor is as controlled by the mechanisation of rehearsal and repetition as the 'moving' image. Even if it is not seen as such, the same hand moves to the same place, at the same angle, through the same axis at every performance.

By plotting the ways in which neither cinema nor theatre are live, I want then to consider exactly the opposite proposition: that in thinking cinema and theatre together, they might be the means by which liveness could be further described both as and not only as the product of an extraordinary kind of negation, and to indicate what has been or might be at stake by doing so.

One (Cinema)

Two people face each other. One speaks a line to the other: 'I love you', for example. The person opposite repeats it, inverted from the first to the second person:

'You love me.'
One: 'I love you.'
Two: 'You love me' and so on.

262

Each time the person speaking inflects the phrase with a different emotional nuance: tenderness, defiance, desperation, horror, declaration, surprise, rhetoric, disbelief, question, accusation and so on. A linguistic face-off until one person cracks or changes tack, what seems like a game is actually a popular training exercise for actors devised by Sanford Meisner. It is also an accumulation of incremental non-responses or an absolutely, repetitively constructed and incrementally evacuated present for the sake of portraying an emotional truth, or Truth itself: what Meisner might call the means for *Living Truthfully Under Imaginary Circumstances,* by which he means acting defined as re-action rather than agency, and proposed as a worry-free suspended state of happiness, which is also the title of a 2011 video installation by Anja Kirschner and David Panos. The artwork maps such exercises and contextualises them with documentary material and a show-reel of actors in Hollywood feature films deploying their learning. Emanating from two experiences of loss – the death of his brother and the economic crash of the 1930s that led to World War II – Meisner's technique is proposed as both the product of and a palliative for the moment in which it was conceived. Reframed in this work, it becomes a metaphor for the artists' own reading of a state of contemporary crisis. The dividing lines (is/is not, have/have not) usually marked by the difference between spectator and representation, the self and another and between subject and object are collapsed, embodied here as both a practice and a theory of acting. Or as a depoliticised state of in-action and in-conclusion, of participants and spectators subjugated in/by capitalism as image-play. The work echoes Dan Graham's analysis of the consumer constructed by a shop window, through a window that is also a screen, seeing their own face reflected, superimposed onto a commodity, indivisible from the empty, cold field of glass that purposefully flattens and contains (becomes) them both: 'Inseparable from the goods the consumer desires is the illusion that buying them will "complete" that which is "incomplete" in himself. This desire is never satisfied (as the market system must continue to function)...'[2]

Two (Theatre)

Your sensation as one in the audience in relation to the play played
before you your sensation I say your emotion concerning that play is
always either behind or ahead of the play at which you are looking...
your emotion as a member of the audience is never going on at the same
time as the action of the play. This thing... is what makes one endlessly
troubled about a play.

Gertrude Stein, 'Plays'[3]

Considered as a picture, the stage of a proscenium theatre functions
according to the principles of Renaissance perspective. Like the lines
that can be drawn from the central figures of Plato and Aristotle in
Raphael's fresco *The School of Athens* (1510–11), in the theatre power
emanates from the focal point of the presented image to the audience
by virtue of the fact that it organises or reorders – distorts, constructs
– space, bodies (in the picture and of its surroundings) and time. And
emotion. This power persuades, and our nervousness in the face of
it is what Stein describes as the symptom of its endless trouble – the
nag of our own lack and our repeated, frustrated attempts to catch up,
to enter, to be fulfilled by. The contemporary theatre maker Robert
Wilson organises his stage as a picture designed and choreographed
to be viewed from the middle of the stalls (from where it was directed)
for optimal impact, that is, greatest visual pleasure, or less 'trouble'.
And so sitting at the back of the auditorium, on the end of a row – in
a cheap seat – throws the picture into radical relief. The power structure breaks down because the lines of persuasion effected by perspective are broken. A swivelled picture plain reveals the apparatus of the
work like exposed cogs in the back of an analogue watch, a mechanism that does not tell us the time but measures it.

A fixed perspective inscribing time – not its machinery (the time-
line of history) – is the metaphor deployed by the artist Lis Rhodes in
her essay for the Hayward Gallery exhibition *Film As Film* (1979):

> ... history represented ... is the illusion of a philosophical ideal, the
> meshing of moments to prove a theoretical connection. It is as
> though a line could be drawn between past and present and pieces

of a person's life and work pegged on it... an inflexible chain, each part in place. The pattern is defined. Cut the line and chronology falls in a crumpled heap. I prefer a crumpled heap, history at my feet, not stretched above my head.[4]

Perspective is there, too, in shop windows. Dan Graham:

> The showcase window as a framing or optical device replicates the form of the Renaissance painting's illusionary, three-dimensional 'space'. Like a painting's perspective, it frames a determined view (determines a view), creating a point of focus – meaning – organized around a central vanishing point. The customer's gaze is focused upon the centered object's external form; focus creates value.[5]

The conditions of the not-live of both cinema and theatre infect each other along the axis of the architecture of reception and its history that they also share and of which they are also an aesthetic, economic, critical and political function: the auditorium.

Three (The Idea of the Live)

If the auditorium – definitively idealised (realised), let us say, in Wagner's opera house at Bayreuth in Germany since 1876 as a perfect, 'pure' space for total immersion (sound, light, image: invisible apparatus) – functions against a construction of liveness, the obvious and easiest way to initiate its reintroduction would be to remove this architecture and its paradigms as a possible location. The history of performance art is often read as such. Positioned most recently by Claire Bishop as a de- or re-skilled subset of theatre where the proximity between performer and audience is recalibrated (intensified) by the same-time, same-place effect of the fully lit white cube of the gallery space, which replaces the immersive, black box of the divided theatrical auditorium (lit stage, darkened auditorium), it is also characterised by a rejection of virtuosic display that accompanied such a shift. But might not the theatrical auditorium also be a location for the same mobilisation of desire that Bishop ascribes to de-skilled performances?[6]

Leaving aside an argument based on reading experimental film as a subset of industrial ('Hollywood') cinema as proof of its coincidence with performance art as a subset of theatre – their similar histories, entering into the discourses of contemporary art via a challenge to the institution by the politics of the dematerialised art object and conceptual practices of the post-happenings, film co-op-spawning Golden Age of the late 1960s and 70s – the auditorium becomes a productive limit or a dialectical location containing all the potential of a crumpled heap. Far from being eliminated, it is the function by which a set of terms are generated, however wildly, that pertain to the live, peculiarly defining it as the product of a cross-feed between cinema and theatre, proposing, however perversely, a certain kind of cinema *as* live. What then is liveness? Where do we find it?

Before cinema assumed the fully industrialised form in which we receive it today (in the form of a post-Wagnerian *dispositif*), early descriptions of what happened there – its potential – differ significantly from those of the subjected, gendered, manipulated or disciplined bodies of its audience. Consider, for example, the cinema reportage of Dorothy Richardson's column 'Continuous *Performance*' (emphasis mine) in 1928:

> ... here we are and there she is. In she comes and the screen obediently ceases to exist. If when finally she attends to it – for there is first her toilet to think of, and then her companion, perhaps not seen since yesterday – she is disappointed, we all hear of it ... her conversation proceeds uninterrupted. And to this we do not entirely object.

> ... all her bad manners that will doubtless be pruned when the film becomes high art and its temple a temple of stillness save for the music that at present inspires her to do her worst, she is innocently, directly, albeit unconsciously, upon the path that men have reached through long centuries of effort and of thought. She does not need, this type of woman clearly does not need, the illusions of art to come to the assistance of her own sense of existing. Instinctively she maintains a balance, the thing perceived and herself perceiving ... She takes all things currently. Free from man's pitiful illusion of history, she sees everything in terms of life ...

[She] testifies that life goes on, art or no art and that the onlooker is a part of the spectacle.[7]

Richardson had more aspirations for this new situation: 'Cinema... is a medium, or a weapon... The new film can, at need, assist Radio in turning the world into a vast council chamber...'[8] She answers, a few months prior, Bertolt Brecht's frustrated desire for that other medium: 'As for the radio, I don't think it can consist merely in bringing back cosiness to the home and making family life bearable again. But quite apart from its dubious functions, radio is one-sided when it should be two.' Richardson echoes Brecht's suggestion to: 'change this apparatus over from distribution to communication... to receive as well as to transmit... to let the listener speak as well as hear... [to] bring him [*sic*] into a relationship... [to] step out of the supply business and organize its listeners as suppliers...'[9] And this is a sentiment no less reflected by his own model of a new type of theatre to replace 'the theatre as we know it [which] shows the structure of society (represented on the stage) as incapable of being influenced by society (in the auditorium)' with one 'which not only releases the feelings, insights and impulses possible within the particular historical field of human relations in which the action takes place but employs and encourages those thoughts and feelings which help transform the field itself'.[10] And it is this model of theatre that informs Peter Gidal's 'Theory and Definition of Structural/Materialist Film', perhaps also, now, the model of a cinema:

> Structural/Materialist film attempts to be non-illusionist. The process of the film's making deals with devices that result in demystification or attempted demystification of the film process.... In Structural/Materialist film, the in/film (not in/frame) and film/ viewer material relations, and the relations of the film's structure are primary to any representational content.[11]

Read, then (again), Alain Badiou, summarising the 'collective dimension of theatre' during the introductory conversation to the art exhibition 'A Theatre Without Theatre':

Theatre is the exemplary artistic form of an immediate liaison
between temporal form (the present) and spatial form (the presence
of a crowd in a place). The idea of performance, anticipated as it was
by Meyerhold and several others throughout the twentieth century
(like Agit-prop theatre and its link to revolutionary experiences),
consisted in treating this liaison as a shared act, as an indistinction
between the time of the idea and the space of the crowd... the intersection between the idea of participation, the construction of
a new collective, and another requirement of contemporary art;
that of the importance of improvisation and openness to chance.[12]

Badiou's theatre and *a particular kind* of cinema are constituted as
a political threat. Not because of the power of persuasion implemented
by an architecture of control but because of a capacity for facilitating instability, that is, a shared world creation predicated not on the
evacuated, depoliticised present represented by *narrative* cinema but
by the construction of an immediate, inevitably politicised, unstable
present in which, as a matter of form, of a form *in use*, viewers are
complicit as Badiou suggests. Dan Graham describes such complicity
as the property of another medium also – video:

Video is a present-time medium. Its image can be simultaneous
with its perception by/of its audience (it can be the image of its
audience perceiving). The space/time it presents is continuous,
unbroken, and congruent with that of the real time which is the
shared time of its perceivers and their individual and collective
real environments.... In a live-video-situation, the spectator may
be included within the frame at one moment, or be out of the
frame at another moment... video feeds back.[13]

The model then for this model of the complicity of video (cinema, theatre) as a feedback loop with political potential is located by William
Kaizen in yet another medium: television – in spite of its ideological
operations – *because* its template is an idea of the live.

Kaizen argues that video was always already coded as 'live' because
of its use in broadcast television and that since its inception in the
1950s television generated 'its reality effect from always seeming to

be live because it always opens onto the possibility of continuous live transmission... even when not live, television seems live'.[14] He continues: 'in live television, no matter how carefully scripted or composed the presentation, the threat of disaster lurks':[15]

> ... it is as if it [television – etymologically 'far-seeing', tele-vision, bringing something far away close to] were a window that tunnelled through to another place, opening directly onto the event shown. In this it is closer, both rhetorically and technically, to the present tense of theatre than to film.[16]

The event shown is in the room. And the room is in the event shown. At which point a material hallucination under pressure of which those perspective lines of the proscenium theatre are radically re-imagined, their function challenged and reconstituted... Imagine for example, a diagram of the Greek amphitheatre. It looks like a fan, the pivot of which is the circular stage surrounded by its banks of grandstand seating that span out around it. In the diagram, the steps by which the seats are accessed are radial struts, their fulcrum the middle of the circular stage. Read (backwards) from the perspective of the Renaissance, the centre of the circular stage, in diagram form, is revealed as a focal point. It is the vanishing point of the lines of perspective into which the bodies of spectators are themselves organised by the architecture of their seating in relation to the stage. Such an arrangement might subject an audience to the power of persuasion, of the story being told, but the story was often already known, perspective as an optical device was not, the stage is not framed like a picture but experienced as a 'perspective' field in which the audience is actually also sat, able to see the actors and also each other. The time and space of the auditorium extends into that of what is being shown, it is organised into it, not reorganised by it. Performer, audience, mirror.

This diagram we have imagined is mirrored in the auditoria of the Baroque: you are sat inside a box in the dress circle of the theatre; your own curtain is swept back along the lines of the arch that frames the front of your box, your view. This view almost exactly replicates the proscenium arch of the stage, its own curtain swept back to reveal an on-stage architecture that repeats the stone columns of the auditorium that also frame it, illusorily diminishing in size to a vanishing point the lines of which extend directly from you, uninterrupted, let us say, into the stage-space to an imaginary focal point, at an impossible distance away that is also absolutely present as if you yourself have been tunnelled through space and time or what is shown tunnels to you – subject of an immediate present. And you realise that actually you are sat inside an eighteenth-century feedback loop that comes from materialist film, and/or (strange, I know) video, via television, as cinema, in the theatre. Like it, you are live.

But I digress. I've made this reading up, based on a diagram I saw of a Greek amphitheatre and a photograph of the finest of one of Europe's few remaining Baroque theatres at the Český Krumlov Palace in the Czech Republic. But my fantasy is not one of Wagnerian total immersion. It is a model of complicity that is thrown into relief, with revealing irony, by another, altogether more strict model of a cinema – an actual auditorium that did once exist: Peter Kubelka's *Invisible Cinema*, designed by the filmmaker as the first auditorium of Anthology Film Archives in New York, is instructive here for what it mitigates against.

The *Invisible Cinema* is well documented and railed against as being disciplinarian. It was intentionally so. A pure black box where the only light source is the screen itself, spectators are separated from one another by panels dividing their seats at eye level like blinkers so that only the screen can be seen. It is anticipated as a structure by the early French theorist Jean Goudal's description of the ideal auditorium as a place where:

> Our problems evaporate, our neighbours disappear. Our body itself submits to a sort of temporary depersonalisation which takes away the feeling of its own existence... the darkness of the auditorium destroys the rivalry of real images that would contradict the ones on the screen.[17]

If we bristle at the reported austerity of this space, or if this room seems out of step with other developments in experimental film of the time – in particular the practice of expanded cinema – then Kubelka makes its purpose clear:

270

This kind of cinema is not for multimedia, multi-screen, multiple speakers or for live action mixed with film. ... There is nothing really radical in this project, this is normal cinema.[18]

If it looks different, it's because other theatres are abnormal. They are like living rooms equipped with huge television sets.[19]

By this Kulbelka means, I think, that the television set in a living room is seen in a context and watched inattentively – a lack of attention that John Berger alternatively seeks to rectify in episode one of his 1972 BBC television series on art and its mediation, *Ways of Seeing*, by addressing the viewer directly:

> Botticelli's *Venus and Mars* [c. 1483] used to be a unique image which it was only possible to see in the room where it was actually hanging. Now its image [by television] ... can be seen in a million different places at the same time. As you look at [these images] now, on your screen, your wallpaper is round them, your window is opposite them, your carpet is below them. At this same moment they are on many other screens surrounded by different objects, different colours, different sounds. You are seeing them in the context of your own life. They are surrounded not by gilt frames but by the familiarity of the room you are in and the people around you.[20]

Whether we like it or not, the *Invisible Cinema* is, for sure, no feedback loop; and it is not for the kind of cinema that we now call expanded, a practice more literally live than my own assisted speculations about the auditorium. By implication expanded cinema could be defined also as the set of things that the *Invisible Cinema* is not: abnormal, social, physical, personal-political, a room (not a screen), with visible apparatus and operators, plural (multimedia, multi-speakers), a situation of live action and a (Marxist!) television set.

What Dan Graham writes about video and William Kaizen of its template, television, becomes exemplary in this regard. Therefore, expanded cinema could be considered as a practice that extends or multiplies the frame of the screen to incorporate what is happening in the screening room itself, to include space, movement, live speaking, to incorporate the corporeality of the spectator as also constituting the work itself through relative, physical positions in space. Perhaps a literally moving image, an artwork that is contingent upon the instability of performance and meaning that is constituted more by a multifaceted response mediated by these things than visual reception alone, expanded cinema might also be figured as a special case of the feedback loop in which the viewer becomes multiply complicit: complicit because the viewer (the receiver of this work) is also one of the work's prime agents, or actors. Regarded as such – as a medium defined by the limit of the auditorium that it functions against – expanded cinema finds its own apotheosis in the work of art as an instruction, where the frame of the work is multiplied and extended not only into the room where the work is viewed but also disintegrating these physical limits to occupy the world at large – life, itself, material.

There is no clearer an example of this than the work of Orders & Co. that Mike Sperlinger describes in his essay, 'Orders! Conceptual Art's Imperatives'. With no named operators, Orders & Co. sent a series of cards to the President of Uruguay in 1971 that co-opted him, irrespective of his will, into unavoidably performing a work that simultaneously inverted both a separation between art and life and the usual: 'relationship between orderers and those ordered, breaking the vicious circle of power'.[21] The only surviving evidence of these instructions is collected in Lucy Lippard's source book, *Six years: The dematerialization of the art object from 1966 to 1972...*, no primary documents exist:

> Oct 5: Our next order is for the 15th of October. That day you will take special care to button your pants before going out into the street. Oct 30: The 5th of November you will simulate normal walking but you will be conscious that for this day Orders & Co. have taken possession of every third step you take. It is not necessary to obsess yourself with this.[22]

Sperlinger argues that the instruction work, characterised in part as a 'rhetoric of withdrawal', with all the paradoxes that an artwork based on such terms confronts, finds its 'limit-case' in Lee Lozano's *General Strike Piece, Feb. 8th, 1969* (1969):

272

Gradually but determinedly avoid being present at official or public 'uptown' functions or gatherings related to the 'art world' in order to pursue investigation of total personal & public revolution. Exhibit in public only pieces which further sharing of ideas and information related to total personal & public revolution.
In process at least through summer, '69.[23]

Four (___)

The body is a promise. Removing it – its *like*ness – is a political act.
Political cinema, political theatre are live. What is this –

LIVENESS?
MATERIAL
ACCIDENT
SIMULTANEITY
DISRUPTION
DISORDER
THREAT
          COMMUNITY
PROVISIONAL COMMUNITY
VIDEO
FEEDBACK LOOP
VIDEO   RADIO
VIDEO   RADIO   CINEMA
VIDEO   RADIO   CINEMA   TELEVISION
THEATRE
POSSIBILITY
          RADIO   CINEMA   TELEVISION
IMMEDIACY
                  CINEMA   TELEVISION
ABNORMAL
                           TELEVISION
SOCIAL
PHYSICAL
PERSONAL
EXISTENCE
SPACE
VISIBLE
REALITY
PLURAL
ACTION
IMMATERIAL
THEATRICAL
WITHDRAWAL.

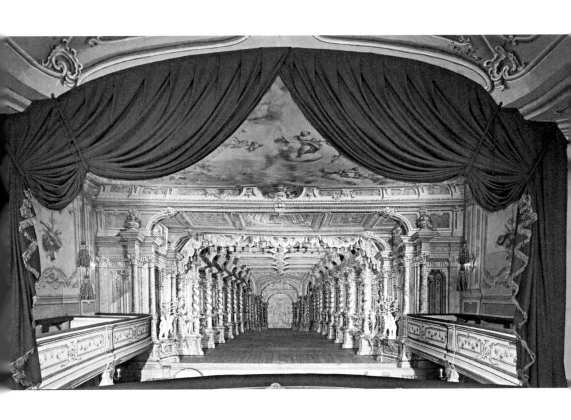

Interior of Český Krumlov Baroque Theatre, Prague.

1. This text is based on two seminar series that I gave in London: '6 or more kinds of theatre', no.w.here, September to October 2010, and 'Performer, Audience, Mirror: Cinema, Theatre and the Idea of the Live', LUX, September to October 2011. As such I am genuinely indebted to all those who participated in both series and to the generosity and versatility of our conversations, which I aspire to reflect.
2. Dan Graham, 'Essay on Video, Architecture and Television' (1979), in *Dan Graham: Video/Architecture/Television: Writings on Video and Video Works 1970–1978*, ed. Benjamin H. D. Buchloh (Halifax: The Press of the Nova Scotia College of Art and Design, 1979).
3. Gertrude Stein, 'Plays', *Look at Me Now and Here I am: Writing and Lectures, 1909–45* (1967), ed. Patricia Meyerowitz (London: Peter Owen Publishers, 2004), p.59.
4. Lis Rhodes, 'Whose History?' (1979), in *Film as Film: Formal Experiment in Film 1910–75*, exhibition catalogue, ed. Deke Dusinberre and A. L. Rees (London: Hayward Gallery, 1979), pp.119–20.
5. Graham, 'Essay on Video, Architecture and Television', op. cit., p.58. 'In the U.S. in the late 1950s, performance art... took place in the actual space-time of the viewer, and these contingencies of location and audience were often factored into the work. The incontrovertible frisson of real life was the steering principle; no suspension of disbelief was necessary because everything was purportedly "real."' / '... the best forms of de-skilling evoke in the viewer something of... spectralization: such works generate in us not a disdainful "I could do that" but the generative energy of "I want to do that!"', Claire Bishop 'Unhappy Days in the Art World', *The Brooklyn Rail* (10 December 2011), available at http://www.brooklynrail.org/2011/12/art/unhappy-days-in-the-art-worldde-skilling-theater-re-skilling-performance [last accessed on 10 January 2016].

6. Dorothy Richardson, 'Continuous Performance VIII', *Close Up*, vol.2, no.3 (March 1928), reprinted in *Close Up, 1927–33: Cinema and Modernism*, ed. James Donald, Anne Friedberg and Laura Marcus (London: Cassell, 1998), p.175–76.

7. Dorothy Richardson, 'Continuous Performance: The Film Gone Male', *Close Up*, vol.9, no.1 (March 1932), reprinted in *Close Up, 1927–33: Cinema and Modernism*, op. cit., p.207.

8. Bertolt Brecht, 'The Radio as an Apparatus of Communication' (1932), in *Brecht on Theatre: The Development of an Aesthetic*, trans. and ed. John Willett (London: Methuen, 1964), p.52.

9. Bertolt Brecht, 'A Short Organum for the Theatre' (1949), in *Brecht on Theatre: The Development of an Aesthetic*, op. cit., pp.189–90.

10. Peter Gidal, 'Theory and Definition of Structural/Materialist Film', in *Structural Film Anthology*, ed. Peter Gidal (London: British Film Institute, 1976), p.1.

11. 'A Theatre of Operations, A Discussion Between Alain Badiou and Elie During', in *A Theater Without Theater*, exhibition catalogue, ed. (Barcelona: Museu d'Art Contemporani de Barcelona; Lisbon: Fundação de Arte Moderna e Contemporânea – Colecção Berardo, 2007), p.25.

12. Graham, 'Essay on Video, Architecture and Television', op. cit., p.52.

13. William Kaizen, 'Live on Tape: Video, Liveness and the Immediate', in *Art and the Moving Image: A Critical Reader*, ed. Tanya Leighton (London: Tate Publishing and Afterall, 2008), p.264.

14. Ibid., p.264.

15. Ibid., pp.263–64.

16. Jean Goudal, 'Surrealism and Cinema' (1925), quoted in Noam M. Elcott, 'On Cinematic Invisibility: Expanded Cinema Between Wagner and Television', in *Expanded Cinema: Art, Performance and Film*, ed. A. L. Rees, David Curtis, Duncan White and Steven Ball (London: Tate Publishing, 2011), p.44.

17. Peter Kubelka, *Design Quarterly*, no.93, 1974.

18. Peter Kubelka, quoted in *The New York Times*, 29 November 1970.

19. Author's own transcription from the television programme.

20. From a letter accompanying the copies of Orders & Co.'s instructions sent to Lucy Lippard, quoted in Mike Sperlinger, 'Orders! Conceptual Art's Imperatives', in *Afterthought: New Writing on Conceptual Art*, ed. Mike Sperlinger (London: Rachmaninoffs, 2005), p.1.

21. Orders & Co., quoted in ibid., p.2.

22. Ibid., p.19.

What is Material?

Is allegory material? Ordinarily not. Published in 1980, Craig Owens's famous essay 'The Allegorical Impulse: Toward a Theory of Postmodernism'[1] telescopes the allegorical from Walter Benjamin's discussion of it in *The Origin of German Tragic Drama* into an observation of artistic strategies and critical theory from which it had been excluded for 'nearly two centuries as an aberration, the antithesis of art' (and by doing so assumes something of the allegorical impulse itself). His argument moves by way of a range of canonical (and other) non-sites, bookended by Robert Smithson: the photographic in Marcel Duchamp, Robert Rauschenberg's copying, the appropriations of Sherrie Levine, Robert Longo, sequence-as-structure in Sol LeWitt, Hannah Darboven, 'dissolution', 'decay', *Spiral Jetty*. That is, its progress is mapped by a specific set of immaterialities, of (art) objects as a double helix of preservation and evacuation that also defines them. Form here is an evacuated one, a gap between the remoteness of the past and its redemption; that collapse of time that is also transitory, a unique and nonetheless impressive type of vacuum. Time, as Smithson writes, as 'a place minus motion'.[2] Categories *and* material in the modernist sense are disregarded, subject to a particular kind of obliteration as a condition of their use, mechanisms of conveyance, that turns them into an outline only, where both it and they are known only by a supplementary act of reading, *in* time – which is also an emptying – and tilts them towards the disposable.

279

A version of this text was first published in *Ruth Buchanan: The weather, a building* (Berlin: Sternberg Press, 2012). The version reproduced here is reconstructed from an earlier draft, and includes an additional section at the end that White wanted to include in the present volume.

Allegory is linked in this way to something like an aesthetics of disintegration, the characteristics of which are also those of Smithson's equally famous borrowing of the second law of thermodynamics (or, entropy) as a model of the contemporary condition, of not only some of the art he saw around him, but also of life itself – to which it is often tied. Smithson's image of it is well known:

> Picture in your mind's eye [a] sand box divided in half with black sand on one side and white sand on the other. We take a child and have him run hundreds of times clockwise in the box until the sand gets mixed and begins to turn grey; after that we have him run anti-clockwise, but the result will not be a restoration of the original division but a greater degree of greyness and an increase of entropy.[3]

Seen in this way, all systems are processes of disintegration, the circulation of parts towards their indivisibility, invisibility. This degenerative spiral into sameness is erasure, producing an inertia even in the act of looking. But move closer. Get really close. Step into the box and bend down. What is there is not what you saw before. The individual grains of sand in Smithson's pit are not grey, but still black and white. The analogy only holds for as long as we occupy a fixed position of inviolable, immaterial perception. 'Greyness' is the impression of a colour from a fixed perspective. Only in this way does looking become blindness.

Let's ask again: is allegory material?

It is a thing of figures. The allegorical figure is something like a vessel, an empty form or a structure that is both a function of and subject to simultaneous orders of preservation and evacuation that depend upon each other. It is the figure of something to be read, an image borrowed for the express purpose of conveying a message and nothing else, no thing. It is a site, constituted by a drive for preservation and an act of evacuation, where nothing exists for the sake of an always-having-existed, that commands the impression of stability from what is in fact a set of contingencies. What its 'message' is, how it becomes known, is contingent upon an act of interpretation, which is

280

to say that its message is not (its) material, but that its material is contingency itself, something subject to time and interaction even as the very refutation of these things might be its form, its outline. Its outline that is no more solid than a cluster of fault lines.

Preservation. Let us say that Bronzino's *An Allegory with Venus and Cupid* (c.1545) is an allegory because it is called so, and that even if you cannot picture it, it is a painting that hangs in the National Gallery in London. Does it matter that you cannot see it? What would you see if you could? A rectangular arrangement of bodies, ordered, shaped, holding things and given character by the frame within which they are painted? Here is what the gallery tells us we would see:

> The picture is *likely* to be that mentioned in Vasari's *Life of Bronzino* of 1568: [...] a nude Venus with Cupid kissing her, and on one side Pleasure and Play with other Loves; and on the other, Fraud, Jealousy and other passions of love. Venus and Cupid are identifiable by their attributes, as is the old man with wings and an hourglass who must be Time (not mentioned by Vasari). The identity of the other figures, and the meaning of the picture remain *uncertain*.
>
> The howling figure on the left has been *variously* interpreted as Jealousy, Despair *and* the effects of syphilis; the boy scattering roses and stepping on a thorn as Jest, Folly *and* Pleasure; the hybrid creature with the face of a girl, as Pleasure *and* Fraud; and the figure in the top left corner as Fraud *and* Oblivion.[4] (My italics.)

Neither they nor I nor you know what you would see even if you did see this painting, *because* it is an allegory, an indeterminacy belied by an otherwise direct address to the viewer. We 'likely' find ourselves, but in difficulty, or at least 'uncertain', 'variously' as the keepers, or measurers 'and' the measure of the picture.

Evacuation. A building or a city might be evacuated of objects or people because of the risk to its contents that are considered to be more

281

valuable or irreplaceable than the architecture which contained them
and which is discarded as useless, or at least is then no longer in use.
Vital contents perhaps because they are what we need to be able to go
on, their removal that of something like human life. Pre-emptive, in
this way evacuation is most literally linked to a guaranteeing of reproduction by which the impulse to preserve might otherwise be known.

But the allegorical form aligns the two – preservation and evacuation – by a different axis. Rather than maintaining or reasserting the
content status of that which is displaced by re-presenting the thing
itself, allegory occupies instead the abandoned container, the 'empty'
structure in the form of a figure, the figure of a building perhaps,
but also that of a lifeless object or a body, and this has implications.
Such, for example, as may be thought about as the difference between
a speaking subject that defines herself, displaced but nonetheless
before us, with the utterance 'I am an evacuee', and the evacuated site
that can only be known by a kind of repurposing, where to say 'it is'
can only testify to something that is not, or is not before us any more
and so can only be relational.

Occupied, the evacuated site is somewhere known – that is,
through its intersection by a re-use or a new use, a re-inscription
that necessarily produces an act of reading, that in turn effects a
renaming. Constituted between what it once was and what it is now,
or what it might be. Many-voiced. Facing opposite directions at the
same time. Self-surrendered. The evacuated site is emptied and by
being so becomes both multiple and contingent, collapsed and/as a
special function of time: an anywhere that could also be somewhere
in particular.

What is important here is that if it is a subject at all, this occupied place I have been describing is a split one, a site of production (it
multiplies) or a location for allegory. Allegory is, in other words, axial
rather than immaterial: an *axis* of disintegration, the metal of which is
both its own material and, by being so, also the framework of a count-
er-proposition to the conditions of entropy with which it has been most
commonly associated. A photograph is allegorical, as is almost any collection, or collecting, or container. A library, for example. Whether all

282

of these are *inevitably* entropic, if one requirement is a kind of invisibility that we could also describe as immaterial, is a different question, or even, simply more of a question than a given. Smithson:

> Like the movies and the movie houses, 'printed-matter' plays an entropic role. Maps, charts, advertisements, art books, science books, money, architectural plans, math books, graphs, diagrams, newspapers, comics, booklets and pamphlets from industrial companies are all treated the same. [Donald] Judd has a labyrinthine collection of 'printed-matter', some of which he 'looks' at rather than reads. By this means he might take a math equation, and by sight, translate it into a metal progression of structured intervals.[5]

That Judd transferred one set of indistinctions (the things he looked at but did not read) into another (the nothing of intervals) is clear. Smithson could also have called such symptomatically entropic circulation 'submission'. But might making (art) in fact be reading by another name, as a different action that is also *resistance*?

The Staatsbibliothek Berlin, read, *re*worked, is the material of this book inasmuch as reading this book is also an action.[6] Matter is made here of three points in time when the institution itself was subject to its own kind of splitting: the temporary evacuation of its own contents, the doubling from its original home on Unter den Linden to Potsdamer Strasse and the interior design of this new building. Intervals perhaps, but *of* time, as a continuous oscillation between doing and undoing, subject to environmental pressure, but not collapsed into a vacuum. Diagrammatically figured as interactions, they are the stuff of a reorganisation of subject positions: inscriptions as opposed to erasures, by which reading is not like looking at a sandpit framed as if it were a picture, but an almost physical relocation into and becoming its raw material, grains of sand *as* seeing. An act of making. Staatsbibliothek Berlin is any library and one library in particular, the emblem of an allegory (preserved, evacuated, disintegrated) and allegory as an evacuated site itself, occupied in the form of a book. Points in its time are intersected as interactions in which the reader is complicit.

This book is not alone.

283

'This book is not alone', as a written sentence that you are reading, is something of a truism. But I mean it as something more determined than a redundant poetic invocation. Not every book, but this one. And not this one considered in isolation, but in the context of an artistic practice and a critical discourse that has so far only provided its shape; a vessel or a structure, a silent mechanism of conveyance.

This is, of course, the artist's practice as a whole that has informed the lines I've attempted to begin to draw through it here, as it is in the instance of this publication. But also a set of ideas in particular that are articulated in an essay by the feminist theorist Karen Barad, whose work extends into the cultural study of science. 'Posthumanist Performativity: Toward an Understanding of How Matter Comes to Matter'[7] pitches against the dominance of the representational, and of a theoretical semiotics, by re-positing the primacy of language as a problem to be questioned:

> The idea that beings exist as individuals with inherent attributes, anterior to their representation, is a metaphysical presupposition that underlies the belief in political, linguistic, and epistemological forms. ... This taken-for-granted ontological gap generates questions of the accuracy of representations. For example, does scientific knowledge accurately represent an independently existing reality? Does language accurately represent its referent? Does a given political representative, legal counsel, or piece of legislation accurately represent the interests of the people allegedly represented?[8]

There is much at stake in 'a *performative* understanding of discursive practices [that] challenge the representationalist belief in the power of words to represent pre-existing things',[9] not only that language might not be the exclusive, exclusively immaterial location of meaning. Barad challenges the equal primacy of the subject position from which we speak in order to know as a hierarchical, pure division: between thought, let's say, and matter, or material; measurer and measured. In her new arrangement this act of division is recast as an impure instance of mutual production (inflection, infection) from a particular starting position. A specifically material 'intra-action' that

284

Barad distinguishes from 'interaction', as perhaps a kind of interaction-with-complicity, a rejection of the implication that two distinct, separate entities could ever exist in the first place. But this is no model of entropy. Instead, the intra-action has a special characteristic in the form of what Barad terms the 'agential cut':

> A specific intra-action (involving a specific material configuration of the 'apparatus of observation') enacts an *agential cut* (in contrast to the Cartesian cut – an inherent distinction between subject and object) effecting a separation between 'subject' and 'object'. That is, the agential cut enacts a *local* resolution.[10]

Which is to say that the agential cut performs a specific kind of measuring that is as such already loaded as an *enactment* (a practice as opposed to a representation) and is the *only* means by which distinctions can be made. In a footnote Barad cites an example that torques the picture-plane of Smithson's sandpit into an altogether different kind of system, one without a frame:

> When light passes through a two-slit diffraction grating and forms a diffraction pattern it is said to exhibit wavelike behaviour. But there is also evidence that light exhibits particle-like characteristics, called photons. ... The diffraction apparatus could be modified in such a way as to a allow a determination of which slit a given photon passes through. ... The result ... is that the diffraction pattern is destroyed! Classically, these two results together seem contradictory [but] the objective referent [here, light] is not some abstract, independently existing entity but rather the phenomenon of light intra-acting with the apparatus. ... The notions of 'wave' and 'particle' do not refer to inherent characteristics of an object that precedes its intra-action. There are no such independently existing objects with inherent characteristics. The two apparatuses effect different cuts, that is, draw different distinctions delineating the 'measured object' from the 'measuring instrument'.[11]

Only in and of the act of measuring itself is a subject differentiated from an object, as 'subject' and 'object', because they are always already equally matter. And the abstract is not superior, or exterior, to the actual – they

285

produce each other, as material. 'Seeing', by this means, is material. Or the weather, a building, for example. 'Things do not have inherently determinate boundaries or properties, and words do not have inherently determinate meanings.'[12] A curtain blows in the wind and this could mark the inside or the outside, but neither is fixed, they are together in a situation where they produce each other. The line is drawn and the line changes. The space on either side of the curtain increases and decreases. The words 'inside' and 'outside' in this instance are performative, not representational, and as such, material. The container is not defined by its boundary, but indeterminate, produced as an action. This library is as much the storm that collapsed a tent as a waterless fountain.

Allegory, reworked into constituent co-conditions, is released from its association with the entropic as an inevitability and recast as a condition of unpredictability that is nonetheless planned for. Time produces place as a temporary arrangement and not as something exterior to that within it, which is also us: performer, audience, furniture, props, signs, proximity, distance, light, air. Body, cupboard, brain, galaxy. Such are the provisional constellations that we could also 'see' here, as functions not of submission but as an arrangement not only in/of time but also as things perceived, the thing of perceiving, as heightened states of observation made. While they might not reverse terminal decline, they nonetheless produce distinctions, which is also political. Resistance occurs at the point of circulation.

This book is not alone. 'Nothing Is Closed', in the book *Lying Freely*,[13] is Part I of the book's three diagrammatic transcripts of performances. This first one is a visit to the Rietveld Schröder Huis in Utrecht, an archive, or a site cut through, during the course of the visit – and like the city itself (the performance began with a bus ride) – by another site, the Hocken Library and Archive of Dunedin, New Zealand, in relation to the work of the author Janet Frame, in the form of images presented and discussed, dissected as a means of dissection. Interpolated are the rules and conditions, preventions, options, physical positions, actions, inactions, perceptions, permissions of our interactions in this space/these spaces, that exist for the already-having-existed. Actually, in my context, here, paraphrasing it or its text seems (I hope obviously) worse than futile. Here are some of its sentences, which even now it is difficult to isolate, but that might be more what I mean. The speaker is a tour guide, the artist:

> ... action, event, memory, daydream, may not occur at eye level
> – rather it may appear, situate itself, slightly behind, slightly
> above, in between. This defiance of eye level demands that we
> act ... to further increase levels of frustration ...

> One holds their head down and holds their breath through
> and in, until the specifics, like the image, are transformed into
> a single point. The archive user is asked to understand material
> in this way, this is the work of the archive, to create an infinite
> amount of fixed points, and each fixed point is fixed, complete,
> and just as we are asked to hold our heads down and look
> at what is now known as a reference, we see the problem. ...

> The reference becomes an inaccurate mirror, the archive
> a space of endless division.

> P a u s e

> But what of this gap? What if one were to try and manoeuvre
> in this gap, to relate to it...

There cannot be a critical commentary, now, but the local present, 'P a u s e'. It is a stage direction. The otherwise incidental is choreographed, a note to self, inscripting:

> M o v e   w i t h   t h e   g r o u p   t o   t h e   b u s ,
> s t a n d   a t   t h e   e n t r a n c e   o f   t h e   b u s .

It is your own map to draw, but 'Nothing Is Closed' stands for the other two parts of the book and their circulations around the space, time and material of two other writers, more places, vacancies, Agatha

Christie and Virginia Woolf, as they stand for each other. As an exhibition stood for them, 'Lying Freely', and a book, and every vice versa. As the bodies of previous audiences (now as readers) are scripted into Part II, 'Circular Facts', stumbled over 'in a group or scattered around the room' by consecutive ones. As 'humans, like animals and buildings' in Part III, 'Several Attentions' are impressed there or embedded into another work, the video *Build A Wall or Be A Room* (2008), as a tiny change of lighting, affected, again, by the wind. As its final words, 'it's wild', were written to be spoken, were spoken, are printed then heard again over headphones as the final words in the performance *Sculptor* (2010), and stand for that work's making matter of a system of communication – perception – by the configuration of three seating areas, an inaudible television clip on a monitor, and others, other people, seen through a screen of equally spaced black slats and a two-way mirror. This circulation is a specific arrest. Here are theatres of separation. It is the direct address of a looking away, already looked away.

Allegory, here, is material. An interval, occupied.[14]

1. Craig Owens, 'The Allegorical Impulse: Toward a Theory of Postmodernism', *October* 12 (Spring 1980), pp.67–86.
2. Robert Smithson, 'Entropy and the New Monuments' (1966), in *Robert Smithson: The Collected Writings*, ed. Jack Flam (Berkeley: University of California Press, 1996), p.11.
3. Robert Smithson, 'A Tour of the Monuments of Passaic, New Jersey' (1967), in *Robert Smithson: The Collected Writings*, op. cit., p.74.
4. From 'An Allegory with Venus and Cupid', The National Gallery website, <http://www.nationalgallery.org.uk/paintings/ bronzino-an-allegory-with-venus-and-cupid> [last accessed on 10 January 2016].
5. Smithson, 'Entropy and the New Monuments', op. cit., p.18.
6. [In the book in which this essay first appeared, *Ruth Buchanan: The weather, a building*, the artist Ruth Buchanan traces three narratives associated with the Staatsbibliothek zu Berlin (State Library of Berlin) – the splitting of the collection during the Second World War, the relocation of parts of the collection due to a major storm and the designing of its new interior – in order to examine the tension between the material contained in libraries and the forms by which that material is contained.]
7. Karen Barad, 'Posthumanist Performativity: Toward an Understanding of How Matter Comes to Matter', *Signs: Journal of Women in Culture and Society*, vol.28, no.3 (2008), pp.801–31.
8. Ibid., p.804.
9. Ibid., p.802.
10. Ibid., p.815. (Italics here and previously are Barad's.)
11. Ibid., pp.815–16n.
12. Ibid., p.813.
13. Ruth Buchanan, *Lying Freely* (Maastricht and Utrecht: Jan van Eyck Academie and Casco Office for Art, Design and Theory, 2010), unpaginated.
14. [In the earliest draft of this text, the 'interval' appeared literally as the last word. Instead of this last line, White had written: 'What is material?
" ".']

Statement for Appropriation and Dedication

I thought this was going to be straight forward, but it isn't.

In writing I am writing about my own work. Which of course is nothing of the sort – neither as a piece of writing, nor as the thing itself to which I am referring. What do I know. In my work, whether it's a piece of writing, a performance or something else, there is often a process of selection at play which is why I am writing about it here, I think.

In my performances in particular what is selected is often blatant – that is, it is either clearly visible (a film is shown, an object or a copy of one is presented) or audible (the radio is on, a recorded bell played) or physical (an action is repeated, a naked man is knitting) or visible-audible-physical (a wind machine is switched on, sentences are broken off artificially) or any other combination of these. In each work, selections are compiled with different senses, or no sense, of purpose. Of course, this isn't necessarily anything other than a general act of making: some things are included, others are not. But what is selected is often borrowed, it can be seen, and how it can be is important: what makes it noticeable might be an unnaturalistic pause between sentences as a text is read, a staged accident, risks or mistakes, contradictions, a proscenium arch. Any frame is a thrown voice. Division.

291

First published (without a title) as part of the programme for the seminar 'Appropriation and Dedication', organised by If I Can't Dance, I Don't Want To Be Part Of Your Revolution at the Goethe-Institut, Amsterdam in January 2013.

This process and its implications are not a strategy, they are more like a condition: not the default of all making, or a strategy *in*, but a condition *of* the work, of work, of conditions in general perhaps, which is what the work is. That's all. But it aims temporarily to reflect-suspend-dismantle that with which we might otherwise be familiar, or conditioned by, by those things being shown in the situations they were in, but are not any more, and the terms or conventions of our encounters. This is political. Nothing is taken exactly, but another situation is established that has characteristics, or maybe loses them, just as we do, or can – thank goodness.

But what do I know. What can I see? Nothing is owned because choices about material, let's say, have been made rather than something having been invented. And this has a lot of implications that have repercussions, two of which might be dependent upon each other: the introduction of time where it might not previously have been, or not in the same way at least, and a subjection to space.

Ordinarily an institution like a museum functions by subtracting time from the things it compiles, ourselves included (e.g. objects are preserved forever and we are reverent, as in silent), as if to subtract life itself. Maybe the time I am talking about introducing is better described as a function: a kind of discussion thought between what has been compiled, ourselves included, that could also be known as a correspondence in the way that the French use this word to describe the place where an interchange between one Métro line and another occurs. If this could be cast as the possibility of chance, and it cannot be.

Ourselves included. By which I mean, this process of selection is not an attempt to prove some*thing* to some*one*. Not taste, not access, not myself. But neither is it an abnegation of responsibility. It is an occupation, which is multiple, not an inscription, which is singular. It does not last, exactly. It is something to do that is also a repositioning against or because of its own grid which is temporary. It is not an address, it is material itself, a condition, etc., e.g. if I am speaking it is not to ask you to witness my feelings or what I am pretending to feel, which is nothing anyway. Here are no confessions. It is because the thing said is to be there, thrown from me, not of me. 'I'm not here'

292

cannot be spoken, stupid. But it is one way of describing agency. And desire. (I'm trapped.)

If objects that ordinarily are removed from time can have time introduced to them (again) for their own erasure, and this is political, so might the opposite be: a thrown voice or subjects subjected to something like architecture, a split. As we are, that is, amongst material.

Here is information. Mobilise.

Such a move-away, a pointing at something other than that which is there – or here – is always, can only be, a kind of comedy.

In. Adequate. Time. (Prisons 1)

Vladimir Nabokov's *Invitation to a Beheading* maps onto Peter Weiss's play *Marat/Sade*. Or it sort of does and it does so because they are both about prisons, of sorts, which is as much to say that they are about hospitals. In *'Beheading* a man is waiting (knowingly) for his execution, although he does not know and cannot find out the date when it will happen. Marat is in his bath waiting (without knowing he is of course) for his execution that is being shown to us in the form of a play directed by de Sade, staged in, and by the inmates of, an asylum. In both death sleepwalks towards and away from its subject, the extension of a kind of circus, a gaggle of cabaret or a chorus, having a laugh, pulled/withheld by forces of which we're sure even though we don't exactly know what they are. Time in this way becomes plastic, something is done, about-to-be-done, undone all at the same time, we move forwards and backwards in time. Now I'm not in prison nor do I feel like this sleepwalker or its subject. But I was in hospital and it was like this. By which I mean that hospitals, like prisons and asylums as they are described by Nabokov and Weiss are theatres of the worst kind.

In hospital doctors wheel through the curtains around a patient's bed as the intendants of C.'s prison in *'Beheading* enter his cell. The doctors and the patient are players to each other. It is a clash because there is no audience or no one who wants to be one. The bed is a stage and only the patient occupies it. And it has a world order, ordered

295

First published on White's blog *Lives of Performers* on 15 October 2012, <https://live-sofperformers.wordpress.com> [last accessed on 10 January 2016]. White began the blog shortly after his diagnosis with lymphoma, describing it as, 'a borrowed title from Yvonne Rainer's 1972 film. An occasional. A bumping into. A few wrong turns, probably. Not really about that film but of what could be got by/as this, as doing and other things, like, reading. A kind of "I'm still breathing."'

by conjecture, superstition, fear etc. That is, it is almost forced into being as much of an imaginary place as any other place represented on a particular kind of stage, with its own laws and its own languages, mainly internal, but there even if they are not spoken in the same way that C. in *'Beheading* does one thing while doing another, his body becoming two where one body acts upon his conjecture, or desire and is immaterial, and the other remains in reality not doing – the one might spit at someone, while the other stays seated.

But the curtains are the curtains and they open, and information is given, or a test conducted, let's say in what is also like an arena of competing persuasions. The doctors wheel through the curtains and they enter, but they do not leave their wheel. The time they spend is limited by its continued turning, irrespective of the information to be conveyed etc. Only in one way like those wooden figures on a Swiss clock. In other ways they have left nothing behind, nothing has changed, they are in their own play still, they smell of elsewhere, their clothes come from the outside, nothing changes in their language, they perhaps are subjects of the other kind to the patient. They are not ill. And to the patient who is us, they are absurd, more absurd because they have logic on their side and that's always kind of humiliating and disorientating, inserted into this other 'world', this other play, the patient's, which has its own order/disorder. Because not only does time become plastic there (nothing happens, everything happens, last Sunday may as well be last year) but the body is plastic too. The relationship to the body is indirect (as the person is an inconvenience between the doctor and the disease), informed, the body is shaped from the inside out by conjecture, imagination, desire even when it is known that these things are a bit stupid, not medical, pitiful and invariably hopeless. And when of course it would presumably be so much better in situations like this to have a direct relationship to the body and not to be inconvenient.

It is under these conditions that it should come as no surprise then that doctors lie. [We all lie, but with a different axis of responsibility.] Of course. How can they not? In a way, to lie is the condition of these conditions. They either lie because they are in the practice of doing so or because they want to get into the practice of doing so. And this is why it's worse than admitting a mistake. So if they'd said those samples we took were sent to the wrong lab rather than the results we got from them were inconclusive and all the other bullshit etc. for a week it wouldn't have made any difference perhaps, but it wouldn't have been consistent with this worst kind of theatre either.

Anyway, the floor of the outpatients is designed by Peter Blake. I nearly photographed my sneaker against it – heart, rainbow, building blocks, red, blue, yellow etc. – but we'd have vomited with the optimism. This is a teaching hospital. I like that, being a teacher sometimes. The doctor takes me into a side room to ask if I am willing to take part in a scheme where they pair a student doctor with a patient undergoing treatment. I feeling like a thinking, living person so I get a bit haughty and decide to say it like it is – that yeh, sure, these doctors could do with some help when it comes to learning how to be patient-focussed in just the way that hospitals need communications consultants (who would make a fortune. We're retraining to do this). I tell the doctor that I'm a teacher and that I believe in education but that as such really if they want me to be paired with one of these students then really that's what's going to happen – education. That I'll not hold back, can't guarantee I won't be awful, that the main problem most times is that these kids in this discipline have no critical relationship to their own methodology, don't imagine that a patient has any intelligence whatsoever etc etc. No doubt parts of this description at least are 'yeh-yeh' familiar to some of you reading this, but what's a boy to do. So, anyway, all this declamation accomplished, caveats issued, the doctor understands, I acquiesce and say that it's fine, I'll be paired.

We walk back into the doctor's room to meet the student with whom I am to be paired. And what do you know. Out flies my position from under me. Ha-ha-professional. Serves me right, or I'm served right... He's only the prettiest, blondest, most sparky-spunky bright-eyed little Bambi thing you ever saw. A slim-fitted, slept-in white shirt and bright turquoise tie like the one Jimmy bought me because it was hard to find. He's bobbling up and down where he's standing and still bobbling around when he sits down. He's blushing, almost

297

and I'm not even going to say that he had a handshake like damp bread. We can't look at each other for a kind of giggling that's too close to the surface. At the end of the meeting he passes me a form to read, and asks if he can come to my next chemo session and ask me questions about my private life. Any bloody time. I only half-turn my head, Marschallin-like and nod, to say he can and then I say that I'll try not to get snappy (he says he doesn't mind) and that if I do get snappy then this is something that we will just have to negotiate between ourselves and the doctor by this time is also in on the game and he says that's fine so long as it's not in his office. I miss Harry.

Chemo Round 2 today. If the floor is designed by Antony Gormley (there is one somewhere in the building) I'm going to write as many nasty things about ageing and his cock as I can.

F R E E (Prisons 2)

While we're on prisons, the other weekend I met my mum, Jackie, and my aunt, Sandra, for a cup of coffee in the Royal Festival Hall. Just for fun the authorities have reduced the number of chairs and tables there by about half which isn't really relevant here apart from in the way that someone in charge was nonetheless somewhere having a kind of laugh at everyone who wanted to sit down, like the laugh that More Power has at None, or at anyone for that matter subjected against their will and by necessity to the minor expression of More Power's petty sadism, including that of criminals, penal or cultural institutions, like for example when one buys balcony tickets in British theatres to feel that the physical pain and/or sensory deprivation we experience when we sit there are nothing less than deserved. Nonetheless and aptly, at the RFH first we were outside, then we were inside (because it got cold). Then we were about to leave but it had started to rain. So we were trapped.

Jackie and Sandra were at the RFH because they'd been to see the exhibition 'F R E E' CURATED BY SARAH LUCAS (by SARAH LUCAS the brand, not just a person with that name in the way anyone has a name). 'F R E E' is a 'showcase' (yep) of 'art by offenders, secure patients & detainees' (i.e. the NOT-'F R E E'-AT ALL?) organised by the Koestler Trust, where visitors (who I can only think the exhibition's title wants us to imagine are themselves The Free being referred to. Ha.

299

First published on White's blog *Lives of Performers* on 29 October 2012, <https://livesofperformers.wordpress.com> [last accessed on 10 January 2016].

Wishful thinking) have the very freedom to vote on their favourite of the works that Sarah (The Most Free) has pre-selected (because The Public/Free ought to be able to judge The Not-Free, after Sarah has of course, because The Public are after all better positioned to do so than the other way round for example, although not as better positioned as Sarah, all of which stands to REASON), and the maker will receive a special award in addition to the ones already distributed by the Trust. That must feel nice, to be in prison and to win a prize. And not to win a prize? Culture. Is it any wonder most of the entries are titled works whose makers share the name Anon?

In previous years this annual exhibition was curated by GROUPS of individuals 'with a close connection to the criminal justice system' (young people from Lambeth Youth Offending Scheme; female prisoners... etc.). But this year is special. Our Trust is 50 so the show is curated by a SINGLE individual, SARAH LUCAS [cue photo of Sarah looking pensive in a room heaped with Arts Stuff. Hold your chin with your hand, Sarah. Look down as if you are considering]. Kudos. If any of this is sounding tainted so far I'm really not doing that much more than re-twitting the accompanying booklet as Jackie, Sandra and I are deciding to go and see the show (for them, again), to do time until it stops raining outside (I was already ranting).

So that's what we did, stumbling onto the tail end of a free exhibition tour I think led by one of the 'ex-offender interns [*really real ex-offenders??! Really? Anyone for a nineteenth-century World Fair?*], all of whom are aged older than the Koestler Trust. Specially recruited... and trained... [for the exhibition, to] challenge the assumption that internships are for youngsters, [quite right, that's just the sort of assumption that it is imperative for us to challenge] *prey upon the older and already also widely reported as discriminated against* and help ~~give a voice~~ *provide cheap labour* to ~~prisoners aged over 50~~ *a self-congratulatory arts project despite its best intentions*' [italics – my insertions, obviously]. I couldn't stop to listen because my ears were too agog with what my eyes and then my mouth were taking in and pushing out, a kind of bodily convulsion/repulsion at being again cast in somewhere I didn't want to be, in the theatre of this theme park.

300

Whether or not she'd chosen the colour of the walls (prison grey) or the carpet (a mustard that convinced no one of sunshine), there were two things that Sarah did for sure introduce to the display: white ceramic toilet bowls, some just empty placed alongside/in between works, some as the support/display structure for selected paintings that spring out of or are being sucked in (either way like waste) to them on the end of coiled metal strips. This is what they looked like:

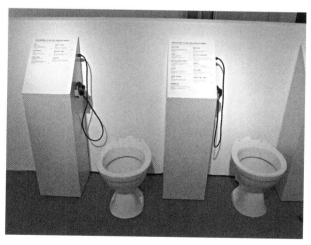

and grey breezeblocks that formed a kind of post-Andre plinth-on-a-plinth platform:

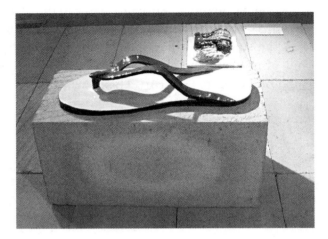

and a wall:

The painting displayed on this wall is called *Hope*:

I guess there's always been something like a revelling in just such a col-lapse that this kind of gimmick suggests in Sarah's own artwork but there, in her work, to me it is often astute, funny, belligerent, accurate – not so much an end of language but something more blatant and also complex to the extent that language just doesn't feel so necessary/useful/worth it. An upfront-ness that is an undone-ness. But the point is that 'F R E E' isn't an artwork. Sure, the checks and balances of cura-torial decisions can be as plastic as we like, but...

On the video documentary in the exhibition where Sarah describes her 'process' (not so dissimilar from the selection of favourites after all) she says that the breezeblocks and toilets are things she always uses in her artwork. So that while some visitors to the exhibition (like me) might think they refer to the construction of a prison theme décor, they are being a bit stupid and reducing them to one-liners, because actually they are not one-liners, because, well, because she always uses them in her artworks (none of which are here). That's alright then. Oh, Sarah.

Just because an artwork can be the site of a strategic 'lapse' of judge-ment of the most disgusting/liberating kind, when you think that art is life or the permission to behave in such a *sloppy* way to the work of others then it is *just* a belligerence, nothing more than privilege. But maybe you're right Sarah – I am simple, and 'F R E E' is actually

303

incredibly clever, because what occurs there is a nasty, insidious kind of inversion. It constructs the visitor as a character who you, Sarah, want us to be while having a laugh at us for being so. What really are you giving to who and who in relation to yourself? Ticketty-tip-toe down the prison corridor, la-di-da a lovely Sunday on the South Bank. 'Look at the little things that those have made who live in grey corridors and know breezeblocks as something other than material for an artwork. Oh I *can* just imagine. It makes me think of little Munchins all busy busy in their little cells. Cheeky little potters. Lovely. I don't know why, I just *like* it.' Of course it wouldn't be surprising if one of these characters moving around the exhibition would say, 'Look at that':

'Who'd've thought that someone in prison could make THAT?' Meaning, it's really good ('good'). Which actually didn't make me laugh but made me really angry and I wondered why the-person-in-prison is not us, or, me. Or could as easily be me as anyone else. Why not? It could be. And what might I make? Well, 'why not' here, in this show, is specifically because the prisoner-artists are also cast, they are also characters, definitely Not-Me's, subhuman, elsewhere, subjectless, encased, as in incarcerated, as figuratively as literally. And so I said to Jackie and Sandra, 'Maybe [the reason why such a thing could be made is because] all artists are now in prison. That is where they all are.' By which I meant that none of us are not in prison.

304

'F R E E 's construction of the visitor-as-character is a gross mediation, the smug rhetoric of this 'F R E E' and of all frees. As such it is a total misrecognition of what is actually brilliant in the artworks on display, which might generally be seen as a rebuttal, a refusal, a disregard of the standard kinds of mediation that otherwise condition artistic production and its associated economies that make 'Sarah Lucas's into brands rather than people and that of course are, by necessity and display reinscribed here by not much more than the holding power of Blu Tack or parcel tape made into a loop and used sparingly.

Right now, I couldn't care less about fighting any kind of art-ethical war over these things, about art as social work, rehabilitation, the ignorant lauding of personal expression or whatever else and all the fucked-up other lies the framing of this show spews in which you have more than a part and that ought to be stopped by the mark of respect on a common ground. You can get on with it. I can't be bothered/haven't got time. What's important to me is what there might be of use in all of this.

In the same way, two days ago I looked for something of what was advertised in Tate Modern's Collection Displays: 'Energy and Progress'; 'Structure and Clarity'. I'd like to say I found none of these things there because the idea that I was really looking for them is pretty funny, but that really wouldn't be true. I found again for the first time in years Matisse's late collage *The Snail* (1953):

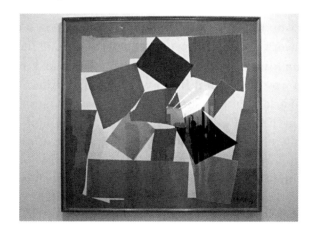

305

At school I scoffed and mocked this picture as if it were nothing. But now I don't. The story its wall text tells is much the same as the one I remember: 'Confined to bed through illness, [Matisse] had assistants paint sheets of paper in gouache which he then cut. [Which was the only thing he could do because his hands were so mangled with arthritis]. The shell of a snail inspired ['inspired'? *really*?!, 'inspired'?! Oh, please] the spiraling arrangement... '"I have attained a form filtered to its essentials" [Matisse] remarked.' Oh right – 'essential' – to....? But what clicked two days ago with what I am writing, its answer-without-a-question, was/is that in this picture it is Matisse's INability that we are looking at, and that also it cannot be seen by the institution without qualifying the work as 'inspired' (plain stupid: what isn't, then, or what is and when do You decide it is so?) and in the artist's own words as 'essential'. And this says more to me about who the institution(s) (museum/artist) want the viewer/reader to be than it does about anything like what this picture could mean – and by implication, who I do not want this person to be, who I do not want to be and where I might find meaning. Which is to say that there might be something to be said for something I've started already to say more often: that from this, ignoring all this other stuff, I propose regardless to take the thought that snares me, that

LIMIT IS MATERIAL.

Is to be in prison to be a player, in a play, a patient on a hospital bed, a player to players, the condition of this/my condition? In one way perhaps I am in a kind of prison defined by a particular kind of theatre, but there is a way out from it that I would prefer, different to the way where oneself is left behind, somewhere (i.e. escape/ism). This way out is not found in 'F R E E', which is really, precisely about this opposite and is not only made so by an act of reading, but by money, of course: 'F R E E' is supported by The Co-operative and 'The Co-operative's support for art and other offender rehabilitation projects has changed the lives and direction of a significant number of offenders...':

306

Visitor:	Oh really, in what direction has this change occurred?
Booklet:	...[The Co-operative's support] has contributed to a reduction in reoffending.
Visitor:	Oh good. That makes me feel nice about myself and all the non-offending values by which I already do and will continue to live, as if I have done this self-validating work too by coming to see the exhibition. Thank you very much.

This other escape that I think might be there or here may be no less of a fiction (because it is written), but it is urgent and hangs upon what this writing might in the end get to/be getting at, to be read as, do[?]: to be a description, a model for use, to work, of another particular kind of theatre that I have still to understand (even if it is nothing new) and still to write for myself. Of, but finally not to be described as a set of 'no's' or 'nots', because what there is to be jubilant about is that limit is everyone's material and it is always here. And this is where to start.

Points of information

1. Sorry this is a long one. Harry came to visit last week, which was great – he is my metronome – but obviously what there is to say built up.
2. For an absolutely excellent alternative way of organising exhibitions like 'F R E E' you might want to check the catalogue/evidence of 'Beyond Reason: Art and Psychosis' which was at the Hayward Gallery in the old days, Dec 1996–Mar 1997.
3. I am now pretty much bald. I don't mind it and once I'm past the slightly patchy ostrich fuzz it'll work just fine, but I know that there's a moment of digestion for some the first time they see it. Take this as prior...
4. A return to a little bit of GORMLEY'S BALLS and more of BAMBI L. THE STUDENT DOCTOR in the next post, I promise.

Removing the Minus

Another way of saying why it's OK in the Cancer Centre is because I do not feel like a subtraction there. And I am writing this not only to explain here the gymnastics involved in trying not to be a subtraction outside of the Cancer Centre, but also as a part of those gymnastics themselves which maybe existed already before any of this, for other reasons. But with regard to now what I mean is that if you don't watch out there's a default position in this game that infects your own life and the lives of others whereby:

$$\text{life} + \text{cancer} = -\text{life}$$

(as in, life plus cancer equals minus life)

Let's not do this. For one thing, life is always lived under some condition or other. But what's more is that this would be too much like not doing anything at all even though 'minus life' is no more 'death' than life without the minus is 'liberation'. I am not experiencing either of these right now anyway. Rather, it will be totally familiar to anyone who has had chemotherapy that we might better call this 'minus life' 'treatment'. There's nothing new in me writing this. This treatment determines the subtraction (nausea, sleep, crash, slowness, half-days etc.) so that when you go to the place where you have the treatment this place can only and obviously be the experience of a double negative, i.e. no longer a minus. Ironically, at that moment, it is something to do, being done.

309

First published on White's blog *Lives of Performers* on 22 November 2012, <https://livesofperformers.wordpress.com> [last accessed on 10 January 2016].

Similarly, it is exactly at this time of year when I make something physical happen to my own perception, like a jerk: because leaves change colour. Forever I have had a default position in my own mind game about this whereby:

leaf – life ≠ colour

(leaf minus life is not a colour)

But this is simply not the case and every year I remind myself of this – it takes some work – and this reminding also feels physical because of the way it commands the eye to look, to work as a muscle, not through conjecture, fear, morbidity or by any other psychological infection. *The Mind Is A Muscle.* Look at the leaf. It is not dead as in nothing. It is yellow. Or red. Or even if it is brown it is still not no-colour. Look at the colour. The colour is real, it is something to do and it can be done. *War is over IF YOU WANT IT.* WANT IT. These are acts.

Which is like what I've been thinking about Robert Smithson's model of disintegration that he uses to characterise modern life in the 1960s as an inevitable decline that might nonetheless be celebrated, his famous picture of entropy:

> Picture in your mind's eye [a] sand box divided in half with black sand on one side and white sand on the other. We take a child and have him run hundreds of times clockwise in the box until the sand gets mixed and begins to turn grey; after that we have him run anti-clockwise, but the result will not be a restoration of the original division but a greater degree of greyness and an increase of entropy. (Robert Smithson, 'A Tour of the Monuments of Passaic, New Jersey', first published as 'The Monuments of Passaic', *Artforum* (December 1967))

Seen in this way, all systems spiral degeneratively into sameness, all of life, all of production is an incremental inertia, even the act of looking and for sure making art. But we can *do* something about this. Move closer. Get really close. Step into the box and bend down.

310

What is there is not what you saw before. The individual grains of sand in Smithson's pit are not grey, but still black and white. The analogy only holds for as long as we occupy a fixed position of inviolable, immaterial perception. 'Greyness' is the impression of a colour from a fixed perspective. Only in this way does looking become blindness.[1]

The Mind Is A Muscle. MOVE.

Not to celebrate decline and yet it is not stopped exactly either, but stayed, in/of time and space, a temporary _____, for as long as..., as a muscle moves, as something provisional but still some *thing*.

So, in general then removing the minus is really about whether or not there are things to do that can be done, which is also what there is to be bothered about for me in anything made and in making it. Things that take time in one way or another and please, I don't mean craft. It is what to me is so magnetic about what these two paintings by Nicolas Poussin in the National Gallery lead me to, and the gallery itself (though I'll write more on that place next):

Landscape with Travellers Resting, c.1638–39

and

Landscape with a Man Scooping Water from a Stream, c.1637

The paintings are not considered to be Poussin's most interesting or remarkable, according to the gallery – they are non-literary, figures (primitive) popped into a landscape, not thinking, like nothing to think about, as an excuse for the particularly Roman landscape to be studied, its painting practiced for another purpose, for the benefit of another picture which would be literary. The figures are described as if they are an excuse, but they are not an excuse. They are there doing things that can be done. In relation to each other. Like sitting in a gallery.

Who *wants* to be trussed-up like this lot adoring the Golden Calf of their own palava just to get told off?

When one can be undone, doing things like this

and this

at the same time as each other, but without that being the motivation as such, told to us by not touching, not looking, like klar, like facts.

I am exhilarated. What is being done? We are told and then we look and this is the thing: it is not, or not only. I do not know and yet I do and these things combined are like that dead clean ravishing of Michael Clark. These paintings mobilise my desire to a regularity. They remove the minus, or they offer this as possible and how. This is not a picture but a body plotted, nothing more nor less is told than by anyone anywhere sitting or walking, framed even if only by the look as an act too: a stage space and a scene of stages. Of ours, or mine, or one that I want, or all I want, or the only one, really. That I am reading backwards and into for a purpose, to go on:

Ian White (in white) performing *Trauerspiel 1*, HAU1, Berlin, March 2012.

Into/of time and space and/as the function of something done. Love and time. It is basic.

314

1. This paragraph is a slightly altered version of an extract from an essay I wrote called 'What Is Material?' for Ruth Buchanan's new book, *The weather, a building* [see earlier in this volume].

First, Six or so People

If you're playing a real drama like Hedda Gabler, you just kill yourself and go home and it's over. But a soap like this is day after day and it stays with you

June Brown on playing Dot Cotton

Lest by this that anyone thinks I'm depressed, I'm not. Actually to me what June Brown says is magic and funny. It is also how these forms function – it's not only playing that counts: looking is a being-done-to, but also a kind of doing, like reading and breathing. So through lung fog I think about everything we go through and how. Tragedy/soap opera. Melodrama, another thing. Tragedy isn't misery. About what is sustaining. What is day after day. What stays and how we get out of it. What moves and how against the lack of resolution. An ask to show me the show versus a frame rubbed out. The threat of the visible frame or the danger of its invisibility. The proscenium arch/one kind of television: this kind of television is a rubbed-out frame, but we're already done with it because we found others that are even more so. And then that really we all or this or me or art ought to be Hedda, but that it is or we are *only because* it is or we are the Dot who produces her. . .

⸕

First published on White's blog *Lives of Performers* on 20 December 2012, <https://livesofperformers.wordpress.com> [last accessed on 10 January 2016]. Dot Cotton is a character on the BBC soap opera *EastEnders*.

Thus Brandon in Brighton. Harry and I are in the Queens Arms because I wanted something to do and it is KKK: Kamp Kevin's Karaoke. Smashing. Two halves of Fosters and we stand at an island table. It's not late and there are just a few smeared around the edges. KK is sloping in a chair in the DJ booth, looking like it's sophisticated and powerful yet entirely hopeless, emitting that really complicated kind of nasty you could also call spineless but that doesn't necessarily mean what it seems. On the ledge in front of him is a small pile of paper slips face down with curled up edges like they've either been re-used or filled in and flicked with a damp thumb and an empty plastic jug for the spent ones.

Things get underway. I like it. Harry wonders how I know the lyrics without reading the words and I remind him of when I lip-synched 'The Greatest Love of All' in Kumpelnest on Kerstin's birthday and his total horror and almost walking out. Go figure. Anyway, KK announces 'Now, if you're thinking about slitting your wrists tonight here is the perfect suicide song... perfect suicide song, if you're feeling miserable, here's the song.... Would Brandon please come to the stage. Brandon. Where's Brandon, come to the stage Brandon. Brandon...' And what it was in this was, sure, the suspense and the excitement at such a song, but also just what KK's relationship to Brandon might be – like, it was indeterminable if KK knew Brandon, though I thought he must to try and get away with high camp negative capability/corporality but really it could have been a genuine irritation, karaoke fatigue exasperation and mild general contempt, fondness and familiarity, playing with a kitten you don't like or possibly just spite.

Brandon mounts the stage. He came from nowhere and has no supporters in the room. Jeans and a sweatshirt, Reeboks but not fashionably so, just plainly with a peaceful face and mid-length, washed, mid-brown hair, a soft 1970s. These solo karaokers are incredible to me. To give and what to get? To sing and hear. To see and do. To act and witness. Call and response. What's the request, to who? To be with...

'My Way' strikes up. Brandon gives a fair-enough account. He's no SuBo but he holds his line and it's smooth. We variously join him but he doesn't need it. The song ends and before you'd imagine KK is on.

He reads out the telephone numbers for the Samaritans and the LGBT Helpline and I do not know what register of reality we are on, but we are. Brandon leaves the stage and comes back to a half-full/ empty pint glass that he'd left on the table where Harry and I are standing without me noticing before. I tell Brandon that he sang beautifully and that it wasn't suicidal at all. Brandon rolls his eyes and drinks and goes off.

Time passes. A vaguely bedraggled trannie in her 60s arrives to 'It's Raining Men', polyester, throws some moves on the way to her seat like a pro, neat tight sharp small uplifts of the arms, hup-hah, kind of. Within 15 mins she's having her photo taken with students who were out the back smoking until now. They're all over the dancefloor like the kids at the end of *Der Rosenkavalier* accosting Baron Ochs: 'Papa! Papa! Papa!', only here I wished they wouldn't because it's got nothing to do with being human this kind of photograph which should be banned *because it IS death*. At least those kids who accosted Gregor and I when we were drugged by the mafia in that bar in Odessa actually wanted something real even though they were ten years younger than these ones – drinks, passports, kidneys, and they themselves could have been boys or girls and they were selling sex with their friends and we couldn't feel our legs but we managed still to 'run' away... 'Papa! Papa! Papa!'... and crawled up what were not the Odessa steps although they were just as many and only round the corner from the real ones and found our senses playing pool in Mick O'Neill's Irish Pub. Wild dogs, lilac minks from limousines and packs of stray kids: scavenging alike. *Happy Days*. But I digress...

KK had a rest then started up again. A few numbers in... 'OK... time for another depressing song. Brandon please... where's Brandon...' the opening strains of the song are starting... Brandon, Brandon... we're thinking, we're all sort of looking around... is he... smoking?... 'Brandon' [hesitantly, to self]... the opening strains repeat... Brandon doesn't appear. No Brandon. No. Brandon has left the building. The song? The song he would have sung. 'Let's listen to it anyway.'

'The Winner Takes It All'.

'Encore une journée divine.'

320

I'm going for a CT scan at the Cancer Centre where they are very efficient. I'm there on time as are the two other contenders with their chaperones. I'm the youngest and on my own. We all get called together and it's follow-my-leader down the corridors. Leading is Marysister, the sister of Mary 1. Mary 2 follows, followed by Maryniece – Mary 2's her aunt – then me.

Marysister is extraordinarily androgynous like someone out of Chaucer. Flaxen hair bobbed, kind of lank, trousers, all practical and chirping like Tourette's of forced happiness as shrill as you like. It's utterly unreal verging on psychopathic. The nurse says 'Turn left', Marysister loves it, 'Oh yes, yes, left, that's it, turn left, ok, ok, lovely' and she turns left chirruping. And she's chirping like this to infect the rest of us and it's dangerous to rise to this bait. Maryniece does and soon they're in league about journeys to get here, how everything's on time, oh yes, very efficient here, always efficient etc. and they're all pleased and proud at it all. And this continues as we sit in the corridor.

Maryniece is blocking Mary 2, but I can see Mary 1 in profile then Marysister at the end of the row. Poor Mary 1. She's like benefiting from/the victim of Marysister's psychopathic chirps and her pain is visible and it's hard and extreme. Her face is absolutely fixed, half-bowed and her mouth is open. There are hardly any lips and it is hooked up into a totally frozen smile that is no smile at all, cut like a crescent moon and only occasionally might she say 'yes' as thinly as you could imagine and not a muscle moves and she is there, frozen and it is like this, this picture of relentlessness. It goes on for this woman.

In a cubicle I get changed into a hospital robe the behind of which of course I can't do up on my own and normally I wouldn't care but what with all the Marys I do, so I have my coat over my shoulders like Larry Grayson or Mr Davis and my little socks still on which are bright green and bags banging around my feet and I come out skitting along and Mary 1 and Mary 2 are already trundled off on trailors for canulas. Marysister and Maryniece are now full flowing mainly because Marysister will not give up and then we hear why, which is what Marysister has been wanting to tell us all the time: Mary 1 not only has cancer but she is also suffering from chronic depression. Who knew. And well, then Maryniece says that Mary 2 is only there because her doctor's receptionist who is a right little upstart rang Mary 2 up and told her she has cancer – Mary 2 lives alone and is in her 80s (Maryniece her 50s or older) – when actually Mary 2 does not have cancer at all, just some polyps on her lungs. I thought wasn't that a plot in *Shameless*, but Maryniece got the first train from Kent to Holborn and gave merry hell at the surgery.

There's more congratulation all round about efficiencies here and then some cussing of the government and what's to become of this medical neatness and Maryniece says something that just stops us dead. What she says about the government, what she says is: 'They have no mandate.' And it is like a radical truth you remember from some time ago when there was politics.

No sooner said than off I have to trot with my bags and my flapping bum and my little socks like a joke tip-tripping to the canula dept. and in it goes and I'm really good when I have a canula in, I can sit there dead still and after ten minutes a kid eating crisps is scrawking down the corridor towards me, his father is out of sight and half shouting but the kid is getting whatever he wants from the crisps and somehow thinks it's his gaff and the kid gets to where I am and there's no curtain and there I am, frozen with the canula and he must be thinking I am a statue because he's looking and he's looking and stuffing his face with crisps and he says to his dad 'How long does he have to be like that'. I am so not going to smile and indicate that I am not like anything, because frankly I'm thinking that's all I need and kids are vermin at times like this and he's uncontrollable this one on crisps and then a nurse comes and the dad doesn't have a pound coin for the locker and the nurse lends him one easy as anything which is amazing, properly nice and the kid is pressing his cheeks against the glass of the office and they put things into a locker out of sight and I overhear and the whole time I'd thought they were there for the dad, but they're not, it's this kid that I couldn't be with who's here for an MRI scan.

I'm called into the X-ray room, lie down and give it my all.

6?

I haven't been to a film screening at the BFI for years. Sold out to the lame, the sick, the half-dead, Rachel and I, we hobble into NFT3 for over 2 hours of some of the most enthralling, stark, spartan and intensive work I've seen in a cinema for a long time. Bliss was David Bowie in a television play of Brecht's *Baal* and a South Bank special introducing three made-for-TV plays by Beckett. Then something happens. Just as the bonus track starts to play – an additional film of Beckett's *Eh Joe*, which both Rachel and I thought was gilding the lily with its simply unnecessary emotion compared to the stringency and depth of televisual humanity at every single material level it could possibly have been constructed on, in everything that had come before – just as this one starts to play, down the left-hand side of the auditorium some of us notice a figure. We see him from the back and it is precisely the figure that we have been watching in Beckett's *Ghost Trio* 45 mins ago, who does nothing to a window, a door and a platform until they lie and creak and show him *nothing more*. There is no doubt because this is not an anyone. The figure in the play and in the room has a severely hunched back, the upper part bent almost at right-angles to the rest of his body. His hair is long and white and he is wearing a floor-length coat. We do not see the face of the man in the room and slowly he is walking down the aisle, descending and he emerges into light and submerges into darkness like the characters in... *but the clouds*... or *Come and Go*. We want to speak about this, we want to talk to strangers and I make the kind of noise that isn't a word to acknowledge this and there are shivers running all over me. I can't remember when I can say the last time was that hairs on my body stood on end but they were, what now I have left of them. I am alive and this is my grave walking over me. The figure is slow and moves forwards like he did on the screen and just before a window appears in *Eh Joe*, a final swift wrist of his in the room opens the Fire Escape stage right and: he EXITS. No alarm sounds but big fat round tears fall out of my eyes and onto my cheeks and I let them, plop plop plop. And there they are, and there we are and there I am and dot dot dot and nothing more.

Division

age. A conversion. I am sat here in the kitchen and open a drawer. I push it closed. It closes every time, with the same deceleration. I am never weak enough to stop it. If it moves, it closes. Converted, I am that same deceleration, never weak enough to stop myself. It is absurd and totally accurate, the first irrelevance. Opening the drawer was the chance operation but the mechanism of its closing is a guarantee, it mitigates against risk and removes all chance. Now there is no mess, no threat, there are no loose threads: there are stories that are circuits, put out, pushed in, tidy drawers. If I am for them, I am also for the birds. I am. Rivers, hairy men and snow only used to be things to do. They were radical flow: an inexhaustible to-be-divided over time, by looking. Action/music for so long as I was only looking at it, as a radical picture. Outside, through the window split into three sections aeroplanes are descending, one after the other. Before one disappears it becomes a dot as the next one is already a shortening dash. They flow in a perfect line, the same deceleration. There I am and there is this line. Through repetition I know it and it looks like there is a lot to be done, like this is information. There is not. It is not. Planes land because they have taken off from somewhere. There is no end, nor even in me, there is not anything like it, I'm making it up. They are a stream. Any extraction is a picture, a story(line), lies. And now there are no stories like that because circulation is logical. I am

329

First published in *Exchange*, exhibition catalogue, ed. Gil Leung
(London: Flat Time House, 2013), p.35.

subject to it. By definition, there is nothing to do. Logic is inevitable. So is a hospital and so is disease. They intersect, these cycles, but being sentient is no intervention, not really. It's cast, a tidy drawer. Tell me lies, I'll tell you lies, it passes the time. It's alright for me because it's something to do, useful as something else to feel, the next irrelevance: to say that I WAS BORN..., *I* think, *I* feel etc. as if it were a truth heard on the radio is not useful to anyone else apart from the extent to which it is contestable. What does it mean to want to be looked at? That it is summer when the concert halls tell us we're stupid, the ones who are left and those who visit. Nonetheless, I am on the bed and the door is closed. Nothing is outside, but people come in and they go out, quickly. Others are around the edges which I do not touch. I am waiting for tear gas. A picture, something written, a whole body in the frame, *that* curtain always inevitably drawn and redrawn. Still pictures. Birdsong. Now, to do anything, even this nothing is division. Figures do not speak. Coming around again. My blood is arriving. Here is my hand, thin as paper, folded over my stomach like a p

(I am) For the Birds

They've got their own thing going on, birds. Whether we see them or not is irrelevant because whether they see us or not doesn't change anything. But on a park bench by a lake we are not asking each other for anything. Behaviour is not driven by looking. Neither mine nor theirs, there is no driving at all. I am looking, but I need not be. It is a trick, a trap, a game – looking, how it would have us do – because actually these birds they do not mind. They do something else instead, regardless. And so do I in fact. And this is the thing. Here we are, both doing. That is what is in this not-looking, looking away. This is what it is: an act of a special kind. Not to be looked at. A one not told. Not the usual drama. I am not figured (I am already so) and am constituted because of it. This, to co-exist, a peculiar balance on either side of the proscenium arch dividing everything.

Balanced there, birds are heard largely by chance. *I* am here by chance, a birdsong. He is on the balcony, a bird on a branch. It is not that one of us is there *for* the other, both and neither of us are pictures. Often when birds *are* heard they are not seen. And they do not see me. Most of the time they don't walk straight either. So it's appropriate that even when I am hearing them I am not being addressed. I am see

333

Originally written for Jimmy Robert's exhibition 'Made to Measure'
at 1857 gallery, Oslo in the autumn of 2013. The text was displayed
over two walls of the gallery space.

ing something like the drift of a catch-all frame producing informa-tion. Peripheral, it's a relief, like the indifferent put-put of a tennis match that I am walking past. It's a release, a rush, no relevance. In *this* room we *all* come and go. He does not see me and neither does any-thing else. I am in a city where adverts do not make any sense. Nothing is talking to me, nobody knows. I am not

Just so, over there the foot doesn't know and neither does the sock. They become both each other and neither at one and the same time, as the same form precisely, all of me, of him. Electric. A something-done-to, put on, but a nothing touched. There's the dumb thrill. In no need. Slightly parted lips, quite far away and no hands. Which is no more clear than when the dirty scuffs of a clay court stay on a white sock for the whole match, unchecked, unknown, the very mark of a not-knowing so extreme that I am up close to it like to the concrete cor-ner of a swimming pool and I talk to it because it cannot be addressed also and I tell it that it doesn't know. Here is information, mobilised as desire, as *high* drama, being ignored. It's a relief, a release, a rush.

The interference of all silence. The sound of a machine, a scratch, dirt or its image. The radio at night. Something – work – somewhere else is being done and it does not need to be done by me and it is being done by me. I have left my body, I am in my body. I am not thinking, no privilege. A flag is flying and there is welding, like smoking, like somebody else smoking. Two things are happening at once. That's all. It is an equivalence that is entirely ordinary. Reorganising suspension. Here exactly at this intersection, *it* is the measure of *me*. I am thrown. Listen. Chance is heard and I am changed. Begin again

334

Afterword: Ways of Writing

Josephine Pryde

The section of Gatwick Airport beyond security has been remodelled since, streamlined and updated, but I can still vaguely identify the bit at the back where I sat and stared at a screen showing the titanic 2008 Wimbledon Men's Singles Final between Federer and Nadal. I'd started watching in London before leaving for the airport, and Ian and I had been texting rapidly in response to the action throughout. We carried on texting once I got to Gatwick and resumed my viewing there. Ian kept a sharp eye on live sport and his commentary was always excellent, and did not stint on important aspects perhaps less immediately connected to the competition in hand, such as fantasy, bodies, desire and what a player might get up to in his or her spare time. We were torn that day between Nadal and Federer, how to choose who to support, who to want. Ian chose Nadal. I think.

After Ian died, I remember being mildly surprised at how many people told me similar stories of intense exchanges enjoyed with him at all times of the day and night. How on earth did he get to do any work? I wondered. I knew his work, he did a lot of it. Writing, reading, curating, teaching, performing. But when did he find the time? And when did he simply do nothing? Of course, sometimes he used his communications directly in what he was doing, as in the email written to Polly Staple from a stay in Ibiza that became a key element of the his piece *Ibiza*. But rarely so directly did something appear out of his friendship world and into his art. He must have had the capacity to know that the talking, the visiting, the texting, the thinking, the loving, the fucking could be part of working, and perhaps part of daydreaming, but he must also have had the ability to know not to relinquish any of it too easily, not to hand it over just like that, not to fall for the

337

easy equations of creativity and value and exchange, not to give in. He could make proper trouble, in a real political present and that meant he sensed as he worked that he was going to have to fight to prevent relations being converted too simply into resources or units of business, even as he sought to expand those relations, open them up to their own joyous, terrifying limitations and excesses.

One Sunday evening at dinner with Rachel and somebody else, maybe Jim, in Song Que, we were talking about sex and Ian drew me a lovely diagram in one of my notebooks of something you could do to a man that the man would like. I studied the drawing after he made it, a light pencil sketch of some cord and some anatomy, and then a few months later realised I could not now find the notebook containing it. Ian refused to recall the instant or to make me a new diagram. I had sort of known he wouldn't, yet I asked him all the same – but he wasn't about making rules, publishing manuals, fixing things in time and space. I'd had my chance with that little nugget of knowledge, he'd given me an insight – and now I'd have to make my way as best I could, with what I might still remember.

Bibliography

Books by Ian White

Kinomuseum: Towards an artists' cinema,
    ed. Mike Sperlinger and Ian White
    (Cologne: Walther König, 2008).
Acid Cut Flowers, Emily Wardill and
    Ian White, play script (London: TEXT
    ART, 2008).
We are behind, Emily Wardill and Ian
    White (London and Amsterdam:
    Book Works and de Appel, 2010).
Ian White: Ibiza Black Flags Democracy
    (Berlin: Deutscher Akademischer
    Austauschdienst Galerie, 2010).

Texts by Ian White

'I kissed him slightly, first, last ...',
    Prodragpinup, ed. Roger Burton, Kate
    Forbes and Ian White (The Horse
    Hospital, London, 1996), unpaginated.
'Suicide Jumpers no.1', *Prodragpinup*,
    no.3, ed. Roger Burton, Kate Forbes
    and Ian White (The Horse Hospital,
    London, 1997), unpaginated.
'The last picture show', *The Guardian*, 6
    October 2001.'Film Art Life (Death, Sex,
    Social History): David Wojnarowicz',
    Untitled, no.28 (Summer 2002).
'ArtFilm: Screen notes' [John Smith;
    'Rodney Graham', Whitechapel Art
    Gallery; Film Framed; Gunvor Nelson;
    kinoKULTURE; Steve McQueen;
    Lux calendar], *ArtReview* (October
    2002), pp.38–39.
'Jet-Packed Nomads: Mark Leckey, Nick
    Relph and Oliver Payne', *ArtFoto*
    (*ArtReview* annual supplement),
    no.1 (November 2002), pp.30–33.
'Information: Suspect, Construction:
    Evident' [John Smith], *Festivalkatalog
    48. Internationale Kurzfilmtage
    Oberhausen* (Oberhausen: Karl Maria
    Laufen, 2002), pp.182–83.
'The Cedar Bar', *ArtReview* (2003).
Exhibition review of 'On General Release:
    Avant-garde and Artists' Films
    in Britain 1968–72', *Art Monthly*,
    no.263 (February 2003), pp.36–37.
'Recording and Performing: Cinema as
    a live art', *art in-sight*, no.8 (insert
    in *filmwaves*, no.21, Spring 2003).
Exhibition review of 'Hey Production!',
    Art Monthly, no.266 (May 2003),
    pp.24–25.

Book review of *The Undercut Reader: Critical Writings on Artists' Film and Video*, Art Monthly, no.267 (June 2003), p.39.

'Rewind and repeat to fade' [Mike Kelley and Tony Oursler, 'The Poetics Project 1977–1997', Barbican; Iain Forsyth and Jane Pollard, 'File Under Sacred Music', ICA], *ArtReview* (June 2003), p.36.

'Romantic, Beyond, Impossible and Heartbreaking: An open response to Tilda Swinton's 2002 *Vertigo* Address', *Vertigo*, vol.2, no.5 (Summer 2003).

Conference review of 'Experimental Film Today', Art Monthly, no.269 (September 2003), p.42.

'Film: Hackers' delight' ['Radical Entertainment', ICA; 'Blinky 1' and 'Blinky 2', Tate Britain; Foxy Productions], *ArtReview* (September 2003), p.38.

Exhibition review of 'The Bogside Artists', Art Monthly, no.270 (October 2003), pp.39–40.

'Film: New points of reference' [Shoichi Chugoku; Takahiko Iimura; London Film Festival], *ArtReview* (November 2003), p.42.

'Piece Work: Yoko Ono', *ArtReview* (November 2003).

'Letter From Jane' (with Mike Sperlinger), *mary kelly* (London: mary kelly project, 2003), p.25.

'Palace Calls Crisis Summit', *Film[lokal]* (Dominique Gonzalez-Foerster, Markus Schinwald, Thomas Steffl, Costa Vece, Albert Weis), ed. Markus Heinzelmann (Frankfurt: Revolver, 2003), pp.40–46.

'Peter Gidal' [original title: 'Yet But If But If But Then But Then: Peter Gidal'], Luxonline website (2003), <http://www.luxonline.org.uk/artists/peter_gidal/(printversion).html>.

'Pull My Daisy', LUX website (2003), no longer accessible.

Exhibition review of 'Mark Leckey: Parade', Art Monthly, no.273 (February 2004), pp.27–28.

'Film: Adjust your set' ['Nothing Special', FACT], *ArtReview* (February 2004), p.44.

Exhibition review of 'A Kind of Bliss', Art Monthly, no.275 (April 2004), pp.32–33.

'Film: All that is solid melts into air' ['Anthony McCall', Mead Gallery], *ArtReview* (April 2004), p.47.

'Film: Small-town stories' ['Double Indemnity: Todd Haynes/Edward Hopper', Tate Modern, London], *ArtReview* (June 2004), pp.49–50.

'Devil in the Detail' [Kenneth Anger], *ArtReview* (September 2004), p.22.

'Film: And for my next trick...' ['Eyes, Lies and Illusions', Hayward Gallery; 'Bruce Nauman: Raw Materials', Tate Modern], *ArtReview* (October 2004), pp.57–58.

'Radical Entertainment', *mute*, vol.1, no.27 (Winter/Spring 2004).

'Not firing on all cylinders' [Gwangjo Biennale], *ArtReview* (December 2004/January 2005), pp.33–34.

'__/__/04 (On Fountains)', *Klaus Weber: Unfold! You Cul de Sac* (Frankfurt am Main: Revolver, 2004), pp.12–21.

'Das projizierte objekt', trans. Gaby Gehlen, *Kurz und Klein: 50 Jahre Internationale Kurzfilmtage Oberhausen*, ed. Klaus Behnken (Ostfildern-Ruit: Hatje Cantz, 2004), pp.191–96.

'Ten Pound Per Head' [Ann Course and Paul Clark], *firstsite papers*, exhibition text for 'No Horizon: Ann Course and Emma Woffenden', firstsite, Colchester (2004).

'Film: Read between the lines' [Margaret Tait; *Two Films by Owen Land* (book);

'Reverence: The Films of Owen Land', Tate Modern, London], *ArtReview* (February 2005), pp.42–43.

'Film: Too much of a good thing' [International Film Festival Rotterdam], *ArtReview* (April 2005), pp.31–32.

'Film: It's a film club, and everyone's invited' [e-flux video rental; Cummings and Lewandowska; assume vivid astro focus; Bernadette Corporation], *ArtReview* (August 2005), pp.46–47.

'Film: Art and film get spliced' ['Oliver Payne and Nick Relph', Serpentine Gallery; preview of first Artists Cinema, Frieze Art Fair (coordinated by White)] *ArtReview* (October 2005), pp.61–62.

'I and I / 12 to 12 – Notes on *UtopiaLive*', exhibition text for 'Cram Sessions at the BMA: 04 Counter Campus' (Baltimore: Baltimore Museum of Art, 2005), p.4.

'These Things Happen', text for DVD booklet, *In Profile: John Wood and Paul Harrison* (Bristol: Picture This, 2005). Reprinted in: *John Wood and Paul Harrison: 124 Minutes*, exhibition catalogue (Cardiff: Ffotogallery, 2006).

'Who is not the Author? Gerry Schum and the Established Order', *Afterthought: new writing on conceptual art*, ed. Mike Sperlinger (London: Rachmaninoff's, 2005), pp.65–83.

'Film: The great experiment' [preview of International Film Festival Rotterdam and 'Satellite of Love', Witte de With and TENT, Rotterdam], *ArtReview* (January 2006), pp.49–50.

'John Cage and Black Mountain College', *The Wire*, no.263 (January 2006), p.80.

'Film 2005' [round-up of the year], *frieze*, no.96 (January–February 2006).

'Liverpool: Documenting urban life' ['Making History: Art and Documentary in Britain from 1929 to Now', Tate Liverpool], *ArtReview* (February 2006), pp.42–43.

'Brian Eno: 14 Video Paintings', *The Wire*, no.265 (March 2006), p.16.

'Film: Frames per second' [no.w.here lab; 'New Work UK: The Chemical Effect', Whitechapel Gallery; 'Le Mouvement des Images', Centre Georges Pompidou] *ArtReview* (March 2006), pp.57–58.

'Film: Frontline voyeurs' [Oberhausen International Short Film Festival 50th anniversary], *ArtReview* (May 2006), pp.53–54.

'On The Road' [interview with David Lamelas], *frieze*, no.100 (June–August 2006).

'Moving pictures: Sergei Dvortsevoy: Documentary is a dirty word', *ArtReview* (July 2006), pp.108–09.

'Nam June Paik: Magnetic Memory', *The Wire*, no.270 (August 2006), p.73.

'Grace Ndiritu in conversation with Ian White', Luxonline website (2006), <http://www.luxonline.org.uk/ articles/grace_ndiritu_in_conversa- tion(1).html>.

'Occupation: Animation and the Visual Arts', *The animate! book: rethinking animation*, ed. Benjamin Cook and Gary Thomas (London: LUX, 2006), pp.120–131.

'The Big Giving', press release text for Klaus Weber exhibition, Herald St, London (2006).

'We would argue: *Argument* now' (with Mike Sperlinger), *Argument: A Project by Anthony McCall & Andrew Tyndall* (London: LUX, 2006), pp.4–5.

'Film and Video: Robert Beavers: Is Film A Site-Specific Artform?', *ArtReview* (February 2007), p.76–77.

343

'The Body Politic: Mary Kelly in conversation', *frieze*, no.107 (May 2007).

'Beginning, Middle, End', *John Bock: Films*, ed. Esther Schllicht and Max Hollein (Frankfurt and Cologne: Schirn Kunsthalle Frankfurt and Walther König, 2007), pp.91–92.

'Broken Windows', exhibition text for 'Emily Wardill: Sick Serena and Dregs and Wreck and Wreck', Picture This, Bristol (2007).

'Camera Obscura', text for booklet accompanying Richard Squires's film *Programme* at the Old Operating Theatre, London (2007), unpaginated.

'ContinuousPresent', text for DVD booklet, *Alfred Leslie: COOL MAN in a GOLDEN AGE – Selected Films* (London: LUX, 2007).

'Crystal Gazes', exhibition text for 'Ursula Mayer: The Crystals of Time', Lentos Kunstmuseum, Linz (2007).

'Feelings Are Facts: A Life by Yvonne Rainer', *Afterall* website (2007), <http://www.afterall.org/online/feelings.are.facts.a.life.by.yvonne.rainer#.VpGFjza9FE4>.

'Ian White and Jimmy Robert: *6 things we couldn't do, but can do now*' (with Jimmy Robert), *Keep On Onnin': Contemporary Art at Tate Britain, Art Now 2004–07*, ed. Catherine Wood (London: Tate Britain, 2007), pp.34–39.

'Jean-Gabriel Périot', Animate Projects website (2007), <http://www.animateprojects.org/writing/essay_archive/ian_white>.

'Kinomuseum', *Festivalkatalog 53. Internationale Kurzfilmtage Oberhausen* (Oberhausen: Karl Maria Laufen, 2007), pp.81–86.Reprinted (in expanded form) in: *Kinomuseum: Towards an artists' cinema*, ed. Mike Sperlinger and Ian White (Cologne: Walther König, 2008), pp.13–27.

Reprinted (in abridged form) in: *Moving Image (Documents of Contemporary Art)*, ed. Omar Kholeif (London and Cambridge, MA: Whitechapel Gallery and MIT Press, 2015), pp.92–94.

'Richard of York Gave Battle In Vain: museums without walls, walls without corners and words with no edges', exhibition text for Nick Relph & Oliver Payne exhibition, Herald St, London (2007).

'Stuart Marshall' [original title: 'Intervention: Stuart Marshall'], Luxonline website (2007), <http://www.luxonline.org.uk/artists/stuart_marshall/ essay(printversion).html>. Reprinted in *Afterall*, no.41 (Spring/Summer 2016), pp.48–53.

'One Script for *9 Scripts from a Nation at War*', *Afterall*, no.18 (Summer 2008), pp.100–07.

'Art on Television', *Art Monthly*, no.319 (September 2008), p.36.

Exhibition review of 'Stephen Prina: The Way He Always Wanted It II', *ArtReview* (September 2008), p.132.

'Blank Space', exhibition text for 'Gail Pickering', Gasworks, London (2008).

'History Is Written for Historical Reasons', *Festivalkatalog 54. Internationale Kurzfilmtage Oberhausen* (Oberhausen: Karl Maria Laufen, 2008), pp.115–17.

'Recording and Performing: Cinema as a Live Art/Becoming Object', previously unpublished (2008, originally commissioned for a proposed issue of *Cinemamatograph*, the journal of the San Francisco Cinematheque, on the subject of 'live cinema').

'Rosa Barba', *Camera Austria*, no.101 (2008), pp.21–26.

'Crowd Control', blog post on LUX website (10 September 2009), <http://

www.lux.org.uk/blog/artistcurator-ian-whites-new-berlin-blog-crowd-control>.

'Baum im Herbst', blog post on LUX website (8 October 2009), <http://lux.org.uk/blog/baum-im-herbst-artistcurator-ian-whites-latest-blog-berlin>.

'Hello/Goodbye Jack Smith/Berlin', blog post on LUX website (19 November 2009), <http://lux.org.uk/blog/hello-goodbye-jack-smithberlin-artistcura-tor-ian-whites-latest-blog-berlin>.

'Ecstatic Resistance, Jingle Bells', blog post on LUX website (18 December 2009), <http://lux.org.uk/blog/ecstat-ic-resistance-jingle-bells-artistcura-tor-ian-whites-latest-blog>.

'Architecture is the Act of Looking', *The Sheffield Pavilion 2009*, ed. Jannine Griffin (Sheffield: Sheffield Contemporary Art Forum, 2009), pp.6–9.

'As thin as they could be and as strong as they could be: Isa Genzken's *Chicago Drive* and *My Grandparents in the Bavarian Forest*', *Isa Genzken: Open, Sesame!*, exhibition catalogue, ed. Iwona Blazwick (London and Cologne: Whitechapel Gallery and Museum Ludwig, 2009), pp.108–15.

'Death, Life and Art(ifice): The films of Sharon Lockhart', *Painting Real: Warhol Wool Newman / Screening Real: Conner Lockhart Warhol*, ed. Peter Pakesch (Graz: Walther König, 2009), pp.149–57.

'I am not an archive', exhibition text for 'Videorama', Kunsthalle Wien, Vienna, 2009.

'Köken Ergun: Personal Works of Public Ceremonies', *Anywhere But Now*, exhibition catalogue, ed. Samar Kanafani, Munira Khayyat, Rasha Salti and Layla Al-Zubaidi Ars (Beirut: Heinrich Böll Foundation, 2009), pp.87–89.

'Life Itself! The "problem" of pre-cinema', *Film and Video Art*, ed. Stuart Comer (London: Tate, 2009), pp.14–25.

'Signs of the (Other) Times: Television, video, representation', *Be nice, share everything, have fun*, ed. Stefan Kalmár and Daniel Pies (Munich: Kunstverein Munich, 2009), pp.1–5.

'The time is now 10 seconds or greater', blog post on LUX website (11 Feb 2010), <http://lux.org.uk/blog/artist-curator-ian-whites-latest-blog-time-now-10-seconds-or-greater>.

'A blog's not a tweet, but London is the Île de Vassivière', blog post on LUX website (1 July 2010), <http://lux.org.uk/blog/blogs-not-tweet-london-ile-de-vassiviere>.

'Someday Soon', blog post on Guggenheim website (10 September 2010), <https://www.guggenheim.org/blogs/the-take/someday-soon>.

'On Yvonne Rainer', blog post on LUX website (12 November 2010), <http://www.lux.org.uk/blog/artistcurator-ian-whites-latest-blog-yvonne-rainer>.

'Situation Cinema: Models of spectacle, empty spaces and *The Saints*', *Paul Pfeiffer: The Saints*, exhibition catalogue, ed. Britta Schmitz (Heidelberg: Kehrer Verlag, 2010), pp.24–36.

'Where do you stand, colleague? Art criticism and social critique', blog post on LUX website (9 March 2011), <http://www.lux.org.uk/blog/where-do-you-stand-colleague-art-criticism-and-social-critique>.

'Not Based in Berlin', blog post on LUX website (21 June 2011), <http://www.lux.org.uk/blog/not-based-berlin>.

'Invisible Cinemas', blog post on LUX website (21 July 2011), <http://www.lux.org.uk/blog/invisible-cinemas>.

'A Life, and Time: Alfred Leslie s letter to Frank O'Hara + Roland Barthes on

Racine', previously unpublished (originally presented as a performance/reading at Kino Arsenal, Berlin, 11 May 2011).

'All That Melts is Solid', exhibition text for Emily Wardill, Art Basel Statements (2011).

'An Idea in Three Dimensions', *Rosa Barba: White Is An Image*, ed. Andrea Viliani and Chiara Parisi (Berlin: Hatje Cantz, 2011), pp.7–39.

'Foyer', *Poor Man's Expression: Technology, Experimental Film, Conceptual Art – A Compendium in Texts and Images*, ed. Martin Ebner and Florian Zeyfang (Berlin: Sternberg Press, 2011), pp.97–98.

'Hinterhof', previously unpublished (originally presented as a talk at a Jack Smith symposium at the ICA, London, 9 September 2011).

'Inevitably Making Sense' [with Martin Gustavsson], *Martin Gustavsson: In No Particular Order*, exhibition catalogue (Gothemburg: Gothemburg Museum of Art, 2011), pp.10–51.

'On Access and Exclusion' (interview with Köken Ergun), *Who Am I Anyway? – Three Interviews with Köken Ergun*, ed. Oliver Kielmayer (Winterthur: Kunsthalle Winterthur, 2011), pp.62–81.

'The hole's the thing...', *Gerard Byrne: Images or Shadows*, exhibition catalogue, ed. Pablo Lafuente (Dublin: Irish Museum of Modern Art, 2011), pp.199–210.

Untitled blog post on *Lives of Performers* (7 October 2012), <https://livesofperformers.wordpress.com/2012/10/07/what-can-be-sai>

'In. Adequate. Time. (Prisons 1)', blog post on *Lives of Performers* (15 October 2012), <https://livesofperformers.wordpress.com/2012/10/15/in-adequate-time-prisons-1>.

'F R E E (Prisons 2)', blog post on *Lives of Performers* (29 October 2012), <https://livesofperformers.wordpress.com/2012/10/29/f-r-e-e-prisons-2>.

'Lube', blog post on *Lives of Performers* (13 November 2012), <https://livesofperformers.wordpress.com/2012/11/13/lube>.

'Bambi L. and I', blog post on *Lives of Performers* (16 November 2012), <https://livesofperformers.wordpress.com/2012/11/16/bambi-l-and-i>.

'Removing the Minus', blog post on *Lives of Performers* (22 November 2012), <https://livesofperformers.wordpress.com/2012/11/22/removing-the-minus>.

'The Trouble With Pictures', blog post on *Lives of Performers* (6 December 2012), <https://livesofperformers.wordpress.com/2012/12/06/the-trouble-with-pictures>.

'First, Six or so People', blog post on *Lives of Performers* (20 December 2012), <https://livesofperformers.wordpress.com/2012/12/20/first-six-or-so-people>.

'Performer, Audience, Mirror: Cinema, Theatre and the Idea of the Live', *The Sensible Stage: Staging and the Moving Image*, ed. Bridget Crone (Bristol: Picture This, 2012), pp.30–43.

'Preface', exhibition text for 'Ruth Buchanan: Put a curve, an arch right through it', Krome Gallery, Berlin (2012).

'Time/Form(s)/Friendship' [with Jimmy Robert], *Jimmy Robert: Vis-à-vis*, exhibition catalogue, ed. Kate Steinmann, Sarah Kramer and Molly Zimmerman-Feeley (Chicago: Museum of Contemporary Art, 2012), pp.61–74.

'What is Material?', *Ruth Buchanan: The weather, a building* (Berlin: Sternberg Press, 2012), unpaginated.

'Wishful Thinking: Morgan Fisher at the
    Ziegfeld Follies, or, Oliver Husain and
    the Potential of Theatrical Excess',
    Oliver Husain: Spoiler Alert, exhibi-
    tion catalogue, ed. Emelie Chhangur
    (Toronto: Art Gallery of York
    University, 2012), pp.34–40.
'Statement for "Appropriation and
    Dedication"', text for seminar
    organised by If I Can't Dance, I Don't
    Want To Be Part Of Your Revolution,
    Goethe-Institut, Amsterdam (January
    2013).Reprinted in: *Rereading
    Appropriation*, ed. (Amsterdam: Idea
    Books, 2015), pp.13–14.
'His Name's Not Bambi', blog post on
    Lives of Performers (13 February
    2013), <https://livesofperform-
    ers.wordpress.com/2013/02/13/
    his-names-not-bambi>.
'Thought & Behaviour (Matthew, Piano...',
    blog post on *Lives of Performers*
    (April 18 2013), <https://livesofper-
    formers.wordpress.com/2013/04/18/
    thought-behaviour-matthew-piano>.
'Bodyimage: Lene Berg's *Kopfkino*',
    Afterall, no.34 (Autumn/Winter 2013),
    pp.28–37.
'Animal, Vegetable, Incidental', text
    for Laure Prouvost programme,
    *Festivalkatalog 59. Internationale
    Kurzfilmtage Oberhausen*
    (Oberhausen: Karl Maria Laufen,
    2013), pp.277–79.
'Division', *Exchange*, exhibition cata-
    logue, ed. Gil Leung (London: Flat
    Time House, 2013), p.35.
'(I am) For The Birds', exhibition text for
    'Jimmy Robert: Made to Measure',
    1857, Oslo (2013).

347

Acknowledgments

Any book completed in the absence of its principal author is likely to rely on the efforts and goodwill of a community, and this book is no exception.

I am grateful first of all to all those who have granted their permission to republish texts previously published elsewhere, and their help in tracking down final copy. In particular Lars Henrik Gass, director of the International Film Festival Oberhausen, kindly provided published versions of Ian's many writings for the festival, which was such an important part of Ian's working life. Roger Burton at the Horse Hospital generously gave me access to their archives, and shared his memories of his five year working relationship with Ian. Chris McCormack at *Art Monthly*, another friend and collaborator of Ian's, was also incredibly helpful in providing his articles and reviews from that publication. And Dr. Markus Heinzelmann sent me a published version of 'Palace Calls Crisis Summit', a key text of Ian's which I otherwise had only discovered unfinished drafts for.

I have relied heavily on the support and advice of Ian's closest collaborators throughout the process of this book, and in particular Emma Hedditch, Martin Gustavsson, Jimmy Robert, Emily Roysdon and Emily Wardill. I'm especially grateful to Martin and Jimmy for their help in preparing the versions of the collaborative texts which are reproduced here. Several people also offered me generous feedback on my introduction at various stages of its drafting, in particular Kirsty Bell and Rachel Reupke.

I would like to acknowledge the support of all of the staff of Goldsmiths Department of Art, where Ian had just started working as a BA teacher in the year before his death. I received a Research Support Award for this publication while working on the Fine Art MFA at Goldsmiths in 2015. I also received funding from Akademie Schloss Solitude, where

I was a fellow in 2016; my time there was enormously important in finalising the book and writing the introduction, and my thanks go to M. Joly and all of the staff of the Akademie for the opportunity.

My thanks also go to the Oslo Academy of Art, which has supported me through my research time to edit the book, and in particular dean Vanessa Ohlraun for her encouragement; and to all of the staff of LUX, past and present, who have contributed in different ways.

Above all, I would like to offer my heartfelt thanks to several people without whose support this publication could not have been realised: Benjamin Cook, the director of LUX and Ian's long-time colleague and supporter, whose unconditional commitment to the publication made it possible in the first place; Josephine Pryde, with whom I am working on Ian's artistic estate, who has been an invaluable source of advice at every stage; and Ian's parents, Jackie and Pete White, whose generosity and trust have been unwavering.

350

First published 2016 by

LUX
Waterlow Park Centre, Dartmouth Park Hill
London N19 5JF, United Kingdom

Published in collaboration with
The Academy of Fine Art Oslo/Oslo National Academy of the Arts
Fossveien 24, 0551 Oslo, Norway

Designed by John Morgan studio
Prepress by JK Morris Production AB, Sweden
Printed in Latvia by Livonia Ltd.

Typeset in *Berthe* designed by Charles Mazé
with John Morgan studio

LUX gratefully acknowledges the financial support
of Goldsmiths College, London and Akademie Schloss
Solitude, Stuttgart. Published on the occasion
of Mike Sperlinger's artist residency at Akademie
Schloss Solitude, 2016 www.akademie-solitude.de

British Library Cataloguing-in-Publication Data
A catalogue record for this book is available from
the British Library

ISBN 978-0-9928840-5-5
www.lux.org.uk

KUNSTHØGSKOLEN I OSLO
OSLO NATIONAL ACADEMY OF THE ARTS

 Goldsmiths
UNIVERSITY OF LONDON

AKADEMIE
SCHLOSS
SOLITUDE